VIEWS
from the Pews

VIEWS
from the Pews

Christian Beliefs and Attitudes

Edited by
ROGER A. JOHNSON

FORTRESS PRESS   PHILADELPHIA

Library of Congress Cataloging in Publication Data

Main entry under title:

Views from the pews.

   Bibliography: p.
   1. Sociology, Christian (Lutheran)—Addresses,
essays, lectures. 2. Lutherans—United States—
Attitudes—Addresses, essays, lectures. I. Johnson,
Roger A., 1930–
BX8041.L57   1983   284.1'33   82–18237
ISBN 0–8006–1695–2

9584H82   Printed in the United States of America   1–1695

Contents

Contributors   vii

1. Theology and Social Research   1
   ROGER A. JOHNSON

A. Religious Beliefs and Experiences   9

2. Basic Patterns   10
   ROBERT WUTHNOW

3. Sources of Doctrinal Unity and Diversity   33
   ROBERT WUTHNOW

4. A Theological Perspective   57
   LYMAN LUNDEEN

B. Religious Beliefs and Social-Ethical Attitudes   83

5. Basic Patterns   84
   MARY CAHILL WEBER

6. Religion and Conservative Social Attitudes   103
   MARY CAHILL WEBER

7. Those "Conservative" Lutherans   123
   TIMOTHY LULL

C. Other Views on Belief and Attitudinal Responses   143

8. Continuity and Diversity Among Lutherans   144
   JERALD BRAUER

CONTENTS

9. To Have and To Hold   157
   KRISTER STENDAHL

10. Social Research and the Church   166
    CHARLES GLOCK

Appendixes   181

    1. Religious Beliefs and Experiences Questionnaire   182
       Lay Responses   182
       Clergy Responses   200

    2. Religious Experience Tables   218
       Laity   218
       Clergy   219

Tables 1–24   221

Notes and References   247

Contributors

Jerald Brauer, formerly Dean of the University of Chicago Divinity School, is presently Professor of Church History there. He is the author of *Protestantism in America* and *Images of Religion in America* as well as numerous essays and articles in the field of American religious studies.

Charles Y. Glock is Professor of Sociology Emeritus, University of California, Berkeley. Formerly president of the Society for the Scientific Study of Religion and vice-president of the American Sociology Association, he has written extensively in the area of sociology of religion as well as on the subject of racial and religious prejudice. Most recently, he has coauthored *The Anatomy of Racial Attitudes*.

Roger A. Johnson is Professor of Religion at Wellesley College and consultant to the Office of the Bishop, Lutheran Church in America. He is the author of *The Origins of Demythologizing* and coauthor of *Critical Issues in Modern Religion* as well as essays in the area of theology and the social sciences.

Timothy Lull is Professor of Theology at the Lutheran Theological Seminary in Philadelphia, where he has special responsibility in the area of ethics. He is the author of *Called to Confess Christ* as well as articles in the area of ethics and ecumenics.

Lyman Lundeen is Professor of Systematic Theology at the Lutheran Theological Seminary in Philadelphia. He is the author of *Risk and Rhetoric in Religion* as well as articles and essays dealing with issues in systematic theology.

CONTRIBUTORS

Krister Stendahl, formerly Dean of Harvard Divinity School, is presently Andrew W. Mellon Professor of Divinity at that school. He is the author of *The School of St. Matthew* and *Paul Among Jews and Gentiles* as well as other essays on the subject of New Testament and homiletics.

Mary Cahill Weber received her Ph.D. Degree in sociology from the University of Chicago. From 1978 through 1980 she was Director of Research in the Office of the Bishop, Lutheran Church in America.

Robert Wuthnow is Associate Professor of Sociology at Princeton University. He is the author of *The Consciousness Reformation* and *Experiment in American Religion* as well as numerous articles in the area of sociology and religion.

1

Theology and Social Research

ROGER A. JOHNSON

Theology has been engaged in dialogue with the social sciences for most of this century. Conversations with psychology, especially the several schools of psychoanalysis, have been going on since Pastor Oskar Pfister's correspondence with Sigmund Freud, and have resulted in an abundance of publications. Theological interest in sociology, while far more limited in earlier decades than the interest in psychology, has grown dramatically in the last ten years. Liberation theology, drawing extensively on Marxist social theory, and sociologically informed historical studies, especially of New Testament Christianity, suggest two of theology's most prominent and recent interests in sociology.[1] In both of these cases, however, theology has been primarily concerned with social theory, not social research. Conversations between theologians and sociologists engaged in empirical studies (for example, through survey questionnaires) are still relatively rare.

This book offers a modest contribution to a dialogue between theology and social research. Half of the chapters are written by theologians and half by sociologists. All of the chapters have their focus on the empirical data gathered by a series of questionnaires administered to a sample population of lay and clergy members of one denomination, the Lutheran Church in America (LCA).[2] Moreover, the collaboration between theologians and sociologists was not limited to the writing of these chapters after the data had been gathered, but extended back through every stage of the research project. Theologians were involved in the initial design of the questionnaire, as well as its subsequent review and revisions.[3] In a formal consultation involving the several authors of this volume, as well as a larger group of other theologians and social scientists, there was opportunity for dialogue in response to first drafts of what became chapters in this

1

book.[4] From the beginning to the end, this study has involved the joint endeavors of these two quite disparate disciplines.

The study as a whole had two major foci, developed in each of the first two parts of this volume. The religious beliefs and experiences of laity and clergy constitute the subject for part A; the social-ethical attitudes of laity and clergy are the subject of part B. In both parts, A and B, the opening chapter provides the descriptive summary of questionnaire results; both these chapters also make reference to the appropriate tables that are printed near the end of the book. Thus, chapter 2 lays out the different patterns of religious belief and experience which are visually portrayed in tables 1 through 14; chapter 5 surveys the social-ethical attitudes of church participants as depicted in tables 15 through 21. These two descriptive chapters, together with their tables, constitute the core of the book, and all other chapters refer back to these descriptive materials.

In addition to the two descriptive chapters, each of the first two parts also offers a sociological and theological analysis of the data. Robert Wuthnow in chapter 3 explores the social sources of religious commitment: What are those social conditions or experiences that appear to be most closely linked with a strong religious commitment? Mary Weber in chapter 5 explores the social consequences of religious commitment: In relation to individual morality, political, socioeconomic, and church advocacy issues, what are the effects of religious commitment? What religious beliefs or practices are most closely associated with a compassionate, or discompassionate, attitude toward others? Following Wuthnow's explication of social sources for religious commitment is Lyman Lundeen's account of theological sources for religious commitment: How do the beliefs of present members reflect the confessional heritage of the Lutheran church? In a similar manner, Timothy Lull explores the social-ethical attitudes of present church members in relation to the public teaching ministry of the Lutheran Church in America: On what social and political issues do member attitudes and the church's Social Statements agree? On what issues are they far apart?

Part C provides three responses to the findings of the questionnaire as a whole, without regard to the distinction between beliefs and social-ethical attitudes. Jerald Brauer reflects upon the diversity of member beliefs in light of both the European origins and American development of the several churches which joined together to form the Lutheran Church in America. Krister Stendahl, presently

2

as concerned with the education of preachers as with the New Testament, pursues the theme of sermon topics (those most and least frequently chosen by clergy) in relation to questions for which lay and
clergy member responses are significantly different, and in relation
to issues central to the ministry of Jesus. Finally, Charles Glock concludes this volume with a summary account of social research, its
goals and procedures, and its potential contribution to the church.[5]

After this overview of the book's structure, I now turn to some of
the general issues and specific findings raised by this study, especially as they impinge on the practice of theology and ministry. As I
am not a sociologist, I will note only in passing any contribution of
this project to social research. Instead, I will focus on the contributions of social research to theology and ministry, as well as some of
the abiding points of tension between theology and social research.

In the first place, social research may be an effective antidote to
the theological heresy of Docetism, especially in relation to the
church. In its original form, Docetism was the christological heresy
which regarded Christ as a purely spiritual figure, not a person in-
carnate in a physical body. In later forms, the docetic heresy appears
as the denial of any essential embodied quality of Christian faith.
For example, a docetic ecclesiology regards the church as a transcen-
dent or spiritual reality, but *not* also as an organized social movement. Social research, in contrast, makes explicit the "this-worldly"
identity of the church as a body of believers, firmly embedded in the
vicissitudes of social history and composed of members whose beliefs
are as likely to be informed by social conditions as by the word of
God. By realistically portraying the actual mixture of member beliefs
and social-ethical attitudes, social research reminds us of the fallibil-
ity of the church as a social institution and so makes less tempting
the tendency to idealize and spiritualize the church.

Second, social research provides a challenge to the religious
privatism so prevalent in contemporary American churches. As a result of both secularization and religious pluralism in our society, a
growing number of American laity, and some clergy, have come to
understand religion as primarily, if not exclusively, a private matter,
involving internal spiritual or psychological concerns of the individual and interpersonal relationships, but not legitimately extending to
include the public domain of government, business, and so forth.

Lay responses to three questions in this study project illustrate this
privatistic posture. In a question concerning God's influence on

3

worldly events, over 60% of lay persons are not sure or believe either that God exercises no influence or acts only through individuals. Only 31% believe that God acts not only through individuals but also "through nations and social affairs"* (L–Q12). In a similar manner, slightly less than half of all respondents regard their religious views as "very personal and private," not the sort of topic to be discussed with others (L–Q52b). Finally, in response to a question concerning their ideas about a "God of justice," 43% of laity believe this applied to personal behavior, while an additional 13% regard justice as only a spiritual category, not applicable to the behavior of either individuals or the church (L–Q46). Less than a quarter of all lay respondents identify justice with the responsibility of the church for supporting "groups working to end inequality and oppression."

Theologians and clergy tend to dismiss this sort of privatism as alien to the official theology of their church. In his essay Stendahl raises the question of whether the operative theology of the church may itself be contributing to the pervasive privatism of the laity. He suggests that a theology limited to grace, love, and forgiveness —topics which rank highly on both preachers' sermon subjects and member beliefs—is quite consistent with a privatistic faith, devoid of corporate concerns. Whether Stendahl's observation is correct or not, the church cannot theologically address the issue of privatism until it recognizes how pervasive it is.[6]

Third, social research can clarify the mix of beliefs within a church as well as the different social sources of those beliefs. For example, Robert Wuthnow describes in chapter 3 how a strong faith commitment in agreement with church theology is primarily associated with active participation in congregational life, a personal quest for meaning and purpose, and close social relations with people for whom religion is also important. The theological consensus shared by laity and clergy, which unites members in common beliefs and which is grounded in the theological traditions of that church, is reinforced by congregational activity, including worship, sermons, and fellowship.

---

*All references to specific questions refer to the complete text of the questionnaire on Religious Beliefs and Experiences, both lay and clergy versions, printed in appendix 1. Usually, the same question has a different number in each of the two versions, and hence question numbers for both lay and clergy versions will be cited in the text. In the abbreviation used above, L– stands for laity followed by Q for question number and the number itself; C– will stand for clergy in future references to clergy question responses.

In addition, however, there are other beliefs derived not from the church itself but from popular forms of American Protestantism—for example, biblical literalism or certainty of "being saved and going to heaven." Such beliefs are not closely linked to congregational participation, but rather to social variations extraneous to the church, such as differences in age, gender, region, level of education, and especially susceptibility to the influence of TV.[7]

For purposes of congregational ministry, Wuthnow's conclusions have two implications. First, ordinary church activities—sermons, worship, adult classes, and fellowship—do make a difference.[8] Adult religious commitments are supported by participation in religious communities; we are as interdependent in the exercise of our religious life as we are in other expressions of our existence. The one-sided self-understanding of traditional Protestantism—that religious commitment is constituted in the lonely encounter of the isolated individual before God—needs to be tempered by the measured impact of congregational participation on religious commitment. Second, the congregation is not the only community to which church members belong and which informs their religious beliefs. We all participate in multiple communities of meaning, communities which reflect our cultural preferences, social neighborhoods, friendship circles, and professional roles. There are no unbridgeable walls which divide these communities from each other in the social world which we inhabit outside or in the self within. As a result, our congregations reflect not only the consensus of belief that is formed and nourished by the church but also the diversity of beliefs supported by the multiple communities outside the congregation to which its members also belong.

Theological pluralism is, therefore, not only a characteristic of our society as a whole, but also a characteristic of the internal life of individual churches in that society. The exploration of the pluralism of beliefs within a confessional church like the LCA is a major theme in several of the chapters of this book. Wuthnow explores the social sources of such pluralism, Brauer examines its historical sources, and Lundeen reflects upon the implications of this pluralism for the future task of theology. In Lundeen's view, the discovery of such a pluralism is not an occasion for fear but for celebration, as theology abandons its monolithic conceptual models from the past.

Fourth, social research makes visible the otherwise invisible connections between beliefs and social-ethical attitudes or behaviors. I

5

will not summarize here the complex analysis of the relationship between beliefs and social-ethics developed by Weber in chapter 6, but I will note some of the more striking findings reported there.

1. Those members who hold strongly to the confessional beliefs of the church do not differ significantly in their attitudes toward any social issue from other members of the church. In the sphere of social ethics, a confessional belief stance appears to make no difference.

2. Members who believe that the Bible is literally true, word for word, are also far more likely to hold consistently conservative views in relation to politics, social and economic issues, and church advocacy roles.[9]

3. The small minority of members who understand extreme instances of human suffering—like the Holocaust—to be the result of God's punishment for sins also extend their theology of a punishing God directly into the social realm. They are far more likely than others to approve of the death penalty and an increase in police power, and they are far less likely to support government assistance for the needy. In their view, society, like God, should give people what they deserve, especially when what they deserve is punishment.

4. On the opposite side of the social and political spectrum are a group of members whose liberal views appear to be closely linked to their particular church experience or roles. People who have been members of youth groups and people who are volunteer (*not* elected) leaders in their congregations are far more likely to adopt a consistently liberal position on political, social-economic, and church advocacy issues.

In all these examples, social research is able to identify connections between beliefs and ethics through computer analysis, which correlates the beliefs and ethical attitudes of respondents.

These positive contributions of social research to theology should not suggest a relationship of harmony between the two disciplines. Within this volume, there emerge at least two issues which at the level of presuppositions dramatize fundamental tensions between the two disciplines.

First, social research and theology are in fundamental disagreement concerning both language and logic. Responses on a questionnaire are designed to have one meaning, and one meaning only; the language of theology is symbolic, with a "surplus of meaning," to use

Paul Ricoeur's phrase. Similarly, the logic of social research is that of exclusion: if this, not that. The logic of theology is dialectical and paradoxical: if this, then also that. As a theologian, Lundeen presents most vigorously his theological objections to both the style of language and the logic of questionnaire construction and analysis. Also as a theologian, Stendahl observes that ambiguous language and dialectical logic appear to mark the theologically trained mind of the clergy. Laity appear to prefer those unambiguous and straightforward response options which theologians like Lundeen find so objectionable. If Stendahl is correct, the difference in the understanding of language and logic, which separates theologians from social researchers, is also a difference separating clergy from laity.

A second tension involves the deterministic presupposition of social research. The findings cited above presuppose a lawful connection between a person's social biography and his or her beliefs, and between beliefs and ethical attitudes. In social research, human beings are not assumed to behave in arbitrary or spontaneous patterns, but according to social roles, class norms, and so forth. Glock believes that this deterministic presupposition, which is so prominent in explanatory types of social research, is alien to church leaders and theologians, who would prefer a more "humanistic" emphasis on freedom.

While determinism is certainly alien to a prevalent American view of life, it may be less of a stumbling block for theology than Glock suggests. Luther, at least, was quite clear in his conviction that human beings were driven either by the divine or by the demonic; there was no neutral third option. Luther was also clear in recognizing the "orders," or "masks of God," through which God exercised his rule in human affairs. On the face of it, there appears to be no valid reason why the structures of social class (or the structures of a Freudian unconscious) could not also serve as *larvae Dei*. But even to evoke the authority of Luther may not be sufficient to ease the tension between theology and social research at the point of determinism, though I suspect that this tension has its locus more in American culture than in church theology.

One final issue separates social research and theology. While not specifically addressed by any of the authors, this difference is visually apparent in this text and may be the underlying source of other difficulties. Social research states its descriptive findings and analytic results in numbers; theologians are trained in the medium of the word which most definitely does not include percentages, tables, and so forth. Among the social sciences, psychological theory and more recently social theory may have become attractive conversational partners for theologians precisely because they are expressed in a verbal, not numerical, medium. This text has been written as an introduction for theologically trained readers to that "other" culture of statistics. Percentages and tables are here, but always accompanied by an explanation in ordinary language.

Social research is clearly no substitute for theological reflection. Nor would any of the authors of this book recommend that the church, faith, and love be reduced to the measured percentages of responses to belief and social-ethical attitude items on a questionnaire. But social research is also not an enemy of the church and its faith, nor should theologians dismiss its work as superficial or irrelevant because they have not exerted the effort to understand the language of statistics. In these chapters, a real conversation begins which recognizes both the limits of social research and its contributions to theology and the ministry of the church.

PART A

Religious Beliefs and Experiences

2

Basic Patterns

ROBERT WUTHNOW

Do most, some, or only a few members of the Lutheran Church in America subscribe to the confessional teachings of the church? Are the traditional teachings about Christ, the crucifixion, faith, and the sacraments still affirmed or have they become neglected? Are there significant discrepancies between pastors and laypersons in the interpretation of these teachings? And beyond the teachings themselves, is faith an element in people's lives? Are people witnessing God's presence, love, and forgiveness? These were the central questions informing the design of the study.

In the past, studies of religious belief and experience have relied heavily on simple, standardized questions (for example, Allport's 1960 intrinsic-extrinsic religiosity scale; Glock and Stark's 1966 orthodoxy index; and Gallup's 1978 questions about belief in God, life after death, and biblical inspiration). These questions have proven valuable in cross-denominational studies because of their simplicity. Since they have been used in a number of studies, they also provide a convenient tool for comparative purposes. To this end, some of these questions were included in the present study. For instance, a question about belief in God was borrowed from a study by Glock and Stark (1966), a question about life after death was taken from a study by Wuthnow (1976), and a question about the Bible was worded exactly as it appears in recent Gallup polls.

These simple, standardized questions, however, have come under increasing criticism, particularly from theologians and denominational leaders. In the eyes of their critics, these questions tap only the most simplistic religious orientations, seldom capturing the rich confessional teachings of particular religious bodies. For this reason, we decided to develop our own questions rather than relying, except in a small way, on questions from previous research.

The following procedure was used to develop the questions on confessional beliefs. First, a series of preliminary questions and topic areas was formulated. This task was conducted in close consultation with denominational staff and in conjunction with denominational literature, including one of the church's main credal statements, Luther's Small Catechism. Second, the preliminary questions were discussed with a number of systematic theologians (thirteen in all) from the denomination's theological seminaries. The purpose of these discussions was to develop question wordings that would reflect a variety of recognizable theological interpretations and include at least one option representing (in the theologians' view) the traditional teachings of the denomination more fully or accurately than any of the others. Third, a semi-final version of the questionnaire was completed by more than fifty volunteers (most of whom were pastors) at the church's 1978 biennial convention in Chicago. These responses assisted greatly in identifying ambiguities in the questions, which could then be clarified with minor rewording. Finally, the structure and format of each question were reviewed in detail by the denomination's Planning, Research, and Evaluation department, both as a check on clarity and to maximize the overall utility of the questions for denominational programs. During the latter phases of this process, drafts of the questionnaire were also administered to several groups of lay volunteers to gain their comments and suggestions.[1]

The questions developed with this procedure were designed to elicit beliefs concerning the central tenets of Lutheran theology. In combination, the questions provide evidence on the following: first, commitment to the doctrine of God's provision of grace to humanity in its condition of sin; second, an understanding of Christ's humanity and divinity and of God's provision of forgiveness through the crucifixion; third, an understanding of faith as the believer's trust in God's provision of grace; and fourth, an appreciation of the sacraments as one of the direct means of receiving forgiveness.

Although different questions employed different formats, the typical question offered respondents four to eight options from which they were asked to choose the one that came closest to expressing their own feelings. (They also had the option of rejecting all of the responses provided.) The options presented gave respondents a wide range of alternatives with which to characterize their beliefs, including varying levels of salience or commitment, alternative doctrinal formulations from within the church's own tradition, and doctrinal interpretations given prominence in other theological traditions.

The three sections of this chapter report: first, the responses of laypersons and pastors to the basic questions concerning confessional beliefs; second, their responses to other questions about religious belief; and third, their responses to a series of questions about religious experiences. The purpose of the chapter is to summarize the response data. This summary will provide the basis for some conclusions about the extent and nature of consensus and diversity within the membership of the LCA. An examination of the reasons behind this consensus and diversity will be the focus of the following chapter.

CONFESSIONAL LUTHERAN BELIEFS

Questions that dealt directly with the confessional teachings of the church (that is, questions that were developed in consultation with denominational theologians and that focused on the doctrinal tenets summarized above) elicited signs of both doctrinal consensus and doctrinal diversity. Consensus or near-consensus was expressed on several of the questions that asked about the believer's concept of his or her relationship with God, beliefs about Christ and the crucifixion, and the meaningfulness of the Apostles' Creed. Greater diversity of interpretation, especially among laity, was evident on questions about the meaning of faith, the "best" description of one's relation to God, and the nature and role of the sacraments.

Beliefs about the Individual's
Relationship to God

One of the questions about the confessional beliefs asked respondents to indicate how well a variety of statements expressed their feelings about their relation to God.[2] It read: "Some of the ways in which people describe their relation to God are listed below. As far as you are concerned personally, how well does each description express your feelings about your own relation to God?" The question was followed by six statements, and respondents were asked to give an answer to *each* of the statements, indicating whether it expressed their feelings "very well," "fairly well," "not very well," "not at all," or whether they were "unsure." Among the six statements (shown in table 1), one read: "I know that I am a sinner but God loves me and is giving me new life." This was the statement that had been formulated in consultation with the theologians as the most accurate single expression of the church's traditional position. Virtually all of the clergy (98%) and nearly all of the laity (86%) indicated that this statement described their relation to God "very well" or "fairly well."[3]

The question also revealed that other descriptions of the believer's relation to God were subscribed to in relatively large numbers. About three-quarters of the laity indicated that the statement "As long as I do the best I can, I feel that God cares for me and watches over me" described their relation to God at least fairly well. Among clergy, however, only a quarter said this statement expressed their views very well or fairly well. Another statement that evoked positive responses from many respondents (both lay and clergy) read: "I am absolutely certain that I am saved and that I will go to heaven when I die." A majority of the laity (55%) said this statement described their relation to God very well or fairly well. The proportion giving this response among clergy was even higher (81%).

Two other statements attracted "very well" or "fairly well" responses from about a fourth of the laity. These were "I am a helpless sinner under the wrath and judgment of God" (28%) and "I am not sure what my relation to God is" (21%). Fourteen percent of the clergy gave this response to the former, but only 4 percent did so in response to the latter. Finally, 8 percent of the laity (but none of the clergy) indicated that the statement "I don't think of myself as having any relation to God" described their relation to God very well or fairly well.

Overall, the responses point in two directions. First, there appears to be widespread agreement with the church's traditional view of the believer's relation to God. In this respect, the belief that one is a sinner but that God is a loving source of new life seems to be akin to some of the beliefs about Christ that will be discussed next. All of these beliefs elicit a high degree of consensus. Second, there is also diversity in members' beliefs about their relation to God. Some members seem less certain about this relation than do others. Some attach greater emphasis to the idea of doing one's best than do others. Some appear to feel more comfortable with language about being saved and going to heaven than do others. There are also significant differences between clergy and laity in the proportions who subscribe to these different beliefs. We shall return to this diversity in a moment.

Questions about Christ

Another question on which there was a high degree of unanimity dealt with the teaching that Christ was fully God and fully human during his life on earth. It was discovered in preliminary versions of the questionnaire that laity usually subscribed to this belief and that few seemed to hold any clearly defined alternatives to it. Consequently, the final version of the questionnaire asked respondents simply to indicate how certain they were about this teaching and how important it was to them. The question read: "Traditionally, a central belief of the church has been that Christ was fully God *and* fully human during his life on earth. Is this a belief about which you have no doubts, some doubts, or serious doubts?" Seventy-five percent of the laypersons and nearly nine out of every ten pastors (86%) responded that they had "no doubts" (see table 2). The second part of the question asked, "In your own life, how important is this belief to you?" Eight out of ten laypersons and virtually all of the pastors said they regarded it as either "very important" or "fairly important." Only 2% of the laypersons and none of the pastors said this teaching was not at all important to them (table 2).

These questions were followed by an item concerning Christ's crucifixion which read: "The church has also held that Christ was crucified on the cross. Is the crucifixion meaningful to you?" Ninety-one percent of the laity and 98% of the clergy responded "yes" (table 2). The next question offered a variety of reasons for Christ's crucifixion and asked, "In your opinion, which of the following statements best expresses the main reason why Christ was crucified?" The options listed were: "to forgive our sins," "as a protest against social injustice," "to show us how to love our neighbor," "the main reason was the disbelief of the Jews," "I'm not sure that Christ was crucified," and "other." The first option ("to forgive our sins") was the one that had been developed in consultation with the theologians as an expression of the church's traditional position. Nine out of ten laypersons and eight out of ten pastors selected it (table 2). The reason why the percentage for pastors was somewhat lower than the percentage for the laity was that a larger portion of the pastors wrote in answers other than the ones supplied.

The Apostles' Creed

The foregoing responses suggest that an overwhelming majority

14

of the laity and clergy surveyed subscribed to the church's teachings about sin, God's provision of grace, the nature of Christ, and Christ's crucifixion as God's means of forgiveness. A summary item that supported this conclusion asked about belief in the Apostles' Creed. Since the Creed is a normal part of the Lutheran worship service, it seemed important to ask respondents their feelings about it. The question asked, "Which one of these statements comes closest to your feelings when you say the Apostles' Creed?" Among the options provided, one stated, "I believe in what it says and regard it as a meaningful confession of my faith" (table 3). Better than 80% of the laity and clergy selected this option. Of those who didn't, the majority indicated that they nevertheless regarded the Apostles' Creed as meaningful ("I do not believe in everything it says, but saying it is still meaningful to me"). Only 5% of the laity and 2% of the pastors indicated that the Creed was not meaningful to them (table 3).

The Meaning of Faith

The remaining questions concerning commitment to confessional teachings showed considerably less consensus than the questions thus far. The diversity manifested was probably due in part to the way in which the questions were worded (more options to choose from), but question construction is not the only difference. For instance, the questions concerning reasons for Christ's crucifixion and views of the Apostles' Creed offered a wide variety of response options, but respondents' answers still showed virtual unanimity. On the questions that follow there appears to be genuine disagreement over rival doctrinal interpretations.

One question that evoked much diversity was an item about the meaning of faith. Although "faith" is a central concept in Lutheran theology, preliminary interviews and discussions with theologians suggested that laypersons and pastors held several different views about the exact meaning of the term. It seemed useful to examine these alternative interpretations. The question read: "Faith has meant many different things to people. Which one of the following statements *comes closest* to describing your own view of faith?" Of the options provided (shown in table 4) the one that gained the greatest assent was the statement that had been developed in cooperation with theologians to represent what they regarded as the most adequate, simple definition of faith: "my trust in God's grace." Forty percent of the laypersons and 74% of the pastors selected this op-

15

tion. It perhaps bears underscoring that even though this was the most frequently chosen option, it was chosen by fewer than half of the lay sample.

The second most frequently chosen option was one that had been designed to indicate a somewhat more active or responsive role on the part of the individual: "a life of commitment to God that I demonstrate by trying to do what is right." About a quarter of the laity and a tenth of the clergy selected this option.

These were the only options that attracted any sizable number of the pastors. Most of the remainder of the pastors chose to write in other, more complex answers. Among the laity, however, two other options were selected by fairly significant numbers. One was phrased in language more common to evangelical or fundamentalist denominations: "my decision to accept Christ instead of going on in my own sinful ways." This response was given by 9% of the laity and by 4% of the clergy. The other option that attracted a visible minority of the laity (10%) stressed sincerity as an attribute of faith: "As long as people are truly sincere in their beliefs, they show faith."

Best Descriptions of One's Relation to God

Another question that evoked a diversity of response—a follow-up section to the question reported in table 1—concerned relationship to God. Table 1 illustrates that sizable numbers in both samples felt that *several* of the statements described their relation to God at least "fairly well." In anticipation of this response, a second part of the question asked respondents to select the one statement that *best* described their feelings about their relation to God (question and responses shown in table 5). The statement "I know that I am a sinner but God loves me and is giving me new life" again drew the highest percentage of choices. But, while it was chosen by more than eight in ten of the pastors (84%), it was selected by only a bare majority of the laypersons (52%). The next most frequently chosen item stated, "as long as I do the best I can, I feel that God cares for me and watches over me." Nearly a third of the lay members chose this option (compared with only 2% of the pastors). None of the other statements received more than a small percentage of the responses.

Nature and Role of the Sacraments

Questions included in the study to assess beliefs about the sacraments also revealed some diversity in theological interpretations. One of these questions asked about views concerning the manner in which Christ is present in Holy Communion. It read: "In your view, how is Christ present when you take Holy Communion?" The options presented expressed the Roman Catholic doctrine of transubstantiation ("the bread and wine actually become the body and blood of Christ and are no longer bread and wine"), the Lutheran doctrine of Christ's presence in and with the elements ("Christ himself is present in the administration of the bread and wine but they remain bread and wine"), a view emphasizing the mystery of Christ's presence ("Christ is present in some mysterious way that can't be defined"), and an interpretation regarding Communion primarily as a memorial service to Christ ("Holy Communion is a memorial service that helps us remember Christ's life and death, but Christ himself is not present"). Respondents were also given the option of saying "I don't think about Communion in any of these ways." The most frequently selected option was the item expressing the Lutheran teaching of Christ's presence, but it was selected by fewer than half of the laypersons (45%). About two-thirds of the pastors (68%) checked it, however, as the view closest to their own. Most of the remainder of the pastors checked the option emphasizing the mysterious nature of Christ's presence (about a quarter selected this response). A fifth of the laity also held this view, while another fourth subscribed to the transubstantiational interpretation, and a tenth said they regarded Communion chiefly as a memorial service (table 6).

A second question abut Communion asked people how they regarded it in relation to salvation and forgiveness (table 7). A majority of both laity and clergy selected the answer that read: "it is not essential for salvation, but it is a way of receiving forgiveness and new life" (62% and 72% respectively). A substantial minority, however, indicated that they regarded Communion as *essential* to salvation. About a quarter of each sample said, "it is essential in order to receive salvation and everlasting life."

A similarly worded question asked about baptism (table 7). On this question, nearly half of the laity (47%) expressed conviction that baptism was essential for salvation and everlasting life, as did nearly as many of the pastors (41%). Most of the remainder (30% of the laity and 51% of the pastors) responded that baptism was "not essential for salvation, but it is a way of receiving forgiveness and new life." About a tenth of the laity but virtually none of the pastors expressed the view that baptism is merely one of the traditions of the church.

Overall, the questions concerning the confessional teachings of the church revealed a rather substantial degree of commitment to those teachings. Where it was possible for members to indicate how salient or important particular teachings were to them, the vast majority of the laity and virtually all of the clergy gave answers indicating that beliefs about Christ, the crucifixion, God's grace, and associated teachings were significant tenets of their faith. But it is also evident from the data that members, particularly lay members, espouse a variety of different theological interpretations among their religious beliefs. Definitions of faith, of one's relation to God, of the nature of Christ's presence in Communion, and of the meaning of the sacraments varied, often with at least a majority adhering to views closely in keeping with the church's theological tradition, but with sometimes substantial minorities expressing alternative interpretations. Each of these results warrants closer examination and will be taken up in the following chapter.

OTHER RELIGIOUS BELIEFS

Besides the items assessing commitment to confessional teachings, the survey collected information on a variety of other religious beliefs, including beliefs about God, the Bible, life after death, the devil, and attitudes toward non-Christians. These questions were included in the study to provide a richer descriptive profile of the orientations of laity and clergy and to assist in examining the relationships between these beliefs and other aspects of religious faith and practice.[4]

Beliefs about God

Recent national polls show that a vast majority (usually at least 95%) of the public claims to believe in God or in some supernatural being (for example, Gallup, 1978). Surveys asking more detailed questions about belief in God, however, find that many of these believers have some doubts about the existence of God (for example, Stark and Glock, 1968). These studies also show that the proportions of persons expressing doubts vary greatly from one denomination to another.

Theologians sometimes question the value of studies that focus too heavily on the measurement of certainty and doubt, arguing that someone with doubts may be as deeply—and perhaps even more honestly—committed to his or her faith as is someone with absolute certainty. For this reason, we steered away from such questions in

18

our efforts to measure commitment to confessional teachings. Studies examining different levels of certainty and doubt, however, have often demonstrated that these differences may be closely connected with variations in other religious beliefs and practices. From this evidence, we decided that some attention should be given to the question of certainty.

As a measure of certainty about the existence of God, the study included a question originally developed by Charles Glock in his research on church members in the early 1960s and used widely in sociological studies since that time (Glock and Stark, 1965). The question allowed respondents to select from a variety of options ranging from "no doubts" about God's existence to not believing at all in God. When Glock and his colleagues used this question in a survey of the nation in 1964, they found that 79% of the Protestants in the sample claimed to have no doubts about God's existence. This figure was 70% among Lutheran bodies (LCA and American Lutheran Church only; Stark and Glock, 1968).

Judging from the present results, the past fifteen years have witnessed little change. In the lay sample 68% claimed certainty about God's existence (question and response options shown in table 8). Nearly all of the rest said they too believed in God but had some doubts. In the clergy sample the percentage claiming certainty was actually somewhat smaller (61%) than in the lay sample, but the difference was largely due to the fact that more of the pastors said none of the responses accurately reflected their views about God (perhaps confirming the theologians' criticisms cited above). Not a single respondent in either sample expressed atheistic or agnostic views of God's existence—a finding that may come as little surprise, but certainly not a foregone conclusion in light of the results of many church member studies. In interpreting this result and especially in drawing comparisons with Glock's figures from the 1960s, it should be recognized that the present sample was probably somewhat biased toward active church members and, therefore, toward affirmative responses concerning the existence of God.

Since church members in other studies (and, as it turned out, in this one too) usually exhibit relatively high levels of certainty about the existence of God, we decided also to ask whether or not people in the study thought it was possible to *prove* the existence of God. This question has often been debated in the past, and even in recent years theologians in many denominations have been divided over the possibility of using reason to establish the existence of God.

Many have argued that the existence of the divine can be established only by faith and, indeed, that it may be wrong to attempt to prove God's existence.

The survey results, as shown in table 9, revealed that many people think it is possible to prove God's existence. But their idea of "proof" seems not to emphasize the idea of logic. In all, about three-quarters of the laity thought it was at least "probably" possible to prove God's existence, while fewer than one in ten thought it was wrong to try. Among pastors, only 42% thought it possible to prove God's existence, while nearly half said, "We don't have the kind of evidence it would take."

A follow-up question sought to discover what methods of proof people had in mind when they said it was possible to prove God's existence. This question was asked only of those who said it was at least "probably" possible to prove God's existence (table 9). We suspected that some of this group may have had in mind methods such as the inner direction of the Holy Spirit, rather than purely objective methods such as logical arguments. The data show that logical arguments were, in fact, much less likely to be checked as methods of proving God's existence than were other methods. Only about a third of the laity and clergy who thought it possible to prove God's existence said this could be done with a logical argument. Four in ten laypersons and six in ten pastors said it was definitely not possible to prove God's existence in this manner. By comparison, all of the other methods asked about—the Bible, personal experience, and the Holy Spirit—drew positive responses from at least eight out of every ten laypersons and pastors who thought it possible to prove God's existence.

Another question concerning beliefs about God was included to determine the *kinds of influence* that God was perceived to exert over human affairs. It has been observed in previous research (for example, Piazza and Glock, 1979) that people vary widely in their views of whether God influences individuals, social affairs, or some combination of the two, and that these different orientations appear to produce—or be associated with—important differences in political, moral, and social viewpoints. As a measure of beliefs about God's influence, respondents in the survey were asked to indicate whether they thought God shapes human events directly, through individuals, only by setting history in motion, or whether God has no influence over things that happen (table 10). The answers, at least in the lay sample, were divided almost equally between those who felt that

God influences individuals who then shape events and those who felt that God also exerts a direct influence on events through nations and social affairs. Among pastors, the latter response outnumbered the former by a ratio of about two to one.

Beliefs about the Bible

The study included two questions about the Bible. The first, taken directly from Gallup polls, was asked in order to afford a comparison with Gallup figures. This question offered respondents three options ranging from a literalist view to a mythical view of the Bible (table 11). Recent Gallup figures (1978) indicate that nearly half (47%) of all Lutheran laity in America think the Bible should be taken literally, word-for-word. But this figure combines the responses of members from the LCA, The American Lutheran Church (ALC), and the Lutheran Church–Missouri Synod (LC–MS). The present results suggest that LCA beliefs are grossly misrepresented by these aggregate figures. Only one in six laypersons and less than 2% of the pastors gave the literalist response. The overwhelming majority of both laity and clergy said that they regard the Bible as the inspired word of God, but not to be taken literally, word-for-word.

The second question about the Bible asked respondents to indicate their preference concerning biblical and scientific interpretations of the origins of humankind. An option also allowed respondents to say that both views may be correct, each in its own way (table 11). The lay sample divided almost equally between those who preferred the biblical view and those who thought both views were correct. Only 2% preferred only the scientific view. Among pastors, the vast majority (about eight in ten) said that they regarded both views as correct. Almost all of the remainder chose the biblical view (only 1% said that they preferred the scientific view).

Belief about Life after Death
and the Devil

The study also included a question concerning beliefs about life after death and a question about the devil. Both questions had been used in previous surveys (Wuthnow, 1976; Stark and Glock, 1968).

The question on life after death showed that a large majority of laity and clergy hold to some possibility of an afterlife (table 12). Laypersons were about evenly divided between those who thought of an afterlife in terms of rewards and punishments and those who had no idea what it would be like (the latter response held a small edge). It is difficult to compare pastors' responses with those of laity because nearly a third of the pastors wrote in their own answers rather than choosing any of the options provided. Nonetheless, it is interesting to note that pastors were somewhat *more likely* than laity to think of an afterlife in terms of rewards and punishments (nearly half gave this response). It is difficult from the question itself to know where these responses stand in relation to the church's tradition. At minimum it appears that the question warrants discussion, since the church has traditionally taken a guarded view of the idea of rewards and punishments. As for the other options provided, only 1% among both laity and clergy indicated disbelief in an afterlife and only 2% of the laity (none of the clergy) expressed a preference for the concept of reincarnation.

The question about belief in the existence of a devil asked simply whether respondents felt sure that a devil did or did not exist or whether they felt pretty sure in one direction or the other (table 12). This question had been asked by Glock and Stark in their national survey of church members in 1964, at which time 40% of all Protestant laity and 31% of the LCA and ALC laity indicated certainty about the existence of the devil (Stark and Glock, 1968). The present figure was 33% among laypersons and 44% among pastors. As with beliefs about the existence of God, this result (taking into account the limitations that were discussed earlier in making comparisons) suggests that there may have been relatively little change in this belief over the past fifteen years.

Attitudes Toward Non-Christians

The other belief item that was explored briefly in the survey concerned faith as it relates to those who have never heard about Christ or to persons reared in other religious traditions. In response to the question "Which of the following comes closest to your attitude toward people in other countries who have never heard about Christ?" only 2% of the laity and 1% of the clergy expressed preference for an extreme proselytizing response: "if we do not preach Christ to them, they will be damned forever" (table 13). At the other extreme, only 1% of the laity and none of the clergy chose a response excusing them from responsibility: "we shouldn't worry about them because there are many people in this country who haven't heard about Christ." Most of the laity (61%) and nearly all of the pastors (89%) said their response would be "a desire to share the love of

Christ." The only other option that received any sizable number of choices was one suggesting "we should respect their religions and stop trying to impose Christianity on them." One layperson in six chose this option (as did 4% of the pastors).

The second question, also shown in table 13, asked specifically about evangelistic efforts toward Jews. Only a fifth of the laity and a fourth of the clergy indicated that special efforts should be directed toward Jews. A fifth of the laypersons, but fewer than one in ten pastors, said no attempts should be made to convert Jews to Christianity. The largest share of each group felt that people should be told about Christ, but that no special efforts should be focused on Jews.

RELIGIOUS EXPERIENCE

In addition to the questions about belief, the survey also contained questions about a wide variety of religious experiences. Several of these concerned experiences of God—God's love, forgiveness, and presence in a number of different contexts. A second set of questions asked about experiences of grief, suffering, and tragedy. Several other questions on the Holy Spirit and on being "born again" rounded out the section. We shall summarize only the main findings; for further details the reader is referred to the tables in appendix 2.

Experiences of God's Presence

The lay members we interviewed prior to conducting the actual survey convinced us that religious experiences were quite frequently an important part of their lives. They spoke most often in generic terms of experiences involving God's presence, love, and forgiveness. They usually had difficulty with questions asking for more detail about the theological content of their experiences or about more specific experiences, such as events involving Christ or the Holy Spirit. For this reason, we decided to devote the major share of our attention to the more generic variety of experience.

The most commonly reported experience involving God was "a sense of God's love." Overall, 86% of the laity and 98% of the clergy said they had experienced God's love. Slightly more than half of the lay sample and 70% of the pastors said they had had this experience at a specific time that they could remember. And nearly as many (44% and 68% respectively) said their experience had had a "lasting impact" on their lives. Of the small minority (8% in the lay sample) who had never experienced God's love, three-fourths said they would like to.

Another question asked respondents whether or not they had felt God's presence or activity in their lives any time *during the past year*. It evoked responses similar to those concerning the experience of God's love. About half of the lay members (47%) and 88% of the pastors said they had; another 34% and 6% respectively said they were unsure, while 14% and 4% said no.

A third question asked about experiences of God's forgiveness. One may question whether or not it is theologically accurate to call "forgiveness" an experience, but the concept of assurance of forgiveness is central to Lutheran theology. To obtain some information about forgiveness, a question was framed—with some deliberate vagueness—asking respondents whether or not they had *ever* felt God's forgiveness in their lives. Given that close to 90% of the laity said they regarded "forgiveness of sins" as the purpose of Christ's crucifixion and that nearly as many considered the sacraments a means of receiving forgiveness, we expected a high proportion to indicate that they had also experienced God's forgiveness. As it turned out, the proportion seemed surprisingly low. Only 31% said, "yes, it has had a deep impact on my life"; and 4% said, "yes, but it wasn't very important to me." In other words, only about a third of the laity felt that they had personally experienced God's forgiveness. Virtually all of the remainder (all but 11%) said they weren't sure whether they had or not.

In the clergy sample the responses conformed more closely to our initial expectations. Nearly eight in ten pastors (79%) said they had experienced God's forgiveness deeply; another 8% said they had had such an experience but not in a deeply moving way; 8% said they were unsure; and only 2% were sure they had not had such an experience.

One interpretation of the responses given by the lay respondents may be that they interpreted forgiveness as absolution for particular—and often serious—misdeeds, rather than defining it as a more general state of assurance in light of God's grace. For instance, here are some of the examples that respondents mentioned when asked to describe their experience:

> "I prayed for help to stop drinking. I felt a very positive presence. God's help is available in proportion to actual personal need."

"In times of crisis in my personal life when I have asked for and received forgiveness."

"I was troubled about a family argument; during Communion I felt relieved."

"After committing adultery."

"Through drinking. I hated my husband. Through Al-Anon I found God and forgiveness and knew I could find love again."

"During a time in my life when I was searching for answers. I realized that God accepts me even though I am a sinner. No matter what I do, God's love for me does not change."

"During high school and college I turned totally away from God. Several years ago I felt the deep conviction of sin and felt God forgive me."

It may also be that the low proportion of respondents saying they had experienced God's forgiveness was attributable to some unforeseen ambiguity in the wording of the question.

Another question concerning experiences of God's presence or activity asked about "feeling that God was telling you something." Although this question evoked fewer affirmative answers than did the one about God's love, a substantial minority indicated that they had had such an experience. Thirty-seven percent of the lay sample and 61% of the pastors said they had felt God telling them something at a specific time they could remember. Another third of each sample said they had had this experience, but not at any specific time they could remember. About a quarter of the laity and nearly half of the clergy said this experience had made a lasting impact on their lives.

To examine more extensively the nature of respondents' experiences of God's presence, the study also asked about the kinds of *situations* in which they had felt God's presence during the preceding year. The situations that respondents checked most often included "during Holy Communion," "while attending church," and "during private prayer." In both samples, over half of the respondents indicated that they had experienced God's presence "many times" in church or at Communion within the past year and nearly half said they had experienced God's presence often during private prayer. By comparison, time spent reading the Bible was mentioned considerably less often as an occasion for experiencing God's presence.

Only about a quarter of the laity (and only slightly more of the pastors) said they had experienced God's presence many times in the past year while reading the Bible (table 14).

Apart from the more ecclesiastical settings, the study showed that two other contexts were associated with experiences of God's presence relatively often. "In nature" was the most common nonecclesiastical setting for experiencing God's presence. Indeed, laity were about as likely to have experienced God's presence in nature as during prayer: about half said they had experienced God's presence in nature many times during the past year. By comparison, only about a quarter of the clergy gave this response. The other setting that was mentioned relatively often in both samples as an occasion for experiencing God's presence was "while meditating" (table 14).[5]

Aside from nature and meditation, nonecclesiastical settings did not appear to be common stimuli for experiencing God's presence—at least in comparison with the more ecclesiastical contexts. Fewer than a third of the respondents in either sample had experienced God many times while among friends or while having fun. Given the kind of work that pastors do, a majority said they had experienced God's presence while working. But among laity fewer than a third had experienced God's presence many times in the course of their work.

In sum, experiences involving God's presence or activity appeared to be relatively widespread, even though they were more common in some settings than in others. A few respondents had never experienced their faith in this manner, but the vast majority could point to some feeling of God's love, forgiveness, or presence in their lives, and approximately half of the laity (more among clergy) had experienced such feelings either in the immediate past or in a way that had made a lasting impression on their lives. It was also clear from the responses that the church had been a major source of these experiences.

Grief, Suffering, and Tragedy

Although most of the literature on religious experiences has emphasized positive (or "peak") experiences, these are by no means the only kinds of experiences that have religious meaning. Experiences of grief, suffering, and tragedy are such universal occurrences that no religious tradition has been able to ignore them. In the Lutheran tradition they hold prominence in the "theology of the cross," and other research has shown that they are an important focus of congregational nurturing activities (see Johnson, 1979).

We asked respondents, "Has there ever been a time in your life when you have experienced deep grief, suffering, or even tragedy?" Those who responded affirmatively were asked to describe briefly what had happened in order to fix a specific event in mind. Then, a list of statements was presented to determine some of the specific reactions that respondents had experienced during this time of grief or tragedy.

Seventy-one percent of the lay members and 67% of the pastors said they had experienced a time of deep grief, suffering, or tragedy in their lives. Deaths of loved ones, particularly of parents, were listed most frequently. Other events cited included serious illnesses, automobile accidents, miscarriages, divorces, and financial setbacks. Here is a random sampling of the events described:

"The death of a close coworker."

"When my father died."

"While a young girl (preadolescent), my life was threatened in a bathroom by a rapist."

"My husband was killed in a car accident on Christmas Eve '76. It was really hard to get over; but with the help of Christ I can accept it and talk about it."

"When my grandfather died. . . . He had been sick for at least ten years with a disease the doctors could not diagnose."

"Our three-year-old son drowned."

"The death of a very close friend when we were together on a fishing trip."

In the more extensive interviews that were conducted in designing the survey, these kinds of experiences were also mentioned frequently and in many cases had been a pivotal point in the individual's personal religious biography.

The more specific statements concerning reactions to times of grief showed that most respondents—at least in retrospect—were able to think of these times as positive events in their lives. Of those who said they had had such an experience, about three-quarters of both laity and clergy said they had come to be more concerned

27

about others as a result of their experience. About the same proportions said they had felt that God was especially close to them, that they had grown in their understanding of God's love, and that they had gained new insights about themselves. About half of the laity (but closer to three-fourths of the pastors) said they had felt support from other church members.

Less positive reactions to times of grief and tragedy were rarer, but many of the respondents, particularly in the lay sample, said they had had them. Nearly half of the laity and about a third of the clergy said they had wondered how God could let this happen to them. About one layperson in eight indicated feeling this as God's punishment (only 2% of the pastors gave this response).

On the whole, these results demonstrate clearly that suffering, grief, and times of tragedy are events that most laity and clergy have experienced and that religious meanings are commonly ascribed to these events. While the majority of persons seems to have constructed these meanings in a positive way, the results also reveal the extent to which religious questions or doubts may be raised by these events.

Other Religious Experiences

Besides the foregoing, many other religious experiences had been part of respondents' lives. A number of them had been influenced by experiences in nature and by times of Christian fellowship. A few had had experiences such as being "born again," speaking in tongues, and witnessing the Holy Spirit, and some had even experienced a feeling of contact with the dead.

Experiences of being moved by the beauty of nature have been regarded positively in the Lutheran tradition, and in the present sample these experiences were relatively common (see appendix 2, tables A and B). Nearly everyone had had such an experience. Many also felt that these experiences had had an important impact on their lives. But relatively, this feeling was more pronounced among laity than it was among clergy. About half of the laity said their experiences in nature had made a lasting impact on their lives, compared with that response from only about a third of the clergy.

As for Christian fellowship, virtually all of the clergy (98%) and nearly all of the laity (85%) said they had experienced "close fellowship with Christians (other than your own family)"; and three-quarters of the clergy and more than half of the laity said this had happened at a specific time they could remember. About a third of the laity and over half of the clergy said Christian fellowship had had a lasting impact on their lives.

"Born-again" experiences were somewhat less frequent than those in nature or those involving Christian fellowship, but a sizable minority of the respondents had had them. The question used was from a 1977 Gallup poll in which 34% of the American public, including 30% of all Lutherans, claimed to have been "born again." In the present sample, a quarter of the laity and 42% of the pastors said they had had such an experience. The question, however, was broadly worded: "In your own life, would you say that you have been 'born again' or had a 'born-again' experience—that is, a turning point in your life when you committed yourself to Christ?" As a check, we also asked a somewhat more specific question simply about "an experience of being 'born again'." We thought that the term itself without the expanded definition of it provided by the Gallup question might elicit a somewhat smaller percentage of affirmative responses. Overall, though, the responses to the two questions were about the same. On the latter item, 29% of the laity and 46% of the clergy said they had experienced being born again. This item also suggested, however, that the proportion of laity who felt their lives had been changed by this experience was relatively small. Only 13% (compared with 23% of the pastors) said this experience had had a lasting impact on their lives.

The data on experiences of the Holy Spirit and on speaking in tongues suggested that these experiences (particularly the former) are not unknown to Lutherans. To the extent that experiences such as these are in some way linked to or consistent with the charismatic movement, the results also suggest that the impact of this movement has been felt by a relatively small number of Lutherans.

About half of the laity and an overwhelming majority of the clergy (81%) said they had experienced "a feeling of being filled with the Holy Spirit" at some time in their lives—an experience that has hardly been limited to the charismatic movement. About a fifth of the laity and a third of the clergy also indicated that this experience had had a lasting impact on their lives. By comparison, an item much more directly associated with the charismatic movement showed that only 2% of the laity and 6% of the clergy had ever spoken in tongues ("I approve and have spoken in tongues myself"). Those who approved but who had not spoken in tongues themselves represented a relatively small proportion—12% of the laity and 20% of the clergy. Yet, the absence of approval did not mean that the majority disapproved; only 12% of the laity and 16% of the clergy gave this response. The majority took a somewhat indeterminate position, stating either that "speaking in tongues is OK for some people, but it's not for me," or that they weren't sure what speaking in tongues was.

Finally, the data showed that a small but not insignificant number of respondents felt that they had had experiences of contact with the dead. Twenty percent of the laity said they had experienced "a feeling of being in contact with someone who had died," as did 11% of the clergy. About one in ten of the laity, but only 4% of the clergy, said this experience had had a lasting impact on their lives. (See appendix 2, tables A and B for responses to other questions not here summarized.)

SUMMARY

The extent to which laity and clergy currently subscribe to a variety of religious beliefs and the extent to which they have experienced a variety of religious experiences has been sketched in this chapter, drawing on the results of the Lutheran Listening Post survey. The limitations of questionnaires for investigating issues of such complexity are all too apparent. However, several conclusions appear warranted.

First, laity and clergy are in basic agreement with each other and among themselves as far as many of the fundamental tenets of Christianity are concerned. There is near consensus that Christ was fully divine and fully human and that the purpose of the crucifixion was to provide forgiveness of sins. There is also widespread belief in the existence of God, in the teaching that God loves humanity as individuals in their condition of sin and that God is giving individuals new life, and in the truth of these claims as they are expressed in the Apostles' Creed.

Other studies have suggested that formal religious beliefs are not particularly salient when people are actually given a chance to talk about their faith (Johnson, 1979), or that such beliefs may have little effect on the manner in which people live their daily lives (Glock, et al., 1967). For these reasons, we went out of our way in designing the present study to give respondents the option of saying that they weren't really sure about their beliefs or, if they were sure, that these beliefs weren't terribly important to them or that they hadn't thought much about them. The results cause us to suspect that previous studies have told only part of the story about religious beliefs. By all indications, people *themselves* feel that their beliefs are important to them, they know and subscribe to the basic confessional teachings of the church, and their religious experiences suggest that they are not merely giving lip service to their beliefs. There is variation in these commitments, of course. For example, we shall see in the next chapter that some persons hold their beliefs more firmly and more consistently than do others. For the largest majority, however, we can scarcely dismiss formal religious beliefs as a vital element of their faith. Church members may not wear their beliefs on their sleeves, but this is no indication that their beliefs are unimportant.

As far as the core elements of Christian belief are concerned, therefore, the evidence suggests both consensus and relatively high levels of commitment.

Despite this consensus, it is also readily apparent from the data (and this is a second main observation) that much diversity exists. Only a handful of the laity happened to give the same responses that theologians had chosen as the most adequate or accurate statement on *all ten* of the confessional belief questions (2.6%, to be exact).[6] Most of the laity held other views on at least some of the questions. For example, sizable numbers leaned more toward a concept of faith that emphasized "trying to do what is right" rather than viewing faith simply as trust in God's grace. On questions about the sacraments, some held that these were essential to salvation, others that they were valuable but not essential, and others that they were merely traditions of the church. Other questions revealed differences of opinion on the nature of biblical inspiration, on beliefs about life beyond death, and on attitudes toward conversion.

At this point we cannot make further assessments of the nature or meaning of these diverse orientations. It is clear that they exist, however, and we shall return to them in the next chapter.

The remaining observation that appears warranted has to do with the importance of religious experiences. We make no claim to have probed the depth or variety of respondents' religious experiences. But the data are adequate to indicate that religious experiences are widespread among both laity and clergy. Even if the responses were biased by the nature of the sample, they demonstrate that experiences of God's presence and activity occur frequently for many persons and in a variety of contexts. Judging from the frequency with which they were mentioned, these experiences may occur quite commonly in the worship service, during Communion, during private prayer, or in the course of daily activities. The data on grief and suffering also demonstrate that unusual circumstances may have powerful religious meanings.

Since religious experiences have recently enjoyed a revival of interest, perhaps because of the more exotic religious movements among youth, it is noteworthy to discover that religious experiences are not absent among the membership of a mainline denomination such as the LCA. At the same time, some of the findings, such as the responses to the question on experiencing God's forgiveness, indicate that there is probably room for the church to nurture and enrich the religious experiences of its members.

3

Sources of Doctrinal Unity
and Diversity

ROBERT WUTHNOW

Pluralist, polyglot, multicentric, conflictive, divided—with varying connotations these are the terms that have been used to describe the contemporary church. Commentators have characteristically assumed that there is much diversity both among different denominations and—as far as the large, mainstream denominations are concerned—within them as well. Yet the evidence presented has often been less than adequate for proving this thesis.

Where actual differences of opinion have been measured, the measures have usually dealt with social issues, such as civil rights, social justice, and economic policies, or with practical goals of the church, such as relative emphases on witnessing or on proclaiming social principles. Where matters of doctrine have been examined, the evidence has been less direct. Studies have shown that many denominations contain variations in commitment, with some members espousing greater commitment to traditional tenets such as the literal inspiration of the Bible or manifesting greater certainty about God's existence or the devil's existence than others. But these studies have generally shown only that people vary along certain continua—for example, from more fundamentalistic to less fundamentalistic, or from having fewer doubts to having more doubts about supernatural realities. They have not established that people actually hold identifiably different theological positions. Differences have been inferred from the monodimensional variations that have been examined. But the actual variety of theological orientations has not been investigated directly.

The doctrinal diversity uncovered in the foregoing chapter provides a rare glimpse of the actual range of theological options that may be represented among church members. As such, it affords an unusual opportunity to gain a better understanding of the nature of doctrinal pluralism. Diversity is clearly a fact of modern life, but it can be experienced for better or for worse. It can acquire the trappings of divisiveness or it can rest on a foundation of common understanding. The fact that it appears in the survey results makes it possible to examine these alternatives.

The results, however, also revealed a strong base for Christian unity. Certain teachings, such as the crucifixion, the nature of Christ, and God's forgiveness, evoked widespread agreement among both laity and clergy. The presence of diversity on other teachings should not be emphasized at the expense of this consensual core. Indeed, the diversity itself can be understood only in the light of the centripetal forces set in motion by these common commitments.

These commitments pose a different problem for investigation. Though they elicit widespread agreement, they are held with greater conviction by some members than by others. While certain members regard these teachings as central, salient, and important in their lives, other members hold them with less consistency and accord them less significance. If we are to understand the nature of these commitments sufficiently to nurture them, we must examine the conditions that are associated with these varying levels of doctrinal salience.

The first part of this chapter attempts to identify some of the factors that reinforce commitment to basic, consensual Christian beliefs. The explanatory value of four popularly held arguments will be examined: first, that commitment to these teachings is significantly influenced by the programs of the church itself; second, that such commitment is largely a function of early religious socialization; third, that it reflects (and is limited by) certain characteristics of a person's social biography; and finally, that it is rooted in deeper concerns characteristic of the human condition. The second part of the chapter will take up the question of why respondents differed in their views on other doctrinal teachings, such as the meaning of faith, descriptions of one's relationship to God, and ideas about the sacraments.

THE CORRELATES OF
CONFESSIONAL COMMITMENT

The beliefs to be examined in this section are items on which there was a high degree of consensus: having no doubts about the teaching that Christ was fully God and fully human, regarding this belief as very or fairly important, holding the teaching of Christ's crucifixion as personally meaningful, believing that the main reason for the crucifixion was forgiveness of sin, and saying that the statement "I know that I am a sinner but God loves me and is giving me new life" described one's relation with God either very well or fairly well. On the average, 84% of the lay sample expressed their commitment to the confessional teaching on each of these questions.

These beliefs, taken in combination, also reflect an appreciable understanding of the core of the Christian gospel. In them is an acknowledgment of sin, recognition of God's grace, and an understanding of Christ as God's provision of forgiveness through the crucifixion. Our interest is in examining the correlates of these beliefs. We are, in a sense, focusing particularly on "model" church members insofar as their commitment to basic Christian teachings is concerned to discover what conditions reinforce the strength of their convictions. Conversely, we are interested in discovering why other persons hold these convictions less firmly or with less consistency.

These questions are inspired primarily by practical concerns. If beliefs are presently being reinforced by the sermons pastors preach on Sunday mornings, this effect is worth knowing about (both by way of encouragement and so that it may be continued). If, however, one's basic belief commitments are a function mainly of early religious training, efforts might be directed more effectively toward programs of training or retraining. Or, if still another possibility proves to be the case—that the salience of one's beliefs is largely a function of age, gender, education, or region—then at least program planners will be able to identify more precisely where their efforts need to be focused.

To simplify the discussion that follows, we have created an "index" which classifies respondents in terms of the degree of *saliency* and *consistency* with which they held the five core beliefs.[1] One point was given to respondents for meeting each of the following conditions:

1. saying *both* that they had "no doubts" about the teaching that Christ was fully God and fully human *and* that this belief was "very important" or "fairly important" to them;

2. saying *both* that Christ's crucifixion was meaningful to them *and* that the main reason for Christ's crucifixion was "to forgive our sins";

3. saying that "I know that I am a sinner but God loves me and is giving me new life" described their relation to God "very well."

35

Using these criteria, 35% of the lay sample received a score of 3 ("very high"), 33% scored 2 ("moderately high"), 22% scored 1 ("moderately low"), and 20% scored 0 ("very low"). It should be emphasized that "high" and "low" refer to differences in *strength of conviction* (salience), not to the presence or absence of confessional beliefs, since virtually all respondents subscribed at least minimally to these beliefs. For this reason we whall refer to the index as a salience of faith index (or simply SFI).[2]

The discussion will focus mainly on the beliefs of laity. Pastors' beliefs will be examined to the extent that they help to illuminate some of the sources of faith among laity.

The Church's Role: Clergy, Sermons, and Lay Participation

The finding noted in chapter 2 that pastors overwhelmingly selected the most adequate or accurate theological response on questions about confessional teachings warrants repeating. Ninety-eight percent said that the statement "I know that I am a sinner but God loves me and is giving me new life" described their relation to God very well or fairly well. The same percentage said Christ's crucifixion was meaningful to them. Ninety-six percent said the teaching that Christ was fully God and fully human was very important or fairly important to them. Five out of six said they had "no doubts" concerning this belief. Eight out of ten said the main reason for Christ's crucifixion was to forgive sins. And three-fourths said they regarded faith as trusting in God's grace. In light of these responses, it seems highly possible that the clergy is a significant factor reinforcing the salience of faith among laity. In other words, an obvious place to begin if we want to know why some layperson's beliefs are more salient than others is with the impact of the clergy.

The data show that pastors not only believed in the confessional teachings of the church, but that virtually all of them preached about these subjects as well. One of the questions in the clergy questionnaire asked, "During the past year, did you preach a sermon that dealt mainly with the following topics?" A list of twenty-one sermon topics followed and for each, pastors were asked to indicate: "yes, many"; "yes, at least one"; "no, but touched on it often"; "no, but touched on it some"; "no"; or "not sure." Ninety percent said they had preached at least one sermon on "Christ's crucifixion." Eighty-nine percent said they had preached a sermon on "God's love for us as sinners." Eighty-eight percent said they had preached a sermon on "experiencing God's forgiveness." Eighty-six percent said they had preached a sermon on "trusting in God's grace." And 82% said they had preached a sermon on "receiving God's forgiveness through Holy Communion."

The reason that these percentages were high could have been that sermon topics were dictated by the liturgical calendar rather than by pastors' own beliefs. However, an examination of the relationships between pastors' beliefs and their sermon topics suggested that beliefs did, in fact, make a difference. For example, there was a positive statistical relationship between the belief that "I am a sinner but God loves me" and having preached a sermon on "God's love for us as sinners." There were also positive relationships between this belief and sermons on God's forgiveness and between beliefs about Christ's nature and the crucifixion and sermons on these topics."[3]

But why were these beliefs more salient to some laity than to others, especially if pastors preached on them this much? One possibility is that some persons belonged to congregations whose pastors preached a great deal more than average on these subjects. We were not able to examine this possibility with the data, because the terms of the study prevented us from connecting specific laypersons with their own pastors.

One possibility that we were able to examine was that some persons participated more extensively in the activities of their congregations, were thereby more exposed to sermons about God, Christ, and the crucifixion, and as a result were more likely to hold these beliefs firmly and consistently themselves. The results clearly supported this possibility. Among laity who attended worship services every week, 80% scored high (2 or 3) on the salience of faith index (SFI), compared to 68% of those who attended nearly every week, 41% of those who attended twice a month, and 30% of those who attended once a year or less. Substituting other measures of participation (evenings devoted to church activities, attendance at Bible study classes, and self-reported activity) did not alter the basic pattern.[4] The point is not that participation "caused" people to believe, but the data revealed that the two were closely associated with one another.

We were also able to show that persons who felt that they had been influenced by sermons tended to score higher on the SFI measure than other persons. For example, 82% of those who felt that God spoke to them through the church service on Sunday mornings "most of the time" scored high on the index, compared to 64% of those who felt that God spoke to them this way "once in awhile," 43% among those who responded "never," and only 24% among those who said they didn't attend. There were similar differences between respondents who felt that they had been guided many times during the past year by "what your pastor preaches in sermons" and those who felt they had not been guided by their pastor's sermons.[5]

Taking the results as a whole, it appeared reasonable to conclude that pastors' sermons were significant in reinforcing the salience of their parishioners' faith. Not only did pastors themselves overwhelmingly subscribe to the church's teachings about God, Christ, and the crucifixion, but they preached sermons on these topics, and the more firmly they believed in them, the more often they preached such sermons. Laity, for their part, not only subscribed in large numbers to the same teachings, but those who more often participated in church activities subscribed to these teachings with greater conviction than those who participated less often, and among those who participated often, those who had been influenced by their pastors' sermons were especially likely to express conviction.

If pastors' sermons were one source of reinforcement, there were yet other ways in which church participation appeared to reinforce doctrinal conviction. Fellowship with other believers also played a significant role. For example, among those who had friends whose religious beliefs were "very important," 83% scored high on the SFI measure, compared with only 47% of those whose friends did not consider religion important. Those who had spouses who valued religion were also more likely to score high on the index than were those who had spouses who didn't value religion. There were sharp differences as well between those who said they frequently discussed their religious convictions with their family or who regularly engaged in family Bible studies and those who discussed or participated less frequently.[6]

These results—relating belief to various measures of participation and support—are likely to come as no surprise, but they need to be kept in mind as other correlates of belief are explored. Having begun with the observation that most respondents subscribed to basic Christian teachings, we are now in a position to add that the more one participates in church activities—both formal and informal—the more likely one is to adhere consistently and saliently to these teachings. In this respect, the church appears to be "doing its job." Whatever the various reasons may be for taking part in church services, it is clear that people go away not merely with warm feelings or a sense of having fulfilled their weekly social obligations, but with a stronger sense of conviction about the nature of their relation to God. This conclusion, though compatible with common sense, flies in the face of much theorizing that has ascribed religious convictions to extrinsic social conditions or to early religious training alone. It will help to clarify the role of the church in nurturing belief, therefore, if we turn to these alternative explanations.

Religious Backgrounds and
Social Characteristics

Previous studies have documented that social characteristics such as early religious training, childhood denomination, age, sex, and education tend to be associated with differences in religious commitment. Are these characteristics also operative here?

First, with respect to early religious background, the data show that there are few differences in salience of faith among respondents from different backgrounds. Among those whose mothers were Lutheran, for example, 69% scored high on the SFI measure; of those whose mothers were not Lutherans, 68% scored high. Substituting father's background for mother's, the percentages were 70 and 68 respectively. And taking a different measure of religious upbringing—childhood church attendance—the differences are only somewhat larger; 70% of those who attended every week or nearly every week scored high, compared with 65% of those who attended once a month or less. The data also show that SFI scores differ little between persons who have always been Luthern Church in America members (or members of its predecessor bodies) and persons who have been members of other denominations. Sixty-seven percent of those who had always been LCA members scored high, as did 67% of former American Lutheran Church (ALC) members, 76% of former Lutheran Church–Missouri Synod (LC–MS) members, 68% of former "other Lutheran" members, 67% of former Baptists and former United Church of Christ (UCC) members, and 64% of former Methodists, Episcopalians, and Roman Catholics.[7]

Second, many of the other social characteristics that have been associated with differences in religious commitment in other studies were also only weakly related to scores on the SFI measure. Education—a strong correlate of religious belief in many studies—produced only small differences in SFI scores even between extreme high and low categories. For example, only 11 percentage points separated those who had earned postgraduate degrees from those who had received only a grade-school education (59% versus 70% scored high on the index). Regional differences were also weak by comparison with other studies (66% scored high in the Northeast, compared to 70% in the Midwest, South, and West).[8] The main divergences were between males and females, for which the differences were still relatively small (73% of the women scored high compared with 60% of the men), and between the young and the old. Seventy-eight percent of those over age fifty scored high on the index, compared with 65% of those between ages thirty-one and fifty, and only 54% of those age thirty or younger.

The differences found between age groups correspond to similar patterns that have been documented in other studies, for example, among Catholics (Greeley, 1976), in Gallup's recent study of the "unchurched" (1978), and in Wuthnow's research in California (1976, 1978). In all of these studies, persons who reached maturity after the early 1960s scored lower on religious commitments than persons who matured prior to the 1960s. Various explanations have been put forward to account for these differences, including the effect of identification with the counterculture, changing sexual standards, disagreement with church positions on birth control, and declining confidence in biblical authority.

We attempted to determine which of these various explanations was most effective in explaining the age differences in the present data. One of the theories we tested was that the young were less committed because they were better educated than the old. Modern education has often been singled out as a force at odds with traditional religious commitment. As we have already seen, however, the differences in commitment between the better and the poorer educated in the present sample were relatively small. When we examined the relation between commitment, age, and education simultaneously, we found that educational differences did *not* account for the differences between age groups.[9] Another idea we tested was that the young differed from the old in religious commitment because of differences in early religious socialization. We took into account different levels of childhood church attendance, participation in church youth groups, parental religious convictions, and previous denominational affiliations; however, we found that the differences between the young and the old in salience of faith still remained.[10]

A third theory we were able to test was that biblical authority was weaker among the young, thereby weakening their overall commitment to religious teachings. Differences in views concerning the authority of the Bible were, in fact, evident between age groups, and when we took them into account, we found that they explained part of the differences in salience of faith. For example, when we looked separately at respondents who preferred the biblical story of creation and at respondents who thought both the Bible and science were true, we found that the differences between the young and the old on the salience of faith index were reduced by about a third.[11] We don't know all the reasons why young people were less likely to hold exclusively to the truth of the Bible, but we suspect that exposure to science and to contemporary education in general may be important factors in shaping responses to questions dealing with creation. At least, it appears that differences in views of the Bible may be an important factor bearing on age differences in salience of faith.

A final theory was the idea (documented in Wuthnow's California research) that identification with values associated with the counterculture of the late sixties had led young people to be less committed to the church, as well as to other social institutions. To test this idea we examined the effects of age differences on three attitudes that have been widely associated with the counterculture: feelings about the propriety of attempting to overthrow the government, feelings about smoking marijuana, and feelings about premarital sexual intercourse.[12] Though there were differences between younger and older people on all three attitudes, only the last (premarital sex) was able to account for the age differences in salience of faith. When we took into account differences between younger and older persons in their views about premarital sex, we found the differences in SFI scores between the young and the old were reduced by *half*. Put another way, if there had been no differences between age groups on premarital sex attitudes, the differences in commitment to confessional beliefs would have been only half as great as they actually were.[13]

Several interesting facts about the relationships between age, salience of faith, and attitudes toward premarital sex also emerged from the data. First, there was a relationship between premarital sex attitudes and SFI scores among *single* young people, but not among young marrieds. Second, the relationship was present among both males and females. And third, young people who felt that premarital sex was "always wrong" were just as likely—even somewhat more likely—to score high on salience of faith as older people who held the same views about premarital sex; whereas, by contrast, young people who gave more qualified answers concerning premarital sex were much less likely to score high on SFI than older people who gave the same answers.[14] In other words, the differences between younger and older persons on salience of faith appear to be largely attributable to the fact that young people with more tolerant attitudes toward premarital sex are considerably less likely to score high on SFI than either their counterparts who hold more strict attitudes or older people who hold either strict or tolerant attitudes.

It will perhaps seem simplistic to suggest that the current generation gap in faith may be more closely associated with such a specific matter as attitudes toward premarital sex than with a number of more sweeping social, cultural, or religious factors. But while it may be true that a host of more general factors has been responsible for the recent changes in sexual attitudes, the data show clearly that premarital sex has become a crucial issue as far as larger religious commitments are concerned.

It also bears remembering that the conflict in evidence in the data between strong religious convictions and tolerant sexual attitudes may have little to do with the social statements of the church, with its formal instruction, or with pastors' sermons, in comparison with less formal perceptions of disapproval or discomfort that young people may simply pick up or even read into their contacts with other church members.

Overall, then, our examination of the relationships between religious upbringing, social background characteristics, and salience of faith suggests that young people may be a group to whom particular attention needs to be paid if commitment to faith is to be bolstered within the laity at large. Beyond this finding, the results give little support to the idea that religious commitment is largely a product of early religious training or to the idea that it is mainly a function of one's social position.

These results also lend additional importance to the earlier findings about the relationship between religious participation and salience of faith. Those findings suggested that the church itself was an important means of reinforcing faith. In the end we were left with the suspicion, however, that something else might be going on, namely, that participation and faith might both be products of some hidden factor such as early socialization or larger social conditions. If that were the case, though, we would have found sharper relationships when we examined the effects of these factors on salience of faith. Thus, we are now in a stronger position to assert that church participation and salience of faith genuinely reinforce one another and cannot be attributed merely to some remote characteristics of the believer's biography.

The Appeal to Universal Concerns

Were we to end the analysis at this point, we would have established that sermons and other religious activities reinforce confessional beliefs; but we would have little sense of why this is so or, more specifically, of the benefits that motivate people to believe confessionally and to devote themselves to religious activities. Christian spokespersons, for their part, have always argued that there is a host of benefits to be gained from the Christian faith, including answers to questions about the meaning and purpose of life and a sense of peace with God. It is puzzling that studies of the present kind have seldom seen fit to examine these kinds of benefits as potential sources of religious commitment. As a step in this direction, we asked a number of questions about existential concerns, meaning and purpose, and other benefits so that we could investigate their relationship with individuals' commitment to faith.

The data showed that people who thought more about questions of meaning and purpose in life were more likely to be religiously committed than were people who thought less about these questions. In other words, the more oriented one was toward deeper existential concerns, the stronger one's convictions were about one's faith. One question, for example, asked laity to indicate how much they thought about "what the purpose of life is." Among those who said they thought about it "a lot," 75% scored high on the salience of faith index; by comparison, only 44% of those who said they never thought about it scored high, while 64% of those who said "some" scored high, as did 58% of those who said "a little." Other questions showed similar patterns. For instance, 74% of those who said they thought a lot about "how to live a worthwhile life" scored high on the index, compared with only 37% of those who said they thought about this question only a little. Thinking about questions such as "why there is suffering in the world" and "what happens after death" was also positively associated with high scores on the index.[15]

The data also supplied some evidence on the kinds of existential benefits that tend to be perceived in conjunction with religious faith. A set of items included in the lay questionnaire asked respondents to indicate whether or not they had experienced certain kinds of "benefits" as a consequence of their religious beliefs and activities within the past year. In general, those who scored high on the SFI were considerably more likely to say that they had experienced each of the benefits listed than were persons who scored lower on the index. For example, 85% of those who scored "very high" (3) on the index said they had experienced the benefit of "more meaning in life" many times during the past year, compared with only 44% of those who scored "very low" (0). Similarly, 90% of the former but only 43% of the latter said they had experienced "feeling at peace with God" many times. Benefits such as "freedom in Christ," "more concern for others," "comfort when I'm feeling low," "joy and excitement about being alive," and "guidance in making decisions" showed differences of comparable magnitude.[16]

These results have two rather practical implications. First, if one wanted to encourage commitment to Christian faith, a good way of proceeding, it appears, would be to stimulate thinking about deeper questions of meaning, purpose, and worth in life. The data clearly suggest that one of the reasons why some people are not particularly committed to their faith is that they are so caught up in the rudimentary details of daily life that they fail to reflect on the larger meaning of it. Second, the reason why faith, in particular, is reinforced by such reflection is that it apparently supplies answers—perhaps in the form of cognitive doctrines, but clearly in the form of existential meaning, peace, comfort, and happiness. Commitment to Christian beliefs seems to be reinforced by tangible evidence, both from one's own and from others' experience, that there are real benefits to be gained from one's faith.

In light of the fact that the larger culture characteristically portrays faith as a kind of "commitment," implying costs, sacrifices, responsibilities, and other obligations, it does not seem unreasonable to suggest that the churches could usefully place emphasis on the other side—on the existential benefits to be gained from faith.

Some Implications

The results have shown (a) that particular beliefs concerning sin, God's love, Christ, and the crucifixion are held firmly and almost universally among LCA pastors, are frequently the subject of sermons, and are reinforced by participation in formal and informal church activities; (b) that commitment to these beliefs occurs largely apart from differences in early religious training (recognizing that the present sample is relatively homogeneous with respect to certain kinds of training, such as confirmation classes), and that it cuts

across most social divisions, with the exception of being more characteristic of older persons and women than of younger persons and
men; and (c) that it is associated with concerns and benefits reflecting broad human needs for meaning and purpose in life.

Viewed as a whole, these findings suggest a certain "currency" as
far as the sources of salient faith are concerned. Those who hold
their faith to be an important part of their lives appear to do so not
simply because of having been taught to do so, nor because of having been reared in a particular socioeconomic or regional
subculture, but because of day-to-day or week-to-week participation
in church activities, exposure to sermons, thoughts about the meaning and worth of their lives, and experiences of meaning and comfort from their faith.

By inference, the results also provide a better understanding of
the near-consensus that surrounds these particular beliefs. We observed near the beginning of the chapter that about 84% of the lay
respondents subscribed to the confessional position with respect to
beliefs about the nature of Christ, the crucifixion, and God's love for
sinners (even though some held these beliefs more saliently than
others). We can now list at least three reasons for this high degree of
consensus.

First, a large majority of lay persons attend worship services every
Sunday or nearly every Sunday, and when they do, they are exposed
to sermons about these basic tenets of Christian doctrine. Pastors,
for their part, not only preach about these tenets, but believe in
them personally as well. In addition to sermons, most laity receive
reinforcement for their basic beliefs through informal interaction
with other believers and through participation in other church activities. Since most of the people with whom they interact in these capa-
cities also subscribe to the basic tenets of Christianity, these tenets
are reinforced. They may not always be reinforced by verbal articulation, but they are assumed, provide the context for other forms of
discourse, and—perhaps above all—are not likely to be openly challenged.

Put this way, the basis of consensual belief appears to be extensive
participation in a rather "closed" community of like-minded believers. This image is only partly correct. Although the data showed definite relationships between religious participation and salience of
faith, these relationships were far from perfect and, indeed, were
only moderately strong by social-science standards. Thus, for example, a third of those who attended church only once a year or less

still scored high on the SFI; six out of every ten who participated in no church activities other than worship services scored high; and nearly half of those who considered themselves inactive scored high. In other words, it was scarcely necessary to be a church leader or a constant participant in church activities to be committed to these basic beliefs.

We suspect that this finding may reflect something consistent with Lutheran theology itself. If faith and grace alone are at the heart of the church's teachings, then members need not feel that they must participate heavily in church activities in order to please God. It is possible to adhere to the core of Christian doctrine and yet to be minimally involved in the church. As a result, basic Christian beliefs can be shared consensually by members exhibiting varying levels of participation. In this sense, there is an "inclusive" quality to these beliefs.

A second source of consensus implied by the data lies in the fact that adherence to those beliefs does not seem to be contingent upon particular background experiences. These beliefs are universal enough to be shared by persons of different educational backgrounds, different ages, living in different parts of the country, and from different former denominations. Again, there is an inclusive quality that seems to cut across standard social divisions.

Finally, the evidence on existential concerns suggests that the present beliefs may be held as widely as they are because the concerns that they address are common to a broad segment of humanity. The vast majority of respondents in the study said they thought about questions concerning the worth and purpose of life, and in so doing their commitment to faith seemed to be reinforced. Furthermore, the benefits that were associated with higher levels of commitment were not the kind of experiences that might appeal only to a small subsection of the population (for example, coping with grief, better family relations, success in one's work)—though these were present—but were of sufficient generality and diversity that any person would likely find something attractive about them (meaning in life, joy, comfort, guidance, etc.).

As a major pattern in the data, therefore, we can identify a core of beliefs having to do with sin, God's love, Christ, and the crucifixion as a source of forgiveness—a core that is part of the confessional teaching of the church and is widely shared among pastors and laity alike. Commitment to this core of belief is reinforced by participation in church activities, but not to the extent of excluding those who do not participate actively. While there are many issues on which members register sharp differences (as we shall see next), this core of belief provides a basis for shared experience, communication, nurture, and unity.

SOURCES OF DOCTRINAL DIVERSITY

We are now in a better position, knowing what we do about the sources of consensual commitment, to explore the reasons for dissensus on other beliefs. The beliefs that will occupy our attention concern the meaning of faith, the best description of one's relation to God, the role of Communion as a means of forgiveness, the necessity of baptism for salvation, and the nature of Christ's presence in Communion. On the average, only 46% of the lay respondents selected the option that had been designed to best reflect the confessional view on each of these questions. The diversity of views that was manifest took the following forms.[17]

On the question about the meaning of faith, about a quarter of the laity selected the statement "a life of commitment to God that I demonstrate by trying to do what is right"; about one in ten said, "my decision to accept Christ instead of going on in my own sinful ways"; and another 10% responded, "in my view, as long as people are truly sincere in their beliefs, they show faith." In addition, therefore, to the predetermined confessional response ("my trust in God's grace"), sizable numbers emphasized "commitment," a "decision," and sincerity.

On the question about one's relation to God, almost half of the laity said that the statement "as long as I do the best I can, I feel that God cares for me and watches over me" described their relation very well and nearly a third chose this statement as the best description of their relation. Also on this question, a quarter indicated that the statement "I am absolutely certain that I am saved and that I will go to heaven when I die" described their relation to God very well and 5% chose this statement as the best description of their relation to God. These were the most frequently chosen responses other than the response that had been designed to provide the fullest expression of the traditional view ("I know that I am a sinner but God loves me and is giving me new life").

The main deviations from the predetermined confessional response on the questions about the sacraments were that a quarter of the laity thought Communion was "essential in order to receive salvation and everlasting life" (rather than simply being a way of receiving forgiveness), as did nearly half with regard to baptism, and about a fourth selected a transubstantiation view of Christ's presence in Communion rather than a Lutheran view.

We shall examine the relationships of these various responses to a number of other social and attitudinal characteristics. To minimize repetition, most of our attention will focus on the correlates of the following responses: each of the main responses to the meaning of faith question; saying that being saved and going to heaven described one's relation to God "very well"; saying that doing one's best describes one's relation to God "very well"; and saying that Communion is essential for salvation.

Social Characteristics

As with the SFI, we examined the relationships between these responses and various social factors, including age, gender, education, and region. Since the church's membership is comprised of a heterogeneous social cross section, we wanted to find out if some of the diversity evident in beliefs might be attributable to differences in social backgrounds.

The data revealed that people holding alternative doctrinal orientations did, in fact, differ in terms of social factors. Unlike the beliefs in the SFI (which for the most part cut across social divisions), the present beliefs were more closely associated with social differences.

Doctrinal responses that tended to emphasize salvation were most common among older persons, women, persons with lower levels of education, and persons living in the Midwest and South—in short, among groups that have been identified in other studies as supporters of "fundamentalist" beliefs. For example, the proportion indicating that being saved and going to heaven described its relation to God "very well" was 33% among persons over age fifty, compared with 20% among persons under age thirty; it was 33% among women, compared with 19% among men; 32% among those with a high-school education, compared with 20% among those with post-graduate training; and 33% among persons living in the South, compared with 24% among persons living in the Northeast.

Beliefs that emphasized trying to do what is right, doing one's best, and the necessity of taking Communion were also most common among older persons, among women, and among the less well educated.[18] No relationship was evident between this orientation and region.

48

In contrast to these relationships, the tendency to regard sincerity as a definition of faith was more characteristic of the young, of men, and of persons from the Northeast. There was no relationship between this orientation and level of education.[19]

These findings provide some insight into the doctrinal diversity that was manifest in the questionnaire responses. The beliefs under consideration here appear to be more closely tied to particular regional, educational, or generational subcultures than were the salience of faith items on which there was greater consensus. Holding the present beliefs appears to reflect something of the social position that one occupies in the society, such as background experiences and subcultural values, whereas salience of faith tends more nearly to be a function of one's present religious participation alone.

Religious Background

Since doctrinal orientations differ from denomination to denomination, we also wondered if different denominational backgrounds prior to becoming LCA members might explain some of the diversity in the data on belief. Only half of the laity had always been members of the LCA or a predecessor body.

Some differences by denomination were evident, but they were only partly consistent with predictions based on the particular teachings of the denominations. The most predictable patterns were differences associated with former membership in liberal or conservative denominations. For example, responses emphasizing salvation tended to be somewhat more common among persons who had been members of theologically conservative denominations (for example, former Baptists and former members of the Lutheran Church–Missouri Synod). Former Episcopalians, former Roman Catholics, and former members of the United Church of Christ tended to be somewhat below average in giving these responses. Perhaps less predictably, former Methodists were above average on these items.

Responses stressing commitment or works were most common among former Baptists, former Roman Catholics, former Methodists, and former members of the United Church of Christ; they were given less frequently than average by former members of the Luthern Church–Missouri Synod, former ALC members, and former Episcopalians. The item about the necessity of taking Communion was selected most frequently by former Roman Catholics and by former UCC members, while former Baptists and former Methodists tended to underselect it.

The view that faith could be equated with sincerity was most common among former Episcopalians and former Roman Catholics. It was least common among former Baptists. Other denominational backgrounds produced no significant variations in this response.[20]

Caution should be exercised in interpreting these results. It is reasonably certain that variations in doctrinal orientation reflect different denominational backgrounds to some degree. Since the LCA membership includes persons from many different denominational backgrounds, it is not surprising to find some diversity in theological perspectives. Beyond this general conclusion, however, inferences become risky. While particular orientations can be associated statistically with different backgrounds—as we have seen—the differences are small and the number of persons representing different denominational backgrounds is sufficiently small that one treads on shaky ground in trying to link specific beliefs with specific backgrounds.[21] It is probably best to take the findings as evidence only of a *general* relationship between religious background and doctrinal differences.

Popular Religious Culture

Another supposition that appeared to be worth exploring was that some doctrinal orientations might be associated with exposure to popular religious perspectives in the larger culture, such as those publicized on religious television programs or as part of the recent evangelical movement.[22]

One question in the survey seemed particularly appropriate for examining the effect of the broader religious culture. It asked about "religious TV programs" as one of various sources from which people might have learned about the meaning and purpose of life (the list included sermons, the Bible, Christian books, school, etc.). We suspected that people who felt that they had learned a lot from this source might be more likely to subscribe to doctrines stressing salvation and commitment than were people who haven't been as influenced by this source.[23]

The data confirmed this expectation. Nearly half of those who said they had learned "a lot" indicated that being saved and going to heaven described their relation to God very well, compared with only a fifth of those who said they had learned "nothing" from this source. The former were also more likely (46%) than the latter (27%) to say that they regarded faith as a life of commitment to God involving trying to do what is right. And 50% of the former said that taking Communion was essential in order to receive salvation, compared with only 19% of the latter.[24]

As a more direct test of popular religious culture's relationship with doctrinal orientations, we turned to some of the belief items that were mentioned in chapter 2—the Gallup question about being "born again," the Gallup question about the literal nature of the Bible, and the Glock question about the existence of the devil. These questions all dealt with religious issues that have been widely aired in the broader culture in recent years.[25]

The results indicated that persons who sided with the more "popularly religious" view on these issues were generally more likely to have given responses emphasizing salvation or commitment on the questions about faith, one's relation to God, and the sacraments than were persons who gave other responses. For example, 43% of those who took the Bible literally said they were saved and were going to heaven, compared with only 25% of those who thought the Bible was inspired but not to be taken literally. The literalists were also more likely (62%) than the nonliteralists (47%) to say that as long as they tried to do the best they could, God would take care of them. Again, more of the literalists than of the nonliteralists thought that taking Communion was essential for salvation (54% versus 22%). Similar patterns emerged in comparing those who said they had been "born again" with those who hadn't and in comparing those who were sure of the devil's existence with those who were less sure.[26]

The two findings—on the influence of religious television and the effect of popular religious beliefs—suggest that laity are by no means isolated from the larger religious culture and that their doctrinal orientations reflect this exposure. The data indicate that one of the significant reasons for diversity in doctrinal perspectives is that laity are differentially exposed and differentially influenced by the "pop theology" that is available in American culture.

Religious Participation

The results thus far may appear to say that doctrinal diversity within the church can be laid entirely at the feet of forces outside the church. This is not the case. The church also plays a role in promoting—or at least maintaining—this diversity.

After observing that participation in church activities seemed to reinforce confessional unity, we expected to find a negative relationship between participation and doctrinal responses that deviated from the predetermined confessional position. The data completely upset this expectation. For example, the most active members (using self-reported activity, which correlated highly with more specific measures of participation) were twice as likely as were the least active members to express a salvational view of faith ("my decision to accept Christ"). They were also somewhat more likely to regard themselves as saved and going to heaven (33% versus 21%). In addition, they were somewhat more likely to think that a person had to take Communion to be saved (26% versus 20%).

The responses stressing commitment or works were somewhat *less* common among active members than among inactive members. But the differences were so small that it seemed clear that activity did not particularly lead one to reject these views. A spread of only 6 percentage points separated the most active from the least active on the view that faith was a matter of trying to do what is right (24% versus 30%), and the difference with respect to thinking that God watches over those who do the best they can was only somewhat larger (44% versus 55%). Predictably, the view that sincerity was tantamount to faith was more common among the inactive than among the active.[27]

One conclusion that can be drawn from these findings is that there is as much doctrinal diversity among active laity as there is among less active members. The reason why some persons hold views that differ from the predetermined confessional response concerning faith, their relation to God, or the sacraments is *not* that they are marginally involved in the church. Even the most actively involved are likely to differ in their specific doctrinal views.

By implication, the results also suggest (in support of a conclusion drawn by Johnson, 1979) that doctrinal diversity is probably accepted, and perhaps reinforced, among those who participate in the activities of the church.[28] If there were strong pressure to conform to a particular orientation, it would seem doubtful that active participants would express other views as frequently as less active participants do. This brings us to a final finding that needs to be reported before some broader observations are developed.

The Relation between Diversity and Salience of Faith

What is the relationship between the diverse doctrinal orientations that we have just been examining and the more consensually held convictions that were discussed in the first part of the chapter? Does stronger commitment on the consensual beliefs reduce diversity on the other beliefs? Or do the core beliefs somehow allow different doctrinal orientations to be encompassed?

The data mostly suggest that a high degree of commitment on the consensual beliefs is compatible with responses stressing salvation and works orientations, but not with the response concerning sincerity as a definition of faith. Specifically, persons who scored high (3) on the SFI were more likely than those who scored low (0) to regard faith as a decision to accept Christ (12% versus 5%), and they were no less likely to regard it as a matter of trying to do what is right (23% versus 24%), despite the fact that they were much more likely on the average to subscribe to the view that faith should be regarded as "my trust in God's grace" (50% versus 15%).

The main response that the high scorers did not accept was the idea of being truly sincere. Only 3% chose this option as their definition of faith, compared with 33% of those who scored low. In brief, salience of faith was positively associated with the predetermined confessional response and with a salvational view of faith, neutral as far as a works or commitment orientation to faith was concerned, and negatively associated with a sincerity view of faith.

The other items indicated even more clearly the compatibility between alternative doctrinal orientations and salience of faith. For example, nearly half of the high scorers on the SFI subscribed to the view of being saved and going to heaven, compared with only 7% of the low scorers. Similarly, 59% of the former, compared with 39% of the latter, felt that God watches over those who do their best. And 32% of the former, compared with 10% of the latter, thought that taking Communion was essential for salvation.

The inclusive quality of the basic confessional beliefs that was noted earlier in the chapter appears to be evident as far as diversity of doctrinal orientations is concerned as well. In other words, a significant factor underlying the presence of doctrinal diversity may be the confessional teachings of the church itself. Although these teachings prescribe particular views of faith, of one's relation to God, and of the sacraments, they also provide latitude for other interpretations. In short, the data point ultimately to a kind of paradox. The nature of the paradox now warrants some discussion.

FAITH AND DOCTRINE

The fact that there was a relatively high degree of consensus surrounding certain beliefs and considerable diversity on others led us to conduct separate examinations of the two sets of beliefs to see what might underlie these differences. For the most part, the findings themselves have been predictable. The beliefs examined in the first part of the chapter largely cut across divisions owing to social and religious backgrounds (with the exception of age differences). Those examined in the second half of the chapter turned out to be more closely associated with these social divisions and with the subcultures corresponding to them. Different doctrinal responses were given by members of different educational, regional, age, and gender groups and by persons having formerly belonged to different denominations. The first set of beliefs was closely associated with participation in church activities, such that greater participation seemed to reinforce greater commitment or salience. The second set of beliefs showed as much diversity among active church participants as among inactive members. This set of beliefs also seemed to be susceptible to influences from the religious media and the larger religious culture. Finally, the data suggested that holding alternative doctrinal orientations was not reduced by strong commitment to the more consensual confessional beliefs and, on occasion, was positively associated with such commitment. Overall, the diversity observed in definitions of faith, in views about one's relation to God, and in views of the sacraments appears to be rooted both in factors outside the church and in the character of the teachings and practices of the church itself. It is the latter that is most relevant to theological discussion.

The paradox noted above concerns the relationship between faith and doctrine. It can be described from the standpoint of the church as an institution or from the perspective of the individual believer. In either case, we must, of course, go beyond what the results themselves can demonstrate and enter the realm of interpretation. Doing so will serve its intended purpose if it invites further reflection.

From the standpoint of the church as an institution, the paradox of faith and doctrine manifests itself in a diversity of doctrinal orientations that, on the one hand, may be regarded as clear departures from the confessional teachings of the church, but which, on the other hand, appear to be tolerated if not reinforced by these very confessional teachings. More specifically, the church places fundamental emphasis on "faith and grace alone" and in so doing rejects—unlike many fundamentalist groups—requirements of strict conformity to a list of particular doctrines or beliefs. In consequence, as manifested clearly in the data, there is much diversity of doctrine even among the most active members and among those for whom Christian faith is most salient. The paradox is that some of these doctrinal orientations pose clear departures from an exclusive emphasis on faith (insofar, for example, as they make salvation contingent upon the sacraments, upon works, or upon a discrete conversion experience). In this sense, yet ironically, the doctrine of faith is compatible with the presence of alternative doctrines, even those that appear contradictory to it.

The paradox is genuine at the institutional level—which is the reason for characterizing it from the standpoint of the church as an institution—whether it is genuine at the theological level or not. At the institutional level, it results in a situation that defies ordinary models of generating institutional commitment. These models (as developed particularly in the sociological literature on organizations) regard compliance with institutional expectations as a function of rewards and punishments; that is, an institution encourages its members to conform to prescribed doctrines and values by rewarding those who conform and by withholding rewards from (or punishing) those who do not. The doctrine of faith defies this logic because it strips away the institution's capacity to manipulate the ultimate reward—salvation. If one's relationship to God is based exclusively on faith and grace, then the church can legitimately make no demands of its members concerning this relationship—no demands of participation, no demands concerning proper beliefs, no demands even that one believe exclusively in the church's doctrine of faith.

In this regard, the church that emphasizes faith is much akin to the society that is based on democratic principles. In neither case can the ultimate sanction be used. Salvation cannot be held ransom by the church to promote conformity to faith, nor can freedom be taken away by the society from those who deviate from its norms of democracy. Both, as Luther recognized for faith and as Jefferson proclaimed for democracy, must be built primarily on understanding rather than on constraint. And by implication, of course, the teaching function of the church becomes paramount.

From the standpoint of the individual believer, the paradox of faith and doctrine is also genuine and, the data suggest, precariously resolved. If faith and grace are sufficient for salvation, the believer's participation in church activities and his or her conformity to church teachings must be motivated by "desire," not by fear of losing favor with God, nor by hopes of being able to prove one's righteousness or religiosity. In the culture at large, however, merit (and, in turn, self-

55

worth) is based heavily on performance. This performance-reward mentality, it appears, spills over into the realm of faith, resulting in pressures to participate, to believe properly, and in other ways to demonstrate one's religious commitment.

In keeping with this argument, we have seen two pronounced tendencies in the data. First, there is a tendency for beliefs to be held that "add" other requirements for salvation (works being the clearest example). Second, there is a tendency for these beliefs to be *positively* associated with religious participation. In short, many believers apparently feel pressure to go beyond faith, particularly by adopting beliefs that give greater legitimacy to their own works (including church participation). Accordingly, the data showed that many of the more active laity in the sample departed from purely confessional responses, as predetermined in designing the questions, and selected instead doctrinal options that attached greater emphasis to works and to salvation.

Given the pressures prevailing in the larger culture to prove one's worth by performance, it seems less than surprising to find the same tendencies within the church as well. If the present data are any indication, however, these pressures are not likely to come entirely from outside the church. If doctrines stressing performance of one kind or another are adopted by the most active participants within the church, there will be social pressures to "prove" one's religiosity among church members as well. Again, care in communicating an understanding of the nature of faith appears to be of utmost importance.

A final caveat is in order: by pointing out the paradox between faith and doctrine, we do not mean to suggest that large segments of the laity betrayed a confessional understanding of faith. The data suggest tendencies. But survey results are poorly suited to making judgments about motivations and subtleties of understanding.

4

A Theological Perspective

LYMAN LUNDEEN

Our purpose in this chapter is to initiate some theological reflection on the survey study of religious belief and experience. The concern will be to provide a theological perspective on that research and, in so doing, to encourage discussion of the relevance of such empirical study for the life and program of the church. What is offered is a framework in which the concrete questions and responses can be discussed. Certain issues involved in the use and interpretation of the data will also be indicated. There is no intention to exhaust or provide a finished discussion of these matters, nor even to offer an adequate assessment of the entire theological import of this particular research project.

The task here has been described as an exploration of continuities between the research and our confessional heritage. Therefore, the theological perspective utilized will draw largely on the Lutheran confessional writings and the priorities reflected in them. These confessional concerns can quickly be identified as growing out of the Lutheran Reformation, but they are seen as fundamental Christian claims about God and his relationship to humankind. Such emphases are taken to be central implications of the gospel of Jesus Christ, which are "normed" by the Scriptures and relevant to the entire catholic church. In many instances, these Lutheran concerns are patently Christian ones that are already shared by a broad spectrum of the Christian community.

For the sake of structured progression of this chapter, the discussion will proceed in the following sequence. First, a theological perspective will be developed in which general considerations about this kind of empirical research will be briefly noted. Secondly, certain aspects of this particular study will be assessed and interpreted. In this latter part, Wuthnow's chapter 3 will receive attention as he attempts to sort out and project some implications of the data.

Theological conversation with social-science researchers has always seemed highly desirable. Frequently such dialogue has occurred only after the fact. Here it can be appreciated that theological concerns were raised and discussed even as the project was being formulated. Consultation with representative theologians is a real advance over some previous attempts to gain empirical access to dynamics of faith in the lives of people. One does not want to discount the importance of such cooperation in this particular study. Getting theologians and empirical researchers together has great promise for both parties. Theology has much to learn from the problems it confronts in discourse about specific methods and assessment of results. By the same token, social science benefits from more careful consideration of its use of terms, survey data, and interpretation in the theological arena.

It is also important, however, to recognize how such conversation concerning social-science research is a continuing project. One is not finished with the matter simply by consulting a select group of theologians at the outset and then proceeding to view the procedures adopted and the resulting conclusions as "blessed" with some abiding theological dependability. The dialogue needs to go on. What is learned by this empirical study, then, focuses not merely on the people questioned, but also on the researchers themselves (both theologians and social scientists), their methods and ways of developing conclusions. The value of this study is in fact the grist it provides for further reflection and study—not merely a set of results based on "hard" data.

The comments offered here are intended to further just this kind of ongoing discussion. They will therefore note both positive reactions to the study and concerns about concepts, distinctions, and interpretations. Theological perspective will be seen as opening up questions as well as affirming valid or interesting conclusions.

SOME THEOLOGICAL CONCERNS

Faith and Belief

The phrase "religious belief" figures prominently in this research project. The purpose is to get at the actual beliefs of church members. The first step in dealing with these matters requires a careful look at the relationship of "belief" and "faith." Involved in that relationship is some comprehension of the complexity of human experience and an indication of certain peculiarities of the understanding of "God" in a Christian frame of reference.

In our confessional movement theologians have frequently distinguished conscious, cognitive components of belief or intellectual assent from the deeper and broader reality of faith as fundamental trust. Beliefs about God have not been separated from faith, but they have been treated as important and partial reflections of that basic relationship which determines the whole thrust of human life. So beliefs, while important, are also potentially distortive, as they can be mistaken for faith itself. What people accept intellectually, recognize in propositions, or speak of as more or less certain or doubtful, can become an interpretation of faith which strains out its living dynamics and conceptual inconsistencies.

Working with statements about faith requires conscious recognition of the confessional appreciation of faith as trust, and attention to the relationship with God is not the product of speculation but occurs enmeshed in historical contexts. It is not one factor alongside all the others, but one that, at least eschatologically, moves toward the total domination of all the rest. It has comprehensive, holistic implications. It includes unconscious as well as conscious factors. Therefore, what is said in response to specific verbal queries can reflect very different features of the life of faith. It can indicate misunderstanding of the words. It can draw on perceptions of what might be overemphasized. It can indicate the actual struggle between "faiths" that persists in the lives of Christians.

Faith and Identity

One way of talking about faith is to see it as the shape of human response to the identity questions—"Who am I and what is my place in the cosmos?" Such faith is not necessarily Christian, but some faith is necessary even for those who do not consciously address this question. The issue of faith, then, allows no ultimate neutrality or postponement. It always stretches beyond the available evidence toward the future and toward the boundaries of life and reality. It is risky and partial. As people live out their day-to-day existence they are compelled to trust—in one way or another. In this sense, they have their identity in the world as they take their place and assume a posture toward life itself. The necessity of some kind of faith and the consequent influence of various "functional" gods in human life put the whole business of religious belief in a different perspective.

We can expect belief statements to reveal something of faith posture, but the depth of that reality and the intensity of the struggles involving it will lead us to be quite cautious about smoothing out all the "roughness" or identifying simple causes. Without our ever intending it, faith can be treated as assent to intellectual propositions and such consistency may be expected on this level that the actual character of Christian faith will be distorted. It is therefore of crucial importance that matters of faith not be reduced to the kind of objective cause-and-effect analysis that may suit issues that are somewhat more distant from the core of human identity.

Faith as Necessity

It is fair to say that in the Scriptures the God-relationship is treated as unavoidable. Even when unbelief is spoken of it is in a framework where humans are seen as trusting in idols rather than the true God. Every person is seen as dealing with their creator—whether they like it or not, whether they talk about it in God-language or not. The issue in the biblical witness is then very clearly focused on the *particular* God in which people trust.

Luther picks up this interpretation. He expresses it clearly and influentially in his explanation to the First Commandment in his Large Catechism. For him, the very definition of the word "god" comes down to the focus of human trust. What people depend on, care about, and serve is their "god." By implication, there is no way to live without ultimate dependence and concern with respect to some god. To have faith in Christ, then, is to trust the god we meet in him as the "true God" who does not disappoint our hope but does, in fact, fulfill his promises.

The theological issue is not *whether* people believe in god, but *which* god is gaining dominance in their lives. The necessary relationship to God implies some response, making faith a far more intimate reality than that which can be discussed in terms of intellectual certainty or skepticism. Indeed, from a Christian point of view, until the end of history our identity reflects a struggle between gods, from which not even the most exalted saint is exempt. Faith does not imply fixed positions, certainly not neutrality in contrast to commitment. Instead, we are dealing with a living interplay of struggling influences. As Kierkegaard noted, even Christians are really people who are "becoming" Christian.

This understanding of faith and God has some direct implications for empirical study. It does not deny the value of such study, provided we do not assume access to final judgments. It can be an encouragement for us to look at the concrete reports of individuals concerning their understanding and experience. As evangelical Christians we will be especially mindful of the tendency of rational efforts to slip over into ultimate matters. We will be alert to speculative types of questions that make faith too much like an external, abstract reality. We will attend to the ways in which the search for intellectual consistency can make our treatment of faith superficial—and far more subject to human control than our faith posture allows. We will be suspicious of our own attempts to remove Christians from the concrete struggles of life in which "gods" and "faiths" persist in conflict.

In this broad theological frame, the care of the researchers in some of these matters is notable. The tentative character of conclusions is lifted up. The complexity of the subject matter is acknowledged. Still, as "social scientists" and "theologians," it is well for all of us to be reminded of the way our best concern turns out to delude us on exactly the issues we care about so much. That is a theological caveat that needs to be kept in view.

The Limits of Research

Already we have a positive and negative way of looking at this research in a theological perspective. We can be alert to insights gained as well as temptations to prove too much.

Positively, given the comprehensive importance of the faith relationship, we can expect it to be reflected in our use of words and concepts. Faith is not so inaccessible that verbal expressions are irrelevant. Reports of "what" is believed are significant even if not final. The apparent contradictions in people's lives can serve to advance our understanding while they frustrate pure logic. Further, since the God-relationship is inevitable in some form, we can anticipate (as the study does) that any human being will have significant experience of the God-relationship to express. We will then move from the "propositions of belief" to concern for the alternative forms of faith that may be reflected in both secular and religious encounters.

Negatively, we will not be overly impressed with the fact that these studies were done in consultation with theologians or that they have some "social-science" weight behind them. We will seek to learn more about the distortions of the research at the same time as we seek insights into the situations of the responders. There are theological reasons for not expecting too much from the data—and for being somewhat suspicious of our own exultation over insights apparently corroborated.

Taking these together, the positive and the negative, let me propose that we look for helpful approximations. Let us consider suggestive implications that are interesting ways of looking at the human situation. We may proceed heuristically, allowing data and tentative conclusions to point toward new perspectives. There are plenty of penultimate insights which can be instrumental in serving the ultimate. We can be helped toward responsible decisions precisely because we recognize the limits of our methods. Those limits are not simply given by the current state of social science or computer capability. They are understood in the very faith which frees us to use reason and calculation (as a kind of alien work of God) in order to give order and press people toward deeper realities. Our performance in careful study can never become the fulcrum on which faith rests.

BROAD CONFESSIONAL IMPLICATIONS

The fact that we are working in a confessional framework will give some impetus and direction to this sort of empirical study. The very fact that confession is seen as important shows confidence that faith can be shared and that words about God are of vital importance. What we say about God makes a difference, or no confession would matter. The depth and dynamic character of the God-relationship is not the denial of the importance of conscious, thoughtful speech about God. In our heritage, the fact that so much is made of the apostolic witness, the confessional writings, and proclamation should drive us to talk about faith—perhaps even into careful research into the way people tend to respond to verbally stated questions and alternatives. If faith precludes neutrality, then attention to the way people sort out a set of limited options has the potential for revealing much about their understanding and commitment.

Making much of a confessional heritage has sometimes seemed to mean that faith could be reduced to written statements. Get it put right and you've settled it once and for all. That's the way many people have acted and been perceived when the confessional element was emphasized. Just as some treat the Bible as a collection of infallible sentences, many have taken a confessional posture to mean total confidence in words as exact expressions of divine truth. The understanding of God and faith given above ought to counter this, but explicit reference to certain implications of our confessional posture may carry us a bit further.

Confessions and Experience

Confessing is fundamentally an activity of people. The words people speak or write are important as they indicate intention, deep feeling, and context. What the words say reflects direction and orientation. It indicates a perspective on life. The words count or else silence would take the place of confession. Such confession is clearly dependent on experience. It reports what has happened to people. It is also put forward as capable of leading to further experience as confessing illuminates, challenges, modifies, and even transforms the lives of others. Scripture, creeds, confessional books, preaching, and all forms of Christian witness are essentially testimony about what has been in some way encountered by people and is relevant to the experience of others. In this sense, confession invites inquiry into experience. It does not glorify all experience as equally important, but it does make human experience the arena and medium in which God is revealed. The issue here is not whether we should proceed with empirical study, but how and how much? The conscious emphasis on experience in this study has the potential to assist us in recovering an appreciation of the existential relevance of confessions and other doctrinal formulations.

We could note here the descriptive function of the confessional writings themselves. As reports of what is taught in the evangelical churches of the Reformation period, they are a kind of empirical reference which has since been used as a check on the teaching of the church. In describing the teaching and practice of the Reformation church, these documents elevate both key doctrines and their impact on human life for further consideration. They do not offer the choice of words or reality but hold before us the concrete emergence of verbal formulation from the struggles of life.

Confessions Point Beyond Themselves

It is important here to see how both the confessions and Scriptures relativize themselves. Each points toward relationships which transcend their own formulations. Confessions refer to Scriptures and their central message. What is lifted up is a relationship to Christ that shapes human identity. In a similar way, the Scriptures provide us with a central message that goes beyond their pages. In both cases, the reference beyond verbal formulation makes just

63

those texts important as vehicles and norms. Thus in utilizing an empirical study there are ways to see us pursuing a descriptive function which can be an aid in proclamation. The way we understand the confessions can provide a pattern in which an approach to empirical study of "confessing" Christians can be developed and assessed. This empirical study, for example, can show us certain levels of our contemporary situation. By the questions we ask, the options we offer, and the responses we collect, we can gain partial indications of the current challenge we face to be faithful to God's work in Christ. These empirical approximations can serve as helpful tools for dealing tentatively but also tenaciously with both the realities of our situation and our inherited forms of "confessional" truth.

Confessions as Contextual

Taking the people who confess into account, along with their experience, requires a further appreciation of actual contexts. Confessions (like Augsburg and Westminster) are expressions of the shape faith took in a particular time and place. They interpret faith over against the alternatives then seen as operative. They are limited by the political, economic, conceptual, and linguistic resources of that situation. This ought to free us to look for new resources in our context. It ought to make us particularly alert to the way people perceive the options they affirm or reject. In this sense, the form of multiple-choice questions has a kind of confessional warrant.

Taking contexts seriously presents difficulties for many people in relation to faith. They wonder if all dependability will not collapse in a sea of sheer relativity. It needs to be clear that the confessional appreciation of contexts is not extreme relativism where no positions matter. Instead, it is a way of seeing and expressing stable relationships and truth in changing situations. Our confessions assert that the same faith alternatives can be recognized, articulated, and understood across spatial, temporal, and cultural barriers. The contextualism implied leaves us the task of saying old things in new ways. It frees us to connect up with our experience so that we can trace the outlines of the key alternatives as they touch our own time and place.

Confessions, then, are testimony to a shared experience that allows communal expression and identity. Faith is a reality that we can talk about together. It is something we can identify and which enables us to discriminate rejected alternatives. Documents such as the Formula of Concord express a consensus about faith. They are an invitation into community where a certain range of agreement and variation is anticipated. The character of this agreement and the nature of the limits of disagreement will need to be established anew in each era. Just as the confessions see faith as dependent on daily renewal, so our doctrinal heritage requires reappropriation as we move through radical shifts of culture and experience.

LUTHERAN CONFESSIONAL PRIORITIES

We can also take a look at the specific priorities in the Lutheran confessions as collected in *The Book of Concord* and give further precision to our perspective on empirical study in general and this study in particular.

The simplest summary of Lutheran priorities is the formula "justification by grace." More carefully, this gets expressed as "justification by grace through faith in Jesus Christ." One wants to be very cautious not to make faith itself a work, and to ensure that grace is not an abstract principle but firmly tied to the person and work of Jesus. This central confessional priority is, as many have noted, a claim about the character of the Christian faith and not merely a kind of denominational preference.

For our purposes, this summary needs further development toward a cluster or constellation of priorities. I would put forward four commitments of central importance.

Justification

The centrality of justification apart from works of the law lifts up the law/gospel distinction as a key consideration. The proper distinction between law and gospel is a decisive Lutheran confessional priority, even though many of us may be uncomfortable with the language and use of this distinction. A proper distinction differentiates sharply between works and grace (or law and gospel) as means of salvation. Human wholeness and fulfillment is not accomplished by making performance the key.

A proper distinction also recognizes that law and gospel cannot be separated. What will not work as a means of salvation is still seen as God's word of demand. The law then needs to be retained, but not allowed to usurp God's "proper" work of grace. In other words, the law has a very important place—even for Christians who are in the most important sense freed from any dependence on works. The elevation of grace as God's fundamental will does not take out of that will the firmness of opposition to sin and expectation of love and justice in the human situation. Speak of it as the third use or as the first, the law continues in some fashion to be relevant to Christians—at least insofar as they are still sinners. The proper distinction between law and gospel turns out to be not just a distinction. It is also some kind of future-oriented arrangement of these two words of God in a living dialectic.

The importance of this for empirical study is the continuing tension between sin and grace that is expected in the life of the Christian. This is expressed in the descriptive phrase *simul justus et peccator* (at the same time righteous and sinner). Sin being the tendency to let idols take over the very center of life, you have the most persistent sort of ambiguity in the life of the Christian. Even consistent trust in God's grace seems out of the question. This prohibits any dependence on performance for salvation. It also leads us to expect signs of works-righteousness in the best Christians. It certainly prohibits any exact empirical recognition of "real" Christians on the basis of the consistency of their lives.

What we have here is one central expression of a theology of grace which finds God at work precisely in the residual ambiguities of human life, where dependable achievement and absolute clarity are not reliable. This has epistemological and behavioral implications alongside of the theological. It has led persons in the Lutheran confessional heritage to stress paradox, experiential dissonance, eschatological expectation, and a whole range of positions in a pattern similar to *simul justus et peccator*. We always know "in part," and just that kind of knowledge is seen as sufficient for those who continually depend on forgiveness. The claim of Christ (and the claim of the Christian church) is therefore hidden in weakness and persistent contrast. The depth and dynamic character of the faith relationship will simply not come out of hiding to be put at the disposal of our techniques or turned into a matter of our control and performance.

This concern for the contrast between grace and works is now being intentionally brought into empirical studies. That certainly is an advance over the equation of orthodox faith with a rigid acceptance of the right propositions. It is also a more difficult thing to do than we may have anticipated. Taken seriously, it may lead us beyond the obvious "works" orientations, like pride in a "born-again" experience or one-time decision. It will lead us to look with concern at Christians who take the gospel to mean "doing my best." It will also draw our attention to the ecclesiastical expectation that all Christians should be able to identify "grace" responses on demand, and with a consistency that is overly impressive.

Affirmation of Particularity

A second facet of the confessional content that I would stress is its emphasis on particulars. One could say that in our confessional posture Jesus Christ is the most radical affirmation of historical particularity that we can imagine. To say that God saves "once and for all" on account of Christ's work in an unrepeatable event is both a scandal to abstract reasoning and a liberating new departure. The law always affirms the universal over against the particular. As a tempting form of idolatry it offers sheer conformity as the way of salvation. The "gospel of grace," on the other hand, is the definitive expression of God's capacity and will to appreciate the particular. In Jesus of Nazareth this is made effective in history in the one event on which the salvation of the world turns. The significance of Christ's decisive cross is new life and acceptance for diverse human beings who are no longer bound to coerced conformity but free to live and act in their special context of responsibility.

So one can see confessionally both the unique significance of Jesus and God's dependable appreciation of diversity in the message of grace. It is just this emphasis on historical particularity that gives the gospel message its character of "good news." Justification by grace apart from works of the law is a new kind of liberating authority. Each person is unique in the eyes of God. This is the collapse of destructive comparisons on the basis of behavioral competition. It is a call to let pretense fall and live lovingly in our actual context.

This emphasis on particularity in the gospel gives a strong emphasis to investigate carefully discriminated data. It is theological justification and motivation for looking and listening carefully. However, it also raises our awareness that by treating responses as discrete and separable we wrench them from the context of relationships that make them possible and intelligible.

We can look more carefully at this affirmation of diversity. Since consensus and diversity are key considerations in Wuthnow's analysis in chapter 3, it is important for us to see how they fit with confessional expectations.

There is a kind of interdependence or circularity here that needs to be surfaced. Agreement on the importance of Christ turns out to be the basis for our freedom to disagree and differ on many other items. So consensus about the centrality of God's grace in Jesus liberates one to accept a broad range of variation on all other issues. Consensus and diversity thereby go together. The issue is made more complex than it appears at the outset.

We could say, then, that consensus about the saving Christ event requires an appreciation of diversity on several levels. First, conceptual theological interpretations of Jesus cannot be forced into a single mold. As the four Gospels reflect four theological perspectives, so we can anticipate that a faithful confessional posture will allow and even encourage a variety of conceptual developments. Not all theological differences turn out to be decisive or divisive. The reality of grace in Jesus Christ allows considerable variation in the way we choose to think it through. Consider the contrast between an Aristotelian "substance"-oriented theology and an existential "presence" approach. There are strengths and weaknesses in both these conceptual schemes, and they both have been more or less effective vehicles for the expression of a theology of grace. It turns out that there are no perfect conceptual systems any more than Christians have been able to perform up to an absolute standard in other areas of human behavior. The demand for a single theological mode of expression is in this sense on a par with other forms of legalism encountered and rejected in the history of faith.

This is not to say there are no limits. Obviously some conceptual interpretations of the gospel will be worse than others, some even hopeless deviations. Surely salvation by doing my best is one of these. Nevertheless, the emphasis on justification by grace requires that we not depend on the perfection of a singular "best" conceptual scheme. Confessionally, grace liberates people to think things through afresh, and the result is considerably more diversity than institutions and individuals are inclined to expect.

Secondly, diversity in concept also means diversity in language. Consensus about Christ is the affirmation of convictions that can be articulated in different ways. As the study here surfaces people's tendencies to state things differently, we can conclude that there is some deviation from a monolithic confessional base or we can be led to look again at the complex freedom which our particular confessions offer. Different ways of saying things are not an automatic clue to heresy or doctrinal deviation. We need to be very much alert to the way that words function as "flags" to identify friend or foe, with little understanding of what was actually intended by the expressions. Such a competitive use of "labels" is another way of slipping into a performance-oriented faith. Here I am appreciative of this study's attempt to get some glimpse through personal interviews of the way respondents actually approach the issues.

Such diversity in language need not lead us to give up the task of considering "better" or "worse" statements any more than grace means the total obliteration of "good works." It will mean that we recognize a range of decent answers and that we treat deviance from our norms in a thoughtful way, considering both the individual's context and the dynamic of *simul justus et peccator*. It is important for people to recognize more helpful answers even if they cannot be used as a basis to judge definitely concerning ultimate commitments.

A third form of diversity that our confessions expect is more broadly behavioral and moral. Consensus about Christ does not mean exact agreement about ethical issues or political solutions. It comes as no surprise that there is diversity about social issues and the church's role in them. Indeed, the interesting problem that may be surfaced by this study is the insistent demand for uniformity on ethical issues that seems to come from two directions. One demand for conformity may be seen in a kind of conservatism in the church itself. Another similar demand may come from academic researchers, both social scientists and theologians, who can expect consensus about God's love to lead to very specific social and political postures. The point here is that confessional consensus affirms more diversity than either of the above tendencies.

A fourth form of diversity is of special import in relation to this study. Wuthnow concludes in chapter 3 that consensus on core doctrines is compatible with or at least tolerates deviation on such a central issue as grace and works. It needs to be noted here that confessional theology makes deviation on just this issue something that is expected to persist in the lives of Christians. Sin in the lives of believers is reflected precisely in behavior and statements that reflect their tendency to distort and betray God's grace. The church must tolerate deviation or the message of grace will be lost in another type of works-righteousness. At the same time, this deviation must be continually identified as such or the message will lose its unique meaning.

In our recognition of persistent diversity in concept and expression we need to be reminded that there is one word that stands both in judgment and affirmation of the church's common life. That is the doctrine of grace—which is itself the basis of our freedom to affirm diversity.

One could conclude from the above that diversity and consensus are concepts that are to be filled in with specific content in order to be meaningful. This study may be a partial step in that direction by holding up some empirical examples of both for further consideration.

The External Word

A third aspect of our confessional posture that we need to recognize is the emphasis on the "external word." In this perspective salvation comes through those relationships where God can address us from outside the limits of our personal experience. We are not only dependent on grace, not only saved by a historic event in the past, but also given a new situation by a communication on the lips of our neighbor. It is our theological conviction that faith is dependent on the hearing of the word—not just in the formal context of worship or sermon—but in some kind of contact with the testimony of another person.

This gives a relational character to the Christian faith. It makes the fact of human interdependence an example of the way we are dependent on God's own initiative. We never get to the point where we have our faith by ourselves. When we come together on Sunday morning we make the sermon a crucial focus of our gathering. An ordinary human being is expected to speak God's message. Since it is a message of grace, the preacher can be both human and sinner. The whole person becomes a part of the message. What happens in that churchly context is a paradigm for the way that same word is carried from one to another in the day-to-day "consolation of the brethren."

You have here the elevation of human words as vehicles for communicating the gospel. They are not words in isolation from physical and nonverbal elements, but without the words the particularity of Jesus would soon be lost. So in the confessions both the office of the ministry and the sacraments are constituted by their connection with the word of the gospel.

This elevation of spoken words encourages us to expect verbal and conceptual understanding of the message even if this does not give us final access to the interior life of persons or the "last judgment" on their faithfulness. It enables us in an empirical study to look for such recognition and to take seriously both apparent understanding of the gospel and apparent distortion of it.

Focus on the external word as one message also leads us to be careful about equating the content of faith with a collection of discrete propositions. We are pressed toward patterns of response, the tracing of histories and types, and various ways of seeing unity in the data. There is much more to be said on this issue, but Wuthnow's efforts in patterning the data around confessional priorities is intriguing. This takes seriously the way the precise responses are indicators of living reality at the same time as it anticipates identifiable directions and forms of response.

A stress on the external word theologically also brings in a corrective to the way some questions are asked. The way people come to faith is in fact a matter of faith. They can report what has seemed helpful. However, to assume that people can identify just what led them to certain commitments is its own form of rationalism. In our confessional movement, we believe that people come to faith by hearing the word of and about Jesus. That will put some built-in limitations on the capacity of a study like this to tell us how we might propagate the faith. It may also free us to measure and assess secondary influences that bring people to pay attention to our message. There are many influences we can identify and measure. More often than not, such influences are likely to be preliminary. They answer the question "how can we get people's attention?" rather than providing an empirical technique for bringing people to faith. Confessionally, the expectation that "hearing the gospel" produces faith is itself a "core" doctrine. We believe it whether or not the current evidence seems to run against it.

Universality

Finally, a word about universality in the confessional posture is important. While the emphasis on Christ has an exclusive thrust, the church is viewed as an event which is not exactly coterminous with any given institution or "special" periods of history. In Article VII of the Augsburg Confession there is a clear indication that where people preach, hear, and believe the word—there is the church. Along with this is expressed the conviction that one church exists throughout our history. Article VII has the great advantage of exalting a church that is bigger than any single institutional manifestation and more dependable than any "golden" age that can be isolated. One would expect, then, that confessional Lutherans would be convinced of the importance of Christ but also open to let that conviction lead them beyond the boundaries of institution or denomination. This openness, however, would not be without limits because the claim of Christ does matter and carries its own exclusive edge.

71

We might say that confessional priorities could be expected to make inclusiveness and exclusiveness a contextual and dialectical affair. It will not be simply a question of being open to worship with all others or closed to such collaboration. It is likely to be both, depending on the circumstances and convictions involved. Confessionally, being Christian is surely more fundamental than being labeled Lutheran. However, there comes a point where an emphasis on works and other "lords" will not be easily acceptable.

Similarly, in regard to evangelization efforts, we would expect in a church that prizes grace that there would be at least the hope that God would deal graciously with all people. Confidence in a gracious God would likely set limits so that God would not be overly dependent on our performance and that the message of grace in Christ would also not become superfluous. The very character of our confessions leads us to be very serious about sharing the grace of God which is crucial for salvation. At the same time, that grace is not our possession or strictly under our control. If evangelization means imposing our faith, the element of control is again decisive. A gracious gospel implies more graciousness about evangelistic efforts than has often been the case.

What I have tried to do here is trace some confessional convictions that give us perspective on this study. It is appropriate now to pay more direct attention to our particular research project and its concrete indicators.

FOCUS ON THE
"RELIGIOUS BELIEF AND EXPERIENCE" RESEARCH

With respect to the specific data unearthed by this research project, I will proceed in a very selective way. I have assumed that it is more important for data to be interesting and thought-provoking than conclusive. It has also been indicated that scientific data says as much about the investigators as it does about those investigated. I would therefore expect that responsible consideration of this project would shed light on our ways of researching as well as on the situation of the responders.

Consensus

First, let me pick up the important perception that both laity and clergy in this study manifest a high degree of consensus on crucial confessional items. One can find that consensus on numerous questions where almost all or a majority of the respondents seem to move in a common direction. It is encouraging to see that so many can recognize the more confessionally adequate responses and that they feel these responses describe their faith. The most important consensus I find is on faith as trust and the relationship to God as an ongoing "journey" within God's love (tables 4 and 1). I would also cite the almost unanimous recognition of the cross of Jesus as meaningful (table 2). These points of agreement surely fit with our confessional understanding and give reason for identifying certain "gospel-oriented" reactions on the part of the group studied.

There also seems to be a clear consensus on the relevance of experience in the responders. For the most part they report rich experiential indications of the relevance of faith in their lives (appendix 2). At the very least, they are not adverse to speaking of faith and experience. We can note in this connection the inability of large numbers of laity to translate their experience into the crucial terms of "forgiveness" and rather standard terminology which may indicate that there is a large educational task to be accomplished even where a faith "consensus" may exist (L–Q11). One would also wonder a bit about the role of "nature" as a vehicle for redemptive revelation.

While it is true, as Wuthnow indicates, that nature has sometimes been treated positively as a vehicle for revelation, the standard confessional position is that nature by itself reveals only law or wrath. Seen through the eyes of a Christian, nature can be interpreted redemptively, but there needs to be a crucial distinction made here between two ways that God is present to human beings. In a framework where God is both judge and savior, it is not enough to investigate the experience of God or presence in a blanket fashion. The same sensitivity that is shown in this study on the works/grace contrast needs to be more evident here.

I want to raise some further questions about the apparent consensus. In some cases, what appears to be agreement may be the result of the way questions are framed or the comparative adequacy of the alternatives presented. An example of the first sort of problem is the consensus about "believing that God exists with very few doubts" (table 8). The speculative character of this question either makes one wonder what it is the respondents are agreeing about or whether their consensus is in fact a good thing from a confessional point of view. We can recall that, confessionally, "which" god people worship is the decisive issue. Fortunately, this question is not used to identify a confessional core of beliefs, but the focus on accepting the two natures of Christ with no doubts has a similar difficulty (table 2). An example of the second type of problem can be seen in the answers concerning the reason for Jesus' death on a cross (table 2). Here the alternatives are minimally attractive so that agreement may mean less than it appears to indicate. In other words, even a good confessional answer loses something if the alternatives are not somewhat attractive. Perhaps what is needed is further consideration of the way we ask questions and recognition of the peculiar problems presented by the popular multiple-choice format.

There are broader ways of getting at these problems in apparent consensus. The value of absolute certainty is one of these. It tends to be assumed by the questions as a confessional priority and an indicator of the strength of commitment. It is a problem because it may be in fact the elevation of a narrow scientific concern over the way faith understands itself as involving risk and struggle. If this is the case, precisely what is taken as gospel consensus can reflect something quite different both in the questions and the responses; then the apparent consensus is something other than a cause for celebration. It can have the benefit of driving us back to the drawing boards to reconsider our own way of researching these issues.

The influence of doubt or degrees of certainty has been minimized in the final interpretation of the data, but it still plays a subtle role in the form of questions and in the general scientific framework within which the study proceeds. The two natures of Christ questions (table 2) and the Apostles' Creed sequence (table 3) would be prominent examples.

This issue needs to be surfaced because the contrast of certainty and doubt runs head on into a very central theological problem. A grace-oriented theology has problems with theoretical certainty as a positive indicator of faith and, conversely, the persistence of theoretical doubt is not necessarily negative. It is too easy for theoretical certainty to become a rationalistic works-orientation so that doubt becomes a failure to perform adequately. What is taken to be an indicator of one orientation has a surprising capacity to turn into its opposite. Thus absolute certainty about the existence of God, my own salvation, the literal truth of the Bible, and the two natures of Christ can be seen as hiding a defensive "works" posture.

This same theological issue dovetails with an inherent weakness of scientific methods when applied to matters of faith. Science values predictability, control, and certainty. It is very easy for these norms to usurp those of grace when the methods conflict with crucial features of the data. So, while we can explicitly acknowledge problems with doubt and certainty as indexing factors, those features of this kind of study have pervasive and subtle influences that will need further attention.

Some of the persistent influences of this kind of mind-set are easily identified in this study. For example, in regard to the full humanity and deity of Jesus the suggestion is made in the responses that one either believes it without question or with various degrees of doubt (table 2). Without taking away from the conclusion that the majority count this doctrine as important and subscribe to it, one can still be concerned as to what the certainty/doubt framework does to the issue. At the very least, we can ask some questions of ourselves about alternate ways of dealing with this sort of conviction. It is hard enough to understand the meaning of this doctrine without also having to give an account of one's performance in relation to certainty.

A similar and related difficulty shows up in questions about the Apostles' Creed (table 3). When people are asked if they *believe in* what the Apostles' Creed says, a host of theological alternatives are obscured. The people may believe in the Triune God—or they may believe in the truth of each sentence. More significantly, this sort of question tends to lump together a works-orientation (I can believe more than others) and a "grace" emphasis on personal trust. The problems involved in seeing faith as acceptance of a series of propositions are simply too numerous to ignore.

Theologians have traditionally made a major point of distinguishing between *belief in* and *belief that*. To believe in God is to trust, and it is a different level of confidence than the somewhat external acceptance of sentences as "true." The discussion of the Apostles' Creed could stand some further consideration with this in mind.

Again, this concern may not take much away from the conclusion that most of those surveyed held the Creed in high esteem, but it may make us wonder a little about the value of that conclusion. It may also encourage us in future studies to pursue such matters further.

The broad support for proofs of God's existence (table 9) is a combination of the concern for absolute certainty and an appreciation of experience as some kind of warrant for faith. Here it is the willingness to make some experiential linkage with the reality of God that I find promising. I am intrigued by the possibilities of encouraging people to respond to questions about the experiential connections they have found between faith and life. Our confessional heritage would lead us to expect such linkage, but we have often been disinclined to develop it. The tendency of doctrine to become separated from concrete experience, combined with ecclesiastical reaction to extremes of pietistic movements, may be a part of this picture. Nevertheless, I find this study opening up avenues for exploring the connections of faith and experience.

In exploring the relationship between faith and experience, the concept of "proof" is not very helpful. That's true whether we are talking about arguments for God's existence or the tendency to turn social-science research into "proof."

First, preoccupation with proofs tends to determine the role that experience plays, thereby tempting us to ignore other ways of interpreting it. As some theologians have noted, the very first thing one must do with the classic arguments for God's existence is to recognize that they are not proofs.

Secondly, this proof-oriented role for experience runs counter to a grace-oriented theology. If one persists in trying to use experience like that, it is inevitable that theology will be set against experience in an extremely unfortunate way. Insist that experience is evidence which can be evaluated from neutral ground as a basis for a decision to have faith and all the concerns about the giftlike character of faith will emerge. The concept of "proof" in this sense carries all the problems of the absolute certainty/doubt syndrome that has been previously mentioned. Concern for experience, then, shapes faith so as to treat it as more external and theoretical than is actually the case.

These two problems with proof may explain the responses to questions about the possibility of proving God's existence (table 9). Proof in relation to faith turns out to be a very ambiguous concept. People want to assert the dependability of God, but they don't really mean dependence on logic (as Wuthnow indicates) or dependence on empirical data in a scientific sense. They simply cannot differentiate their concerns adequately because the concept of proof is so central in the questions. What is required is more careful consideration of the relation between faith and experience.

Faith and Experience

The study clearly calls for attention to some different understandings of experience. What stands out for me is the capacity of the respondents to report special experiences of religious significance which they differentiate from all the rest. Granted, the questions asked them to do that, but their willingness to do so holds up for me the reality that they *can* single out particular experiences as closely related to God, faith, and religious significance.

Secondly, the respondents also indicated that they can assign religious significance to extreme experiences of trauma and loss. It seems that their faith does give meaning to the whole range of experience, from beauty to suffering and even death.

These two aspects of the respondents' reports of experience are very productive. They reinforce the conviction that there are many other uses of experience besides that of providing evidence that will support a proof. These uses of experience are important for faith without providing a direct challenge to its giftlike character.

Let me briefly develop two alternate views of experience related to the "special" and "comprehensive" features noted above.

EXPERIENCE AND VISION

Selected experiences which count more than others in a life history have been described as peak experiences. They need not be single events, but they may be a set of experiences or a kind of accumulation of events with special impact. They can be turning points in life, moments of conversion, reinforcement, or clarification. These special, selected experiences influence life by shaping perspective and vision.

For example, standing on a mountaintop looking down on a broad expanse of terrain can give one a feeling for the worth of life and the breadth of possibilities. Kneeling at the altar for Communion during a time of great stress or celebration can give a similar, but more Christian, focus to the eyes of the heart.

In addition to the role of experience as evidence we need to recognize the way selected experiences affect our thought and feeling so as to become key models for our imagination and anticipation. Experience can so jar our minds as to move us beyond the need for evidence. These life-shaping events are not significant because of their frequency or potential for replication on demand. One alone might be enough for a lifetime. As a consequence, this use of experience has about it a giftlike character of its own. It frees us to remember and report—but not to manipulate. Such key experiences would thus seem to be quite compatible with our confessional concern for grace. Indeed, the Scriptures and our confessions would make no sense without discerning this use of experience in the accounts there given.

Insofar as this study lifts up such special experiences and encourages us to look at them, I believe it offers its own corrective to many of the problems of empirical research.

One thing needs to be kept in mind in elevating such selected experiences. Here, too, we need to be alert to the different "gods" experienced and the various faith alternatives emerging from "peak" experiences. If the experiences chosen are uniformly those of "nature's" harmony, for example, one would expect a faith of a "works" type to develop. Similarly, if church members report no "peak" experiences of forgiveness, that would raise questions about a serious deviation from a confessional point of view, or it might be that other levels of misunderstanding are involved. The experience of forgiveness is precisely what the Christian gospel is all about. One would hope that those persons who say they haven't experienced forgiveness in a special way are confused about how this experience is to be identified.

In any case, what is opened up here is a radically different way of relating faith and experience that does not run the same risks as our tendency to use experience as the basis for proof or objective determinations.

EXPERIENCE INTERPRETED BY FAITH

The comprehensive capability of faith to illuminate the whole range of human experience is another alternative surfaced by this study that deserves consideration. Again, the giftlike character of faith can be maintained, and we can ask the question concerning the way this faith assists us in interpreting experience.

In this use of experience the sequence of evidence and conclusion is exactly reversed from the normal "proof" pattern. The experiential developments come in the process of risk, not as a way of excluding such vulnerability.

This approach to experience enables us to assess the ways in which different types of faith (different gods, if you will) actually lead us to read various meanings into what happens to us.

Perhaps we can see here why Christians in this study reported negative experiences as colored with deep meaning. They could have been "peak" experiences of death and resurrection, bondage and liberation. Or, it could be that their vision of life's meaning in

Christ enabled them to put even "defeat" experiences in a context where the threat of loss actually reinforced the value of Christ as Savior.

What is suggested here is the value of seeing how faith enables us to interpret experiences in ways that go beyond what is given in just that moment. Experience becomes not only the medium for God's revelation, but the "matter" to be formed by faith. Conversation and study of the way people use our confessional inheritance to illuminate the struggles and satisfactions of life jumps out at us as a very proper and compelling use of "experience." All the biblical and confessional material on identification with Christ's death and resurrection comes alive in this perspective. In the light of Christ we look for new life to break loose just in those experiences when destruction seems close at hand. In this sense our faith offers its own framework of interpretation for all the experiences of life.

Distinctions and Concepts

These two alternate views of experience may help us in looking at reports of experience in the study more carefully. Confessionally, we expect all people to have some experience of God to talk about. But we need to help them differentiate and develop the alternative paths this opens up. In dealing with proofs of God's existence, questions about presence, and experiences of God, alternate views of God need to be allowed to surface. Is the approach to experience shaped more by a god who rewards performance—like believing with no doubts, accepting the Bible literally, or always doing our absolute best? Or does the intricate pattern of demand transcended by promise shine through so that all events are seen as pointing beyond mere human achievement?

Here more explicit use of the works/grace contrast needs to be developed. People need some common language in which to discuss their experience. One important result of this study, as I see it, is that it presses us toward the complexity of experience and therefore lifts up the need for conceptual and linguistic tools to deal with that. Some of these instruments are given in our theological heritage. They need to be rediscovered in relationship to experience so that we will not argue simply about labels or "flag" words.

The need for consensus pushes us to see that agreement about grace also requires some willingness to share "useful" conceptual conventions and linguistic tools. In this manner, we begin to look not only for ultimate consensus that goes beyond concepts and words, but we recognize that there are other levels where consensus has an operative importance. Just here the works/grace or gospel/law contrast is helpful. We expect grace will make us able to identify more appropriate formulations even if that is not a final indicator of actual faith. This is especially true for preachers of the Word so that the appropriate message will be proclaimed even if the response of faith is not predictably or consistently effective. I take it this is the reason our church has insisted on an educated clergy and maintained a high regard for the office of Word and Sacrament. The study is encouraging just at the point where it indicates that clergy are more adept at recognizing appropriate statements.

So if the identification of confessionally sound expressions is a secondary level of the life of faith, it can be treated in a more demanding and works-oriented fashion without dislodging the priority of grace. This would explain in part why the church tolerates extreme theological diversity in its members as long as that is not allowed to shape the core message around which the community gathers. It would also suggest that the church is not simply at the mercy of democratic determinations concerning the limits of diversity in proclamation.

The diversity on sacramental questions also benefits from some reference to language and conceptual niceties. Answers to how Christ is present in the Lord's Supper and concerning the essential character of the sacraments seem to reflect diversity, but the concepts involved are a part of the problem (tables 6 and 7). In respect to presence, the response stressing mysterious, inexplicable presence seems to me to be quite compatible with the emphasis on the bread and wine remaining bread and wine. The latter may reflect more theological sophistication, but it also is couched in a substantial conceptual frame while the former is in line with more "existential" interpretation. It would seem that attention to widely recognized theological problems with "consubstantiation" language is required before one can do much with the diversity indicated.

Similarly, both the emphasis on sacraments as essential and as aids to faith can be seen to fit with a confessional emphasis on the external word as a means of grace. The problem may well be in understanding "essential" as meaning absolutely necessary or relatively necessary. Even though the confessions say that baptism is necessary for salvation (Augsburg Confession, Article IX) it is not always treated as an absolute necessity (the thief on the cross is the notable exception). Luther sees the problem as the despising of the sacraments when they are, in fact, accessible. Here, too, we need to take another look at the way undifferentiated concepts influence resulting agreement or divergence.

It may be important to note that the need for greater consensus on the distinctions and concepts utilized does not simply apply to social-scientific researchers. The conversations with theological types in the process of this study indicated quite clearly that the theological community has a similar need. If we are going to talk and think about faith we simply have to be more willing to speak some common language for the task at hand. It need not be the "best" language or the "right" language. For me, an important consequence of this study is the recognition that key confessional concerns require reappropriation and fresh articulation on several levels. The people who develop and interpret surveys need assistance at this point. As this study indicates, so do the people surveyed. This certainly identifies communication and educational tasks for clergy and academic theologians.

CONCLUSION

Wuthnow's attempts to move quickly into cause-and-effect analysis in his interpretation offers considerable problems for me. The determination of sources of commitment raises two particular problems. First, the set of core confessional commitments represent a very "small sample" of doctrinal implications of justification by grace. Specifically, they do not include the conviction that faith comes to life in Christian community, through the means of grace. As a consequence, we are led to ask questions like "Does preaching lead to faith?" or "How is it people hear but don't believe?" Both of these questions are answered fundamentally by faith and not by empirical research. The message of grace limits any decisive rational conclusions about this sort of question. In the end we trust that faith comes by hearing the message on the lips of another human being (Rom. 10:17).

What I prize most in Wuthnow's interpretation is his own attempt to come to terms with theological concepts and distinctions. His analysis of the faith/doctrine paradox is largely on the right track. It recognizes the need for somewhat sophisticated language in order to deal with the complex and inconsistent data unearthed in the study. In this sense, he opens the door for us to see both the experience that faith illuminates and the need for enlightened interpretation.

RELIGIOUS BELIEFS AND EXPERIENCES

I would suggest two further steps in that analysis of paradox.

First, the contrast of faith and works is really what's at stake. Doctrinal agreement is one form of works which does not qualify for salvation or produce faith without exception. It is an important level of the life of faith which exists in persistent tension with the "openness" of God's fundamental grace.

Secondly, in the light of the above, churches can exercise *some* control over their life, organization, and members, provided those demands are not allowed to define the ultimate conditions of salvation. Since our faith is seen contextually, members are involved in a particular community that has no choice but to set some boundaries which are at least publicly identified. Discipline with respect to community organization and doctrine may be another problem, but in principle it is compatible with the central paradox or dialectic.

In this perspective, many of Wuthnow's conclusions will stand up. Yes, bring people into the fellowship of a nurturing community and they will have a better chance of coming to faith. Yes, get people to think about deep, existential questions and they may be better able to hear and appropriate the gospel message. Yes, continue to preach a particular message if you want a specific faith in Christ to develop and be reinforced. These are not conclusions based on empirical evidence, but they are truths of faith that can be seen in a fresh way because of empirical inquiry.

The study reminds us of the shape and complexity of our task. Wide diversity does exist in the church. It needs to be recognized so that our message is not mistaken as a call for conformity. Diversity recognized can be appreciated as an implication of the gospel. At the same time, this diversity needs to be identified as potential competition over against that message. What this study offers is a view of what's happening from a different angle. Hopefully, that gives us both perspective and leverage for renewed effort at an old task. Such "good works" are anticipated because of our confidence in the power of God's grace in Jesus Christ.

PART B

Religious Beliefs and
Social-Ethical Attitudes

5

Basic Patterns

MARY CAHILL WEBER

Building on the preceding analysis, we turn now to the relation between religious belief and social-ethical attitudes. This chapter focuses on some of the diverse attitudes expressed by lay respondents to the Lutheran Listening Post questionnaires. The next chapter will analyze the relationship between these attitudes and the religious beliefs, practices, and organizational involvement of respondents.

Four topics provide the foci of this chapter:

1. individual behaviors;
2. political actions;
3. social and socioeconomic policies;
4. church advocacy efforts.

Respondents' social attitudes are presented in relation to these four topics. For each topic, we describe the range of social attitudes on a spectrum from "liberal" to "conservative." For all of the topics, it becomes evident that lay respondents represent a wide range of attitudes. While the majority of responses fall in the intermediate or moderate position, both the extreme liberal and extreme conservative views are represented.

In order to portray the social attitude of Lutheran lay respondents, we have developed a series of indexes combining several questionnaire items. Any index may be constructed from as few as two or as many as six different questions. When each new index is introduced, we give it a name, specify the question items included in that index, and describe the range of responses to the several items in that index. In this way, we are able to provide a broad data base for this profile of social attitudes while focusing only on twelve different indexes.

While this chapter is purely descriptive in its focus, the next chapter will analyze the relationship between these attitudinal indexes and a variety of measures of religious belief, practice, and organizational involvement. In this way, we will be able to delineate clearly the actual relationships between religion and social liberalism or conservatism.

INDIVIDUAL BEHAVIORS
The Authority Index

The first of these attitudinal indexes measures peoples' responses to authority in matters of individual behavior. Three symbols of authority were selected: the Bible, parents, and the state. The authority index was constructed by assigning 1 point for the "always wrong" response to each of the following items:

1. disobeying the teachings of the Bible;
2. showing disrespect to one's parents;
3. cheating on one's income tax.

Thus, the highest possible score for this index would be three. That is, respondents would receive such a score if they chose the "always wrong" response to all three of the items above. The lowest possible score would be 0, for respondents who did not choose the "always wrong" response for any of the three items above. The score of 0 would indicate a liberal attitude toward authority figures, while the score of 3 would suggest a conservative attitude.

Table 15 illustrates the complete range of response options, as well as the percentages of pastors and laypersons choosing each response. Note that "always wrong" was the most absolute and unqualified option available; that is, respondents choosing this option saw no situation in which any of these authorities could be disobeyed "in good conscience." The "always wrong" response is thus qualitatively different from the "usually wrong," "depends on the situation," or "not at all wrong" responses. Note also the rank order of "always wrong" responses for these three items: "cheating on your income tax" (75% of pastors and 75% of laypersons) is significantly higher than either "showing disrespect to parents" (60% of laypersons and 44% of pastors) or "disobeying the teaching of the Bible" (56% of laypersons and 43% of pastors). Finally, it is interesting to observe that pastors tend to choose the less absolute response more often than do laypersons: for example, in the case of both biblical and parental authority. This difference between pastors and laypersons will reappear in several of the other attitudinal issues examined in this chapter.

The range of "always wrong" responses to these three items in the authority index provides us with a spectrum of liberal-conservative attitudes, weighted toward the conservative side. The actual distribution of laypersons is as follows:

Frequency of "conservative" responses	Number of sample responding	Percentage of responses
0	167	12
1	299	21
2	411	29
3	551	39
	1,428	101*

Over one-third of the laity chose "always wrong" to disobey authorities for all three items; a little less than one-third found disobedience to two of these authorities to be "always wrong"; and another third selected none or one to be "always wrong."

The fact that only a small minority (12%) were convinced that none of these items was "always wrong" indicates that, in the total picture, most lay respondents accept the authority of these major institutions of American society in their everyday actions.

The New Morality Index

The second index was built from the "always wrong" responses to issues of the so-called new morality.[1] Three new morality issues were selected for examination: homosexuality, the use of marijuana, and premarital sex. Again an "always wrong" response to any of these items was counted as 1 point:

1. homosexual relations;
2. smoking marijuana;
3. premarital sexual intercourse.

Scores for the new morality index range from a high of 3 (conservative) to a low of 0 (liberal).

Table 15 provides a range of responses for each of these three items. Homosexual relations are perceived as always wrong by two-thirds of the laity and half of the pastors responding to the question-

* Error due to rounding.

naire. Smoking marijuana receives a similar response, although pastors are somewhat less likely to view this as always wrong (64% of laypersons, 39% of pastors). In the case of premarital sexual intercourse, there is a drop in the "always wrong" responses, and the difference between laypersons and pastors is less noticeable (46% of lay respondents and 36% of pastors find this behavior to be always wrong). Once again, however, approximately one-half to two-thirds of the lay respondents to the questionnaire display absolute responses regarding the morality of these individual behaviors.

The range of "always wrong" responses to these three new morality items is distributed as follows:

Frequency of "conservative" responses	Number of sample responding	Percentage of responses
0	285	20
1	237	17
2	374	26
3	520	37
	1,416	100

This means that slightly more than one-third view none or one of these behaviors to be always wrong, while an identical proportion of respondents consider all three behaviors to be always wrong. The intermediate position is taken by about one-fourth of the respondents.

These responses, once again, indicate fairly conservative views on these matters by the overall lay sample. However, in comparison to the first index, a larger minority of respondents (20%) feel that there are circumstances under which all of these behaviors may be considered morally acceptable. In light of the fact that most studies point to relatively large numbers of Americans who practice these behaviors, it is important to note that among lay respondents in this study, reservations concerning these behaviors are the rule, not the exception.

POLITICAL ACTIONS

The Political Change Index

The third index measures attitudes toward domestic political change; that is, a change in the form of government in America. Three topics were selected for examination: overthrowing the government, engaging in political protest, or simply any major change in government. As with the other indexes, the political change index was constructed by assigning 1 point to each of the responses chosen in relation to the items specified below:

1. "always wrong" to work to overthrow the government;
2. "always" or "usually wrong" to take part in political protests;*
3. "mostly oppose" major changes in our form of government.

Scores for the political change index also range from a low of 0 (liberal) to a high of 3 (conservative).

Responses to individual items on the political change index are presented in tables 15 and 16. In the case of "major changes in our form of government," nearly half of the laity and slightly more than half of the pastors voiced direct opposition (table 16). "Working to overthrow the government" received the response "always wrong" from nearly half the laity; however, only 12% of the pastors gave this response. The majority of pastors took a situational view on this subject (table 15). "Taking part in political protests" was far less likely to elicit a negatively charged response from either group: combining the "always" and "usually wrong" categories, only 18% of laypersons and 4% of pastors had fairly strong objections to this behavior (table 15).

These responses may be explained with relative ease. Since the first item ("major changes in *our* form of government") refers directly to the United States or to the Canadian government, and since most respondents would not be expected to support sweeping changes in these democratic governments, it would be expected that a good deal of opposition would be generated. In the case of "working to overthrow the government," the differential responses of laypersons and clergy probably derive from the professional educations of most pastors; that is, most pastors, but only a minority of laypersons, probably read this statement as an abstraction which includes the overthrow of governments founded on undemocratic principles. Finally, both lay and clergy respondents seem to have inculcated the idea that some forms of political protests are acceptable.

The responses to these three items in the political change index are distributed as follows:

*As may been seen in table 15, "taking part in political protests" was viewed as "always wrong" by only 7% of the laity. Another 11% of the laity found this behavior "usually wrong." Therefore, "always" and "usually wrong" responses were totaled in creating the index.

Frequency of "conservative" responses	Number of sample responding	Percentage of responses
0	340	25
1	612	45
2	355	26
3	64	5
	1,371	101*

While one quarter of the respondents find none of these behaviors objectionable, nearly half of them find at least one of them objectionable. About one-third find more than one to be objectionable.

These responses show that lay people are somewhat more tolerant of changes in the domestic political sphere than they are of the individual "deviant" behaviors previously noted. While only a minority of lay respondents find major changes in our form of government to be desirable, the respondents as a group are rather tolerant of political protest as a mechanism of instituting some changes in American[2] institutions. Thus, while not exactly locating themselves on the "left wing" of American politics, the respondents as a group hold the view that some forms of protest may be moral. This is an interesting finding, given the widespread opposition to "cheating on your income tax" above. It is likely that respondents took the word "cheating" quite literally in that context. Rather than interpreting the question as including the withholding of payments in protest, they were biased toward a censorial response by virtue of the illegal behavior involved.

The Human Rights Index

A fourth index summarizes lay responses to questions expressing concern for human rights in other nations. Three issues were selected for this index: support for Soviet dissidents, noninvolvement with South Africa, and taking a tough stand to support human rights in other countries (a general position of U.S. leaders). The human rights index was constructed then by assigning 1 point for each of the responses listed below with their appropriate item:

1. "mostly favor" actively supporting Soviet dissidents;
2. "mostly oppose" leaving South Africa alone to solve its own problems;
3. "mostly favor" American leaders taking a tough stand in support of human rights in other countries.

* Error due to rounding.

89

Because of the positive reference ("mostly favor") in this index, the highest score of 3 signifies a liberal position and the lowest score of 0 a conservative view, with the moderates in between.

Table 16 presents the responses chosen by pastors and laypersons for these three items. Note the large gap between the responses of pastors and laypersons to two of these items. While only a minority of laypersons actively favor support for Soviet dissidents (27%), the majority of the clergy do so (61%). As far as intervention in the South African situation is concerned, similar results apply: 26% of laypersons and 62% of pastors actively favor such intervention. Only support for international human rights is more consistent for both groups: half of the laity and four-fifths of the clergy are supportive of this generally worded item. Note also that for both groups the matters of international politics described here are issues of some indecision; large minorities of both laypersons and pastors indicate that they "don't know" whether they favor or oppose these actions.

When responses to these items by lay respondents are summarized into the human rights index, the results are striking. Giving one point for the liberal responses stated above to each of these issues, the distribution is as follows:

Frequency of "liberal" responses	Number of sample responding	Percentage of responses
0	495	36
1	426	31
2	321	24
3	126	9
	1,368	100

This means that lay respondents can be approximately divided into thirds: one-third favors intervention into none of these areas; another third favors intervention into one; and a final third favors intervention into two or three of the situations described above.

These results are consistent with the responses described in the political change index.[3] There is strong objection to intervention in foreign affairs from about one-third of the lay sample, while a similar proportion of lay respondents find domestic political change to be objectionable. This is not to say, however, that the opposition to these two forms of behavior comes from precisely the same "camps." We will have more to say on this subject in the next chapter.

SOCIAL AND SOCIOECONOMIC POLICIES

After surveying attitudes on individual behavior and political issues, we turn now to social and socioeconomic issues. Because a relatively large number of questions were asked in this area, it was necessary to exclude many items from consideration in this section.
Items included were selected because of their prominence for North
American society in general and for the church and its social concerns in particular.

The Corrective Policies Index

A fifth index summarizes lay responses to public policy issues regarding legal restraint or prolonged economic assistance. Three issues were selected: police power, the death penalty, and welfare.
One point was assigned to each of the responses listed below:

1. "mostly favor" giving more power to the police;
2. "mostly favor" the death penalty;
3. "mostly oppose" spending more money for people on welfare.

For this index, scores range from a conservative high of 3 to a liberal
low of 0.

Table 16 provides the detailed responses of pastors and laypersons to each of the three items in this index. The table shows that
there is considerable opposition to spending more money for people
on welfare, especially among lay people. Three-quarters of the lay
respondents and more than half of the clergy respondents indicate
that they generally oppose such spending. Regarding the death penalty, while only one-quarter of pastors are actively in favor of it, half
of the laity are actively in favor of this punishment. Finally, the likelihood of favoring increased police power is somewhat lower: only
16% of pastors and 39% of laypersons favor this development.

The distribution of lay responses to the three items in the corrective policies index suggests a strongly conservative bias:

Frequency of "conservative" responses	Number of sample responding	Percentage of responses
0	175	13
1	413	30
2	523	37
3	286	20
	1,397	100

One-fifth of lay respondents support the death penalty and an increase in police power and oppose greater spending to support welfare clients. Only 13% take the liberal position on all three issues, with two-thirds of respondents in between.

The Economic Equalization Index

A sixth index measures support for programs to equalize economic benefits. Three issues were examined: international economic inequality, domestic social programs versus military programs, and domestic health-care programs. The equalization index was constructed by assigning 1 point to each response listed below:

1. a more equitable distribution of wealth among all nations in the world today;
2. social programs being given a higher priority in government spending than military programs;
3. a national program to improve health-care services and to curtail rising health-care costs.

As in the human rights index, scores for this equalization index range from a liberal high of 3 to a conservative low of 0.

Table 17 displays the range of responses selected for the three items in this index. Both social program spending and national health care received favorable responses from laypersons and pastors alike, although pastors were somewhat more favorable. Eighty-two percent of pastors and 54% of laypersons indicate that they favor prioritizing social over military spending, and 85% of pastors, as compared to 73% of laypersons, favor programs to improve national health care. Somewhat less favorable responses were received regarding redistribution of wealth between "have" and "have not" countries: 75% of pastors, as compared to only 40% of laypersons, say they are favorable to such redistribution of wealth. Certainly as a group these responses indicate surprisingly broad support for social programs which would equalize societal benefits and resources even among laypersons. This indicates a fairly strong sense of social justice and egalitarianism among the respondents.

The range of responses to items in the equalization index suggests a more liberal bias:

Frequency of "liberal" responses	Number of sample responding	Percentage of responses
0	164	12
1	374	27
2	509	36
3	353	25
	1,400	100

We will have occasion to make further reference to these figures in a later section of the chapter, where these personal views will be compared with views toward church advocacy regarding these policies.

The Congregational Minority Inclusion Index

A seventh index measures the attitudes of respondents toward the inclusion of minority group members within a predominantly white congregation. Two issues were explored: congregational action to increase minority membership, and the acceptance of a minority pastor. The index was constructed by assigning 1 point for agreement with each of the statements below:

1. congregations should be doing more to increase the number of minorities holding membership;
2. a predominantly white congregation should be willing to accept a minority pastor.

Regarding minority membership increases, the responses were distributed as follows: "yes," 47% of the pastors and 23% of the laity; "don't know," 18% of pastors and 43% of laity; "no," 30% of pastors and 27% of laity, with no response coming from 5% of pastors and 8% of the laity. Regarding the statement that a predominantly white congregation should be willing to accept a minority pastor, the responses were distributed as follows: 58% of pastors and 46% of laypersons agreed with this statement; 26% of pastors and 23% of laypersons were undecided; and 12% of pastors and 18% of laypersons disagreed. Four percent of the pastors and 12% of the laity indicated they had no opinion or offered no response.

The "yes" and "agree" responses to these items, when totaled, indicate the extent to which an individual respondent feels that congregations should recruit minority members and accept minority pastors. Since fewer than 2% of lay respondents belong to congregations which are other than predominantly white, these findings are rather important. They indicate only a limited desire on the part of these lay members to increase the number of minority members in their congregations, while also illustrating wider but limited acceptance of the idea of a minority pastor.[4]

The Lutheran Church in America has strong goals regarding increases in minority membership and leadership, goals which have been accepted by the convention of the church. However, these findings suggest a bit of foot-dragging among both laypersons and pastors in the ongoing attempt to implement the goals. When I point is given for positive responses by laity to each of the above items, the following index results:

Frequency of "liberal" responses	Number of sample responding	Percentage of responses
0	617	45
1	528	38
2	236	17
	1,381	100

Nearly half of the lay sample did not feel positively about either item, while only 17% believed that both minority recruitment and the acceptance of a minority pastor are responsibilities of white congregations.

The Women's Equality Index

The eighth index summarizes respondents' attitudes toward women. We use the term "women's equality" as a shorthand expression for changing or strengthening the social status and role of women in society. Three issues were selected: women in politics, society's efforts to change or strengthen women's status, and women's liberation groups. The index was constructed by assigning 1 point for a response favoring each of the following:

1. women becoming more involved in politics;
2. current societal efforts to strengthen or change women's status in society;
3. current overall efforts of the various women's liberation groups.

In this index scores ranged from a liberal high of 3 to a conservative low of 0.

Table 18 indicates the range of responses for pastors and lay-

persons for the items on this index. Nearly three-fifths of the lay respondents and four-fifths of the pastors favor "women becoming
more involved in politics." Half of the laypersons and nearly three-
quarters of the pastors favor "current societal efforts to strengthen
or change women's status in society." Yet, when it comes to "current
overall efforts of the various women's liberation groups," support is
quite limited: fewer than one-quarter of the lay respondents and
only two-fifths of the pastors favor the efforts of these groups.

Creating a women's equality index which gives 1 point for favorable responses to each of the above, the distribution of lay responses
is as follows:

Frequency of "liberal" responses	Number of sample responding	Percentage of responses
0	412	28
1	387	27
2	346	24
3	300	21
	1,445	100

Thus, half of the respondents are favorable toward one or two of
these efforts on behalf of women, while the remainder are divided
as shown above.

Church Advocacy Efforts

A final set of attitudinal indexes taps the area of church advocacy
efforts. It is true that favorable dispositions toward the active involvement of the church in the political, economic, and social arenas
are analytically distinct from attitudes toward political, economic,
and social issues themselves. In fact, there is reason to believe that
some liberals (and radicals, generally) would not lend support to the
advocacy functions of the churches, out of the fear that churches
would not support those causes which they, as liberals, find attractive. However, because the LCA has frequently issued social statements in support of attitudes cited here as "liberal," there is relatively little reason to expect that liberals within the church would
respond in the way just described. There are other reasons to fear
church advocacy, which arise largely from the view that the church
should "stick to spiritual matters and stay out of politics." This is the
attitude called "conservative" in the case of church advocacy. However, it is clearly *not* identical with the other forms of conservatism

we have described earlier. The following discussion must be understood with that caveat in mind.

The Clergy Political Index

A ninth index summarizes the responses to pastors engaged in a variety of political advocacy efforts. Five possible forms of political advocacy by pastors were examined: endorsing candidates, preaching a political sermon, participating in protests, criticizing other nations, and speaking against corruption. The clergy political index was constructed by the addition of 1 point for each lay "no" response to the following items:

1. endorse candidates for office;
2. discuss political issues from the pulpit;
3. participate in protest marches or demonstrations;
4. criticize the actions of other countries;
5. speak out against political corruption.

For this index, scores ranged from a conservative high of 5 to a liberal 0, bearing in mind that the terms "liberal" and "conservative" are used in this context in a somewhat different manner than they have been previously.

Table 19 portrays the range of lay and clergy responses to these five items. Four of these five items receive wholehearted support from pastors themselves (95% view speaking out against political corruption as "all right," while about two-thirds of pastors find discussing political issues from the pulpit, participating in protest marches or demonstrations, and criticizing the actions of other countries to be "all right" for pastors). Here, as elsewhere, there is a significant gap between lay and clergy responses. The lay respondents are more skeptical as a group regarding these activities: while 71% regard it as all right for pastors to speak out against political corruption, only about a quarter find it acceptable for pastors to discuss political issues from the pulpit, participate in protest marches, and criticize the actions of other countries. Like pastors, laypersons are unlikely to feel that pastors should endorse candidates for office; compared to 17% of pastors, 11% of laypersons find this behavior acceptable.

Summing these items into a clergy political index was achieved by allowing 1 point for each item which a lay respondent indicated was not "all right." The outcomes were as follows:

Frequency of "conservative" responses	Number of sample responding	Percentage of responses
0	199	14
1	293	21
2	286	21
3	277	20
4 or 5	336	24
	1,391	100

About 35% of the lay respondents find none or one of these actions to be objectionable; about 40% take an intermediate position; and the remaining quarter find four or more of these to be objectionable.

CHURCH ADVOCACY INDEXES IN RELATION TO SPECIFIC AREAS

The prior index summarized the attitudes of lay respondents toward pastors engaged in political advocacy. It is also possible to examine the range of attitudes toward church advocacy efforts in relation to a variety of specific areas. In the concluding indexes of this chapter, three such areas will be explored: (1) economic equalization, (2) world hunger, and (3) women's equality. Previously we had described respondents' personal attitudes toward issues of economic equalization and women's equality. In this section, our focus falls *not* on their personal views, but on how they feel about the *church's* support for these efforts. As previously noted, an individual respondent may oppose policies designed to increase economic equalization and still support church advocacy efforts in this area. In the following section, the focus falls on the question of support for, or opposition to, church advocacy efforts in each of these three areas.

Economic Equalization
Church Advocacy Index

For this index, the same three issues were included that had been previously discussed as part of the economic equalization index, namely, international economic inequality, domestic social versus military programs, and domestic health-care programs. For this index, however, respondents were asked whether or not they felt that the church should support each of these policies. This church advocacy index was then constructed by assigning 1 point to a positive response for church support for each of the following:

1. a more equitable distribution of wealth among all nations in the world today;
2. social programs being given a higher priority in government spending than military programs;
3. a national program to improve health-care services and to curtail health-care costs.

Scores for this index ranged from a liberal high of 3 to a conservative low of 0.

Table 20 displays the range of responses to these three items. When asked whether the LCA should publicly support social programs being given a higher priority in government spending than military programs, three-quarters of pastors and two-fifths of laypersons agreed that the church should do so. Moreover, church support for a national health-care program received positive opinions from 70% of pastors and 51% of laypersons. Finally, somewhat less favorable responses were received regarding church advocacy for an international redistribution of wealth: 65% of pastors and only 30% of laypersons feel that the church should support such a policy.

In effect, these results indicate that respondents are somewhat less likely, as a group, to affirm church advocacy of these policies than they are to favor these policies personally. Presumably the drop-off from "personal support" to "church support" levels is largely explained by the underlying attitude held by some individuals that the church ought not to engage itself in the political and socioeconomic issues of the day. But, the drop-off is relatively small, and by and large the results indicate that the majority of both laypersons and pastors are favorably disposed to the advocacy of the church for those policies to which they also give their personal support.

The frequency distribution of the church advocacy for economic equalization index is as follows:

Frequency of "liberal" responses	Number of sample responding	Percentage of responses
0	371	27
1	397	29
2	388	28
3	213	16
	1,369	100

Again, this frequency distribution indicates that some respondents who are personally disposed in favor of the policies mentioned above are not in favor of church advocacy in their behalf. While only 12% of laypersons do not personally support any of these policies, 27% feel that the church should not publicly support them.

The World Hunger Church Advocacy Index

The index for church advocacy efforts concerning world hunger contains more items than any of the other indexes in this chapter. Six types of activity were examined, and the index was constructed by combining the two most positive responses ("very much" and "quite a lot") to each of the items below:

1. assisting church members to take an active role in promoting just policies toward food production and distribution;
2. testifying before government committees and agencies about the problems of hunger at home and abroad;
3. assisting hungry people to form action groups so that they have a voice in programs that affect them;
4. participating in lawsuits against the government if public funds authorized for the poor and hungry are misused;
5. speaking to corporations about their ethical and moral responsibilities in pursuing policies which affect hungry people;
6. participating in lawsuits and proxy actions, when appropriate, which urge corporations to face their ethical and moral responsibilities toward hungry people.

Scores for this index range from a "liberal" high of 6 to a "conservative" low of 0.

Table 21 sets forth the range of clergy and lay responses to the several forms of church advocacy on the issue of world hunger. The statement that the church should place "very much" or "quite a lot" of emphasis on a given area of advocacy work varied for laypersons from 52% for the area of assisting church members to take an active role regarding hunger, to 22% for participation in lawsuits and proxy actions against corporations which are irresponsible toward the hungry. In essence, the lay sample, as a group, gives reasonably strong support to those forms of advocacy which assist church members to support the hungry, which testify on behalf of the hungry, and which teach the hungry to become organized in their own behalf. When the topic turns to "speaking to" or taking legal action against offending corporations, however, support is much reduced.

The responses of pastors follow a somewhat similar course, although the level of support for these actions is much higher; it ranges from 80% for assisting church members to take an active role in this area to 44% for participation in corporate lawsuits and proxy actions.

The frequency distribution of the world hunger church advocacy index is created by the addition of one point for the response by laypersons that "very much" or "quite a lot" of emphasis should be placed on each area above. It is distributed as follows:

Frequency of "liberal" responses	Number of sample responding	Percentage of responses
0	389	24
1 or 2	494	31
3 or 4	375	24
5 or 6	331	21
	1,589	100

This distribution is remarkably similar to the index measuring church advocacy for economic equalization. Once again, advocacy is certainly not supported by all those who feel personally concerned about the issue of world hunger.

The Women's Equality Church Advocacy Index

The women's equality index summarized attitudes concerning societal efforts to change or strengthen the role and status of women. This issue is explored along three dimensions of its relation to the church: church support for societal changes, ordination of women, and the biblical witness concerning women. This church advocacy index is constructed by assigning one number of each positive response given to the following three items:

1. current church efforts to strengthen or change women's status in society;
2. the ordination of women;
3. understanding the biblical witness to call women and men to the same discipleship and leadership in the mission of the church today.

Scores range from a liberal high of 3 to a conservative low of 0.

Table 18, presented earlier in relation to the women's equality index, also measures responses to the items on this church advocacy index. When asked for their reactions to current church efforts to strengthen or change women's status in society, half of the layper-

66743

sons and three-quarters of the pastors responded favorably. Similar responses were obtained when respondents were asked whether they favored the ordination of women. Finally, when asked about their understanding of the biblical witness on the role of women in the church today, nearly two-thirds of laypersons and fully three-quarters of pastors responded that "women and men are both called to identical discipleship and leadership in the mission of the church."

These responses, when cumulated for lay respondents, form an index which measures support for church efforts in the area of women's rights. Those respondents who score highly on the measure may be said to perceive the church as called to strengthen the roles and status of women both in society and within the church—particularly in church leadership functions. The frequency distribution on this measure appears as follows:

Frequency of "liberal" responses	Number of sample responding	Percentage of responses
0	225	16
1	334	24
2	413	30
3	430	31
	1,402	101*

This variable provides an interesting reversal to the trend which has been described earlier. Instead of the usual pattern of limited support for church functioning in areas in which respondents have generally more liberal responses, we find that there is as much support generated for the equalization of the roles and status of men and women in the church as there is for such equalization in the wider societal context.

Most of the differential between attitudes toward church efforts and those toward the more general societal participation of women is undoubtedly due to the effect of one item in the composite variable treated above—"women's liberation groups." Therefore, the opposition of many respondents to these women's groups influenced that variable in a negative fashion. In the absence of that variable, support for church and societal efforts on behalf of women would be more constant.

* Error due to rounding.

CONCLUSION

The presentation of attitudinal items above has been a necessary precursor to the further analysis of these attitudes in the following chapter. The purpose of this chapter has been purely descriptive; it has provided information about the extent and content of certain measures of attitudinal liberalism/conservatism. In the next chapter, the attitudinal indexes will be cross-tabulated with a variety of measures of religious beliefs, practices, and organizational involvements of lay respondents. In this manner, the relationship between religion and attitudinal liberalism/conservatism may be studied.

It is probably also important to summarize the descriptive findings by saying that the laity is a diverse group attitudinally. In every case above, we saw that high, moderate, and low values on an index were equally likely to be filled. This means that there is a range of opinion from liberal to conservative on individual behavioral, political, social, and church advocacy measures. Many respondents, usually a majority, take intermediate positions on these indexes; we interpret this to mean that there exists a stronghold of moderate opinion in the LCA.

The importance of moderate opinion in a church which is quite pluralistic cannot be overstated. Without the "mixed" views of the core of the church, there is reason to believe that the "extreme" views of significant numbers of respondents would be detrimental to the continued mission of the church. This is because, on virtually every issue, *both* liberal and conservative "extremes" are well represented. The moderates serve to provide a buffer between discordant opinions, and they also serve as a "center of gravity" for the difficult process of forming corporate identity in a pluralistic church.

6

Religion and Conservative
Social Attitudes

MARY CAHILL WEBER

The relationship between religion and conservatism has been a sub-ject of social scientific inquiry for many years, although the attempt to measure this relationship through survey-research methods has been a fairly recent development. Years ago, the debate was largely theoretical: Marxists argued strongly that religion operated as an "opiate" of the masses, creating a context in which they would accept the very social class system which oppressed them. American sociol-ogy was also likely to view religion as exerting a conservative influ-ence over society by creating shared values and the possibility of so-cietal integration. Thus, whether or not the religion-conservatism link was viewed positively depended upon the analyst's view regard-ing social change. In neither case, however, was the religion-conser-vatism link challenged.[1]

With the development of survey-research methods, it became pos-sible to study the matter at the individual unit of analysis. A large body of findings resulted from these surveys, much of which has been summarized and categorized by Robert Wuthnow, the author of chapters 2 and 3 of this study.[2] He reviewed some 266 reported relationships between religion and conservatism, all of which were drawn from research completed during the decade preceding 1973.

In general, his discussion indicates that the religion-conservatism link is not simply a straightforward, positive one. Rather, fewer than half of the relationships between religion and conservatism were positive. These positive links were somewhat more likely to exist be-tween religion and conservative *social* (46%) attitudes than for the *political* (36%) and *economic* (21%) counterparts. Finally, these rela-tionships also depended upon which dimension of religion was be-ing tapped; this point will be elaborated shortly. In this chapter, many of the same religious dimensions, with some modifications and additions, are examined for lay respondents.

Four types of conservative social attitudes were the foci of the last chapter, attitudes toward: (1) individual behavior, (2) political actions, (3) social and socioeconomic policies, (4) and church advocacy efforts. These attitudinal dimensions have a somewhat broader scope than do those reviewed by Wuthnow, since they also include attitudes toward individual behavior and church advocacy. The religious dimensions with which these attitudinal dimensions will be cross-tabulated include: beliefs, practices, and organizational participation. Religious socialization and the social biography of the individual are also treated, although very briefly. These religious dimensions include most of the variables studied by previous researchers addressing the religion-conservatism link, with a few additions.

One obvious characteristic of this study, which differentiates it from most other research projects concerning religious beliefs, is that it is a scientifically selected cross section of the binational membership of the Lutheran Church in America. By sampling members of one particular denomination, the usual need to measure the denominational affiliation of the respondent is eliminated.[3] Also, and more importantly for our purposes, it becomes possible to consider the relationship between religious dimensions and social attitudes in the context of the particular theological and social teachings of the LCA.

DIMENSIONS OF RELIGION

This section will examine three dimensions of religion to be cross-tabulated with the attitudinal indexes: religious belief, practices, and organizational participation. The first dimension, religious belief, has a variety of subdimensions which are subjected in this section to an analysis which will replace the analysis of religious belief itself. Therefore, rather than asking "What is the effect of religious belief upon attitudinal outcomes?" or "Do believers and nonbelievers differ attitudinally?" this discussion asks these questions for specific *forms* of belief. To discuss the question concerning the effect of "belief in general" is not particularly useful with a sample of whom virtually all are themselves "believers."

The subdimensions of religious belief examined here (there are certainly many others which are not examined here) are as follows:

1. The salience of faith index. Described earlier in chapter 3, this measures the degree of saliency and consistency with which

respondents hold traditional Christian beliefs concerning: the humanity and divinity of Christ, the meaning of the crucifixion, and the relation of the respondent to God.

2. "Orthodox" beliefs.[4] This has been further divided into two categories:

     a. biblical literalism and the related tendency to regard the biblical account of creation as solely "correct";

     b. other "orthodox" beliefs.

Biblical literalism here refers to the belief that "the Bible is the actual word of God and is to be taken literally, word for word." The choice of a biblical account of creation as "correct" is treated as an "orthodox" belief only when it is held in exclusion of the scientific account. Other "orthodox" beliefs include the assertion of certainty regarding the existence of the devil and the belief that there is life after death, with rewards for some people and punishment for others.

3. The orientation of respondents toward individual salvation. Three variations from the traditional position espoused by the church are: the respondent's statement that she or he is "absolutely certain that I am saved and that I will go to heaven when I die"; the statement that faith means "a life of commitment to God that I demonstrate by trying to do what is right" (in contrast with "my trust in God's grace"); and the statement that "as long as people are truly sincere in their beliefs, they show faith." Each of these represents a variation from the traditional Lutheran idea of salvation by grace through faith.

4. Discompassionate theodicies. These are explanations given by laypersons for the existence of evil and suffering in the world but which discourage action to alleviate such phenomena. Such theodicies are apparent in some responses to the question of why God allows terrible things, like the Holocaust, to occur. The belief that such suffering is a punishment for sin is viewed as an extremely discompassionate theodicy, while the belief that "we don't know why these things happen, but we know that God is able to use them for good" is viewed as a less extreme one.

5. God's activity in human affairs. This is measured by the response that God's influence over human history is *continuous* (currently active, not limited to the time of creation) and *direct* (through nations and social institutions as well as individuals).

The belief that God's activity is continuous and direct suggests the influence of God over human affairs.

The religious practices examined in this chapter are as follows:

6. Self-reported frequency of church attendance.
7. Self-described level of activity and commitment as a church member.
8. Level of importance assigned to the church. This may be measured by the statement that "the church is absolutely essential for my spiritual growth" or the more moderate statement that it would be "difficult" to grow spiritually in the absence of the church, as opposed to the statement that the church has no particular effect on one's ability to lead a Christian life. It is also measured by affirmative responses to the question "Do you feel that God speaks to you through the church services on Sunday mornings?"
9. Participation in private devotions, whether alone or with one's family. Individual behaviors of this kind include frequent private prayer and Bible reading, as well as attention to religious radio and television. Family-related behaviors include the frequent inclusion of grace before daily meals, family prayers and devotions, and family Bible reading.

Finally, organizational participation measures included here are:

10. Congregational leadership. This is further subdivided into elected and voluntary positions held by respondents.
11. Membership, whether past or current, in a church-sponsored youth group. This includes both Lutheran and non-Lutheran groups.

Each of these religious beliefs (1–5), practices (6–9), and organizational participation (10–11) variables has been tested for its effects upon the attitudinal variables discussed in the preceding chapter. In addition, religious socialization and the social biography of the individual were considered in the analysis. However, the very limited effect of religious socialization upon the attitudinal outcomes, and the substantive distinction of social background characteristics from the dimensions of religion discussed here, caused these two topics to be relegated to the endnotes of this chapter.[5,6]

Table 22 is a summary table that illustrates the relationships between:

1. The dimensions of religion (belief, practice, organizational participation);
2. The conservative social attitudes (individual, behavioral, political, social/socioeconomic, and church advocacy) described in chapter 5. It should be noted that those indexes for which high scores have previously been described as denoting liberal responses have been transformed for the sake of this analysis. Thus, in table 22 and in the following discussion, *high scores on all attitudinal variables will indicate conservative responses.*

The reader of table 22 will note that the cells are filled with the symbols plus (+), minus (−), or asterisk (*), or they are empty. The plus sign indicates a positive relationship between a religious dimension and a conservative attitude. This means, for example (as in the upper left of the table), a high score on the salience of faith index is associated with highly conservative views regarding disobedience of the established institutional authorities in American society. The minus sign (as in the lower right of the table) indicates that membership in church youth groups is associated with low conservatism (equivalent to liberalism) regarding church efforts to equalize the status and roles of women in the church and in society. An asterisk indicates a curvilinear response pattern. This means that conservative attitudes are associated with moderate religiosity. For example, both those who attend church services weekly and those who attend very rarely are more likely to take conservative views on the new morality index than are persons who attend church services approximately once every six weeks. An empty cell indicates that there exists no statistically significant relationship between the two variables under consideration.*

RELIGIOUS BELIEFS

An introductory note on the structure of the following pages will perhaps be of assistance to the reader. Three dimensions of religion (beliefs, practices, and organizational participation) are presented

---

*A final note about table 22 is in regard to the key printed at the lower right of the table. For the reader who is not acquainted with statistics, the key may be interpreted as follows: positive (+), negative (−), and curvilinear (*) effects reported on the table have less than one chance in one hundred to have occurred simply by chance. Put another way, these findings are 99% or more likely to represent real differences between groups. No percentages reported in this paper fall below this standard, and most of the findings would pass far more rigorous tests.

below. Under each are presented subdimensions (for example, the salience of belief is a subdimension of belief itself). The discussion of each subdimension will focus upon its particular relationship to the various forms of attitudinal conservatism. The order in which the religious dimensions and subdimensions are presented in the text is identical to the left-to-right order of presentation in table 22.

Salience of Faith Index

The analysis of the relation between religion and conservatism will begin with the effects of the salience of faith index upon attitudinal conservatism. First is the case of reactions to disobedience of civil, religious, and parental authorities (measured, as in chapter 5, by the response that such disobedience is "always wrong"). It is quite clear that those lay respondents who find basic, consensual Christian beliefs concerning the humanity and divinity of Christ, the meaning of the crucifixion, and the relation of themselves to God to be highly salient are also likely to take a conservative posture regarding disobedience to these norms. Fifty-two percent of those laypersons who scored high on the SFI (as opposed to only 8% of those respondents for whom those religious beliefs were not at all salient) took the viewpoint that disobedience of civil, religious, and familial authorities is always wrong.

Similar results were obtained for the new morality index. Fifty percent of the laypersons who scored highly on the SFI, as opposed to only 12% of those for whom these religious beliefs were not at all salient, took the viewpoint that all components of the new morality index are always wrong. These components include homosexual relations, smoking marijuana, and premarital sexual intercourse.

Finally, high scores on the SFI were also associated with conservatism concerning domestic political change. Fully 50% of those laypersons who scored most highly on the SFI believe that it is always wrong to work to overthrow the government and that it is always or usually wrong to take part in political protests, and oppose changes in our form of government. In contrast, these three conservative positions were held by only 5% of those laypersons with low or moderate scores on the SFI.

Reference to the table indicates that the SFI is not, however, associated with other forms of conservatism; rather, it is simply unrelated to them. Basically, it would appear that those areas mentioned above are the central areas in which persons holding basic, consensual Christian beliefs are conservative. That such "core beliefs," when consistently held and salient, are associated with proscriptions regarding individual behavior is not surprising. Respect for authority and for traditional norms regarding sexuality and hedonistic behaviors has historically been associated with Christian beliefs. Such attitudes presumably are partially derived from the teachings of the church itself.

Less immediately understandable is the association of the SFI with conservatism regarding political change. It is possible that the political change index taps some of the same opposition to counter-cultural values which appears for the authority and new morality indexes; that is, participation in protests and other attempts to force change from the government has typically been the activity of groups that severely question both institutional authority and traditional morality. Thus, respondents may well perceive that the content of these three indexes—authority, new morality, and political change—is similar. Indeed, it is evident that in the 1960s they were part of a cohesive value system.

As will be seen throughout this discussion, views on authority and new morality tend to "hang together" in the minds of respondents, while views concerning domestic political change are sometimes associated with them. Generally speaking, however, there is a very strong likelihood for religion to influence individual behavioral attitudes to a greater extent than they influence any of the other attitudinal dimensions, political or otherwise. This finding is consistent with those reported by other researchers studying a large variety of Christian denominations.[7]

Biblical Literalism and the
Biblical Account of Creation

Biblical literalism and the associated tendency to choose a biblical account over a scientific account of creation are certainly the strongest predictors of conservative attitudes of every type analyzed here. The results are striking in terms of both the consistency and the size of these effects. Only in the areas of social policy and church advocacy are the results at all inconsistent and, as will be seen below, there are interpretable reasons for this.

Two measures of respondents' views of the Bible produce very similar results when cross-tabulated with the attitudinal indexes. In the first biblical measure, we compare those lay respondents who view the Bible as "the actual word of God . . . to be taken literally, word for word" with those who view the Bible as "the inspired word of God, but not everything in it should be taken literally, word for word" and those who say the Bible is "an ancient book of fables, legends, history, and moral precepts recorded by men." The second biblical measure asks respondents to choose between the biblical account of creation and the scientific theory of evolution as correctly interpreting the beginnings of human existence. Respondents were also allowed to indicate that they found both explanations to be correct "in their own ways," or that they found neither to be correct.

The biblical literalists' responses may be compared to those who treat the Bible in nonliteral fashion, either as God's inspired word or as a book of fables. Interestingly, it is often of relatively little import which of these latter nonliteral views is held. For example, those who see the Bible as inspired and those who see it as a book of fables are about equally likely to take highly conservative views concerning women's issues (25% and 23% respectively). Biblical literalists, however, are much more likely to take highly conservative views (42%). Similar results were obtained concerning several other indexes: political change, human rights, clergy political advocacy, and church advocacy on behalf of women.

However, in the case of individual behavior, as represented by the authority and new morality indexes, the respondents who view the Bible as the inspired word of God differ dramatically from those who view it as a book of fables. Both groups differ even more dramatically from those who say the Bible is to be taken literally, word for word. While about two-thirds of the biblical literalists take the posture that all the items on the authority and new morality indexes are always wrong, only about one-third of the biblical inspirationists take this view. Finally, fewer than one-fifth of those who consider the Bible to be a book of fables see all these behaviors as always wrong.

The results are similar when comparing those who take a biblical account of creation as correct with those who accept the scientific explanation, or both explanations, as correct. Those who choose the biblical account take far more conservative views than do either of the other groups. This is particularly true in relation to individual behavior and political change, but it is also somewhat applicable to social attitudes and in relation to pastoral and church advocacy.

The exceptions to the biblical literacy-conservatism pattern are worth a brief note at this point. These occur in the case of attitudes toward economic equalization, and of church advocacy in this regard, and in the area of church advocacy regarding world hunger. In these cases, it is likely that liberal attitudes are related in part to sympathy for the impoverished, the weak, and the hungry. That these sympathies are rooted in the hearts of biblical literalists is not surprising: the New Testament instructions regarding charity toward such people are clearly stated in the Sermon on the Mount and elsewhere. Because these people may be treated without moral reservation, the reactions of the literalists do not contain the attitudinal negativism which they exhibit regarding the other dimensions tested.

Other "Orthodox" Beliefs

The other "orthodox" beliefs tested, as has been mentioned previously, were certainty of belief in the devil and belief that there is a life after death with rewards for some and punishment for others. In the question concerning the devil, respondents were asked to say whether they were "absolutely" or "pretty sure" that there is or is not a devil. As for views of life after death, respondents were allowed to choose from a variety of options: lack of belief, uncertainty of belief, a general belief "that there must be something beyond death," life after death without punishment, life after death with rewards for some and punishment for others, and reincarnation. Respondents were also allowed to write in alternative responses.

"Orthodox" beliefs concerning the devil and life after death are less consistently associated with attitudinal conservatism than is biblical literalism. However, there does exist a relation between these beliefs and individual behavioral conservatism as measured by the authority and new morality indexes. Also, these forms of "orthodoxy" are related to conservative views regarding societal and church efforts to equalize the social status and roles of women.

These findings illustrate a noticeable trend within the data: conservative attitudes about individual behaviors are often held by those respondents who are not favorably disposed toward the equality of the sexes. An interesting qualifier to this observation is that, while women are more conservative regarding individual behavior, they are more liberal regarding women's equality. Thus it follows that men who hold highly "orthodox" beliefs are very likely to take conservative views regarding women's equality.

Comparing those who believe that the devil exists to those who do not, certainty of belief in the devil is strongly associated with conservative views regarding individual behavior. Nearly 60% of those who express certainty, as opposed to fewer than 20% of those who doubt or disbelieve the existence of the devil, take strongly conservative views regarding the authority and new morality indexes. The analogous figures for societal efforts to change the roles and status of women are 32% and 18%, indicating a somewhat lower correlation, but one which remains highly significant. Just over one-half of those who believe that life after death contains rewards and punishments are highly conservative regarding individual behavior, as compared with only 30% of the rest of the sample.

Orientations Toward Salvation

Although there were several items related to the issues of salvation, three orientaions were isolated: First is the "saved" orientation, measured by the response "expresses my feelings very well" to the statement "I am absolutely certain that I am saved and that I will go to heaven when I die." The second orientation is the "works" orientation, which is measured by the respondent having chosen, among a variety of definitions, that faith means "a life of commitment to God that I demonstrate by trying to do what is right." The third orientation is "sincerity," indicated by the response to the faith item that "as long as people are truly sincere in their beliefs, they show faith."

A glance at table 22 will illustrate that both the "saved" and the "works" orientations operate in the direction of conservatism,* while the "sincere" orientation produces the opposite, or liberal,** result. The reader should also note that the "saved" are similar to those respondents who hold the "orthodox" beliefs described previously (belief in the devil, life after death with rewards and punishments). For the "saved," the certainty of afterlife is strongly associated with prohibitions regarding individual behavior (and, once again, with conservative views regarding women's equality). More than 55% of the "saved" (as opposed to approximately 30% of other respondents) took the most conservative views toward individual behaviors. In the case of women's equality, the figures (34% and 27%) were less startling, but still quite significant.

While the reactions of the "works" respondents are similar to those of the biblical literalists, they do bear some analysis. It is partic-

*Denoted by a plus (+) sign on table 22
**Denoted by a minus (−) sign on table 22

ularly important to stress that these variables join behavioral conservatism with strong political and social conservatism, culminating in the viewpoint that clergy (whom conservative laypersons perceive as liberal) should not engage in political advocacy from the pulpit. As expected, the works respondents are far more conservative than are other respondents on the authority and new morality indexes (nearly 50% of the works respondents are highly conservative, in comparison to about one-third of the other respondents). Political change gets similarly lower marks from the works respondents, of whom 27% are highly conservative, than it does from other respondents, of whom only 17% are highly conservative. A conservative view of corrective policies is more likely to come from the works respondents than from others (67% versus 55%).

Strong conservatism regarding racial integration of congregations is the rule rather than the exception among the "works" respondents, though it is only somewhat more prevalent than among other respondents (52% versus 43%). Finally, women's issues receive moderately or strongly conservative reactions from more works respondents than from other respondents (64% versus 53%). The works respondents are likely to oppose pastoral advocacy (34%, as opposed to 21% of other respondents), presumably because they doubt that pastors would pursue social and political causes which would have appeal for them.

The "sincere" respondents are a particularly interesting group, because they offer some evidence as to the roots of more tolerant attitudes toward individual behavior, as well as to political liberalism. Their responses to the items on individual behavior and political change show them to be in exact opposition to the biblical literalists: they are far less likely than are other respondents to have highly conservative scores on disobedience to authority (22% versus 41%), new morality (16% versus 39%), and international human rights (22% versus 34%).

The data offered thus far suggest that "sincere" respondents are a highly secularized group for whom religious beliefs are not very important or meaningful. This is consistent with the self-definition they have chosen, which implies that the content of religious beliefs is not central to faith. However, there is no evidence that the rejection of "orthodox" beliefs has any particular effect upon social, socioeconomic, and social advocacy variables; that is, the "sincere" respondents do not differ from the rest of the lay sample on these matters of public policy, social justice, and church involvement in both arenas.

Discompassionate Theodicies

Discompassionate theodicies, as mentioned earlier, are explanations for the existence of suffering and evil in the world which discourage action to alleviate these phenomena. It has been hypothesized that such theodices have a major (negative) impact upon support for church social activism, as contrasted to other variables;[8] that is, because such theodicies do not encourage structural change in society, it is to be expected that respondents who hold them would be similarly indisposed to church support for structural change.

Questionnaire respondents were asked to choose one of a variety of statements as expressive of their view as to "how a merciful God can allow terrible things to happen." Some respondents chose views which encourage structural change, notably the beliefs that "people cause these things to happen, not God" or that such evil and suffering "doesn't seem right to me." Others chose what have been termed discompassionate theodicies, such as the view that "God allows terrible things to happen in order to punish people for their sins," or that "the devil causes them," or that "we don't know why these things happen, but we know that God is able to use them for good."

The choice of a discompassionate theodicy is associated with conservative viewpoints regarding the authority and new morality indexes and some of the political and social/socioeconomic attitudinal indexes. However, it has no relation to the church advocacy indexes, a finding which contradicts the hypothesis offered above. The special character of these theodicies apparently does not affect church social activism per se, but affects reactions to behaviors and groups which are labelled as socially deviant.

Regarding the authority and new morality indexes, only about 20% of the overall lay sample (as opposed to nearly half of those who espouse discompassionate theodicies) take highly conservative views. This means that those who believe that evil and suffering are humanly caused, or are simply incomprehensible, are far more tolerant of deviations from norms regarding authority and personal conduct than are those persons who are inclined to provide transcendental explanations for evil and suffering.

The reactions of respondents to corrective public policy supports this interpretation of the data. When asked to comment upon several punitive policies taken by the state (increased police power, the death penalty, fewer welfare dollars), those respondents who chose discompassionate theodicies were more likely than others to take conservative views. This was particularly true of those few respondents (only about 2% of the lay sample) who believe that evil and suffering occur in order to punish people for their sins. Fully 60% of those respondents took the most conservative posture on the subject of corrective public policy, as opposed to about 20% of the entire sample.

God's Influence

One measure of the extent to which lay respondents view God as "active" in human affairs is contained in their descriptions of God's influence upon the world. Respondents were allowed to choose from a variety of statements concerning the way in which God influences the things that happen in the world. Two statements allowed respondents to answer that God does not influence human events, except for having set history in motion. Other responses presented to respondents were: "God influences individuals, who then shape events," and "God influences individuals, but also shapes events directly through nations and social affairs." Clearly, the latter response is most indicative of a God who is active in all dimensions of human affairs.

Once again, those respondents who view God as influencing human events most directly take a conservative position regarding the authority and new morality indexes. Between 45% and 50% of those who believe God "shapes events directly" are highly conservative on these indexes, as opposed to about one-third of those who believe that "God influences individuals (only)" and about one-quarter of those who do not perceive God as influencing human events.

While beliefs concerning God's influence have no apparent bearing on the political or social attitudes of lay respondents, they are associated with views concerning political advocacy by pastors. Here, however, the results are a bit different: those respondents who believe that "God influences individuals (only)" tend to side with those who do not perceive God as influencing the world, in contrast to those respondents who believe that God "shapes human events directly." The latter are likely to approve political advocacy by pastors. This relationship is presumably explained by the fact that the acceptance of pastoral advocacy is in some part due to the belief that pastors speak God's word concerning human affairs.

RELIGIOUS PRACTICES

Because religious practices are not often strongly related to the attitudinal indexes, we will not discuss them as fully as we did the beliefs indexes. We will, however, have occasion to describe the extent to which private or familial religious practice is related to these attitudes, in contrast to church-located practices. The latter, which will be discussed briefly first, include frequency of worship attendance, self-described level of activity in the congregation and in the church, and the view that the church is central to one's spiritual life.

Frequency of Church Attendance

Frequency of church attendance has relatively little bearing on the attitudinal indexes described in chapter 5. Where it is related to attitudes of respondents, frequency of church attendance is related in a curvilinear fashion. This means that those persons who report that they attend worship services only once or twice annually, and those who never attend church services, are more likely to take conservative views than those persons who attend every month or six weeks. However, those persons who attend twice a month or more often are most likely to take conservative views. This pattern holds for the authority and new morality indexes, and for the women's equality index.

Two comments may be offered to explain these findings. First, the curvilinearity of the relationships may be partially explained by the fact that many older and disabled persons, who are quite conservative regarding individual behavior and women's equality, do not attend church services as often as does the average church member due to health, transportation, and weather conditions.[9]

Secondly, the particular areas in which these relationships exist (and do not exist) should not be surprising. Those respondents who report that they attend worship services "every week" are far more conservative than even those persons who report attendance "nearly every week." Almost half of the weekly attenders, as opposed to one-third of those who attend nearly every week, take the most conservative positions on the authority and new morality indexes. This pattern suggests that a certain "works" orientation demanding weekly worship attendance is at root here. This view is supported by the fact that church attendance affects only those variables which are common to the "saved" and to respondents holding "orthodox" views of God, the devil, and life after death.[10]

116

Activity in Church/Congregation

Self-descriptions of respondents as "very active" or "active" in their congregations and in the church are somewhat subjective measures of religious practice. That is, respondents are allowed to choose their own criteria for a decision about their own behaviors. That this variable produces a mixture of positive, negative, and curvilinear results is indicative of the fact that such self-descriptions are composites which include such matters as church attendance, evaluations of the importance of the church, congregational leadership, and other indicators of activity. Thus, these responses will not be discussed here; rather, more objective indicators will be analyzed.

Importance of the Church

Those persons who view the church as essential or important to their spiritual lives, and those persons who believe that God speaks to them through the church, take an interesting set of views. While they are conservative regarding individual behavior and corrective public policies, they are liberal in their attitudes toward public policies, which would equalize economic resources and benefits, and toward church advocacy of these. For example, the most conservative attitude toward church advocacy of economic equalization was expressed by 57% of those who did not attend church, in contrast with only 23% of those who indicated that God speaks to them through the church "most of the time."

Those who stress the importance of the church are, in effect, liberated by the church from the extreme attitudinal implications of the "works" position. This point requires some explanation. In effect, the respondents who find the church important/essential and who believe that God speaks to them through the church offer responses which parallel those of the "works" respondents, but which are more liberal on political, social, and church advocacy indexes. In the cases of tolerant views toward individual behaviors (authority, new morality), the effect of the church is much less pronounced.

Private/Family Devotions

This variable, interestingly, is a far better predictor of attitudinal conservatism than any of the other religious *practices* variables. This is particularly notable in the case of the church advocacy variables. While religious practices which are centered around the church have no effect on attitudes toward church advocacy, private religious

117

practices do have such effects. (So, too, do they affect views concerning individual behavior, political change, and changes in the status of women, but these are occasionally related to church-centered practices as well.)

Private/family devotions include two types of behavior. Individual behaviors of this kind include frequent private prayer and Bible reading, as well as attention to religious radio and television. Family-related behaviors include the recitation of grace before daily meals, family prayers and devotions, and family Bible reading. Each lay respondent was given a score on the private and family devotions indexes, based on his/her perception of performance of these activities. These two types (private and family) need to be understood at the outset, since they operate somewhat differently from one another. In the case of individual behavior, both private and family devotions are positively associated with conservatism. In the cases of domestic political change, church and societal efforts to change the status and roles of women, and political advocacy by pastors, only private devotions have this effect.

An illustration is in order. Of those who scored highest on the private devotions index, about two-thirds also took the most conservative posture on individual behavior; the comparable figure for those who do not engage in these private devotions is about one-fifth. Family devotions are also strongly related. Nearly half of the high scorers on the family devotions index were most conservative concerning individual behavior, as compared to about 30% of those who received low scores. On the political change index, those who engage in many private devotions were about twice as likely to be conservative as were those who do not engage in these (48% versus 24%). Similar results occurred in the area of church (32% versus 12%) and societal efforts on behalf of women (44% versus 21%), and that of political advocacy by pastors (41% versus 20%).

The strong relationship of private devotions to both individual behavioral and other forms of conservatism suggests a relationship between private devotional practice and "orthodox" beliefs, particularly biblical literalism. Family devotions, on the other hand, are not associated with such "orthodox" beliefs.

RELIGIOUS ORGANIZATIONAL PARTICIPATION
Congregational Leadership

Congregational leadership has been divided into the categories "elected position" and "voluntary position" for this analysis. This was necessary because elected and voluntary leaders have quite different attitudinal patterns; this may be seen by reference to table 22. The elected congregational leaders in this sample are more conservative than are respondents as a group toward the new morality and toward punitive policies exercised by the state. They are more likely than average, however, to encourage intervention of American governments into matters of human and civil rights across the globe. These differences are small and uninteresting when compared to the distinctive portrait of voluntary leaders which arises from the data.

Voluntary leaders at the congregational level are a consistently liberal group on social issues and in regard to church advocacy. However, they are not more liberal on individual behavioral and political issues than is the remainder of the sample. Rather, they reflect "average" views on such matters. What this indicates is a strong social conscience and a strong belief that the church should take an active role in implementing that social conscience. Some of the findings are as follows: Regarding corrective public policies exercised by the government only 17% of the volunteer leaders, as opposed to 24% of nonleaders, took extremely conservative positions. Volunteer leaders were less likely than nonvolunteers to take very conservative views regarding government policies which would equalize economic resources and benefits (10% volunteer leaders versus 15% nonleaders), church advocacy for these government policies (25% versus 30%), integration of local congregations (41% to 50%), changes in the status and roles of women (25% to 34%), church efforts on behalf of women (15% versus 18%), and political advocacy by pastors (22% versus 27%).

Since they are not terribly large, these percentage differences may not appear to be of much significance but—when coupled with the facts that they are remarkably consistent, that the number of volunteers in the sample is very large (more than half serve in a congregational voluntary leadership capacity), and that these figures represent only one end of a response continuum—they are highly significant indeed.

Membership in Church Youth Groups

A second measure of religious organizational participation is membership in church youth groups, past or present. Like volunteer leadership, membership in church youth groups exerts a liberal effect on the social attitudes measured here. However, the effect is

119

slightly less consistent. Once again, membership in church youth groups, past or present, exhibits no relationship with the individual behavioral indexes. However, fully 45% of those who had never been members of a church youth group were strongly opposed to American intervention in behalf of international human rights; in contrast, only 34% of those who were members of Lutheran church groups, 32% of those who were members of Lutheran and other groups, and 30% of those who were members of non-Lutheran groups opposed such intervention.

Using the four options of membership in church youth groups, (1) for non-youth-group members, (2) Lutheran youth-group members, (3) Lutheran and other denominational youth-group members, and (4) non-Lutheran youth-group members, the following percentages emerge in relation to these social issues: opposition to minority inclusion in congregations: 49%, 42%, 43%, 42%; conservatism regarding changes in the roles and status of women: 36%, 27%, 22%, 22%; church advocacy on behalf of women: 20%, 14%, 15%, 18%; and church support of public policies which would equalize economic benefits and resources: 32%, 24%, 23%, 37%. These figures should make it clear that there is a tendency for those persons who have not engaged in any church-related youth groups to be less positive in their reactions to some rather controversial church-supported social positions than are persons who have engaged in such groups. Also, there is no evidence that affiliation with Lutheran youth groups produced more conservative responses than did affiliation with groups composed of members of other denominations.

CONCLUSION

These data have illustrated quite clearly that religious beliefs and practices are strongly associated with conservative attitudes toward the individual behavioral indexes measuring disobedience of authority and the new morality. Not only "orthodox" beliefs, but basic, consensual Christian beliefs, as measured by the salience of faith index, are so associated. The one exception to this pattern is in regard to the "sincere" respondents, who tend to be liberal on matters of individual behaviors and political actions.

Attitudes of other types, which are removed from the individual behavioral level, are not affected by such basic, consensual Christian beliefs. Rather, biblical literalism (and the related tendency to choose the biblical over the scientific account of creation) and the "works"

orientation (faith means "a life of commitment to God that I demonstrate by trying to do what is right") are the only forms of belief
which are strongly associated with conservative political and social/
socioeconomic attitudes. While generally these are not strongly associated with the church advocacy indexes, they are related to a negative view regarding political advocacy by pastors. Essentially, this was
interpreted as an indicator of the belief that the church should "stick
to spiritual matters and stay out of politics."

With the exception of private/family devotions, religious practices
were found to have very little relationship to the political, social/
socioeconomic, and church advocacy indexes. Private devotions,
however, were associated with conservatism in many of these matters—particularly those associated with the "orthodox" and "works"
belief structures. In contrast, religious practices which are centered
around the church displayed few relationships of any strength with
any of the attitudinal indexes.

Finally, religious organizational participation operated quite differently than did religious beliefs and practices. Particularly in the
cases of volunteer leadership positions and membership in church
youth groups, organizational participation was found to have no relationship to the individual behavioral indexes, but to be consistently
related to liberal attitudes on political, social/socioeconomic, and
church advocacy indexes.

These findings suggest that the relationship between religion and
conservative social attitudes is rather diversified: "orthodoxy" affects
such attitudes more often and more extensively than do basic, consensual Christian beliefs; practice (particularly public practice) is of
lesser importance; religious organizational participation (at least of a
voluntary sort) works in a pattern which is the reverse of that associated with "orthodoxy." Clearly, judgments about the morality of individual behavior are more often affected by religious beliefs and
practices than are other attitudes. Social ethics, on the other hand,
are less likely to be treated as directly related to the religious beliefs
of individuals. Where they are so related (as in the case of biblical literalism and the "works" orientation) they are related to a conservative direction.

Some readers may respond to these data by stating that the LCA is
characterized neither by "orthodoxy" nor by a "works" orientation.
Nevertheless, it must be stressed that significant minorities, and
sometimes majorities, of respondents associated themselves with "orthodox" beliefs and/or "works" orientations. While only 16% of the

121

lay respondents took a fully literal view of the Bible, about half of the laity chose the biblical account of creation as correct, in exclusion of the scientific account. Two-thirds of the respondents believed in the existence of the devil. More than one-third believed in life after death, "with rewards for some people and punishment for others." More than one-quarter chose the "works" view of faith over the traditional Lutheran response "my trust in God's grace."

Because these responses are not simply characteristic of a small segment of the lay sample, and because they affect attitudinal outcomes, they should be regarded with interest by the leadership of the church. Probably the most important findings, should we wish to single out two which have major significance, are these:

1. The salience and consistency with which basic consensual Christian beliefs are held influence attitudes toward the morality of individual behavior, but have no effect on attitudes toward social issues.

2. Biblical literalism and the related belief in the biblical, as opposed to the scientific, view of creation are very good predictors of conservatism of a more pervasive and general sort.

7

Those "Conservative" Lutherans

TIMOTHY LULL

What are we to make of the portrait of Lutheran social and ethical attitudes that emerges in this study—is it predictable? I find the resulting image of the church to be recognizable, mildly reassuring, and full of implications for future work to be done. I would not like to be misunderstood on the question of predictability. The research described here is fascinating and well deserving of careful study. It has revealed a number of trends, insights, and connections which must be surprising to all. Nevertheless, the place to begin is with the fact that the Lutherans described in the two previous chapters are a great deal like what one would expect Lutherans to be. Let me try to be specific.

A CLASSIC LUTHERAN PORTRAIT
The Conservative Heritage

The Lutheran ethical heritage is, I think, rightly characterized as basically conservative. By this I do not mean that Lutherans vote in a certain way in American elections, but rather that the teachings of the Lutheran church contain a number of characteristics that are conserving or stabilizing in the social and ethical realm.

One of these is the high regard for the role of the state. In Article XVI of the Augsburg Confession the state is assigned a positive and important role in human life:

> It is taught among us that all government in the world and all established rule and laws were instituted and ordained by God for the sake of good order, and that Christians may without sin occupy civil offices or serve as princes and judges, render decisions and pass sentence according to imperial and other existing laws, punish evildoers with the sword, engage in just wars, serve as soldiers, buy and sell, take required oaths, possess property, be married, etc.[1]

The state has its legitimate role directly from God. Therefore, I am not surprised to find Lutherans in North America reluctant to overthrow the government and even, surprising as it may be to others, reluctant to cheat on their income taxes (table 15).[2]

The basic impulse toward government is negative. In a fallen, sinful world violence lives potentially in each person, and the state has a very important role to play in restraining the evil within each one of us and in establishing a minimum of good order. Perhaps the state also has a positive role to play, if one speaks not simply of restraining evil but of establishing justice. Yet, most Lutheran theologians have tended, until recently, to put the emphasis on the police role of the state. Therefore, it is not surprising to find large numbers of Lutherans supporting more power for the police and the death penalty (table 16). These functions of the state are reflected in the above quotation from the Augsburg Confession.

I find H. Richard Niebuhr to be correct in saying that the basic thrust of Lutheran ethics runs in this culturally conservative direction since the state is seen more as a restraining force than as a positive instrument of justice. Short of the return of Christ, justice in the fallen world will always be partial and imperfect.[3]

Nevertheless, this tendency to characterize Lutherans as conservative can easily be overstated. The Augsburg Confession itself, in the same Article, goes on to note the limits of obedience:

> Christians are obliged to be subject to civil authority and obey its commandments and laws in all that can be done without sin. But when commands of the civil authority cannot be obeyed without sin, we must obey God rather than men (Acts 5:29).[4]

This "escape clause" has received much attention in Lutheran ethics since the time of the perceived bondage of the German churches to the Nazi regime. Pastors especially, having been trained in such revisionist Lutheran ethics in their seminary days, can be expected to uphold the right of Christians to work to overthrow the government—at least under certain conditions.[5]

Respect for Authority

Classic Lutheranism also has tended to stress the legitimate role of authority in the family, in the church, and in society. Luther's explanation of the Fourth Commandment was, perhaps, the popular key to that attitude. Christians were instructed not only to honor and obey their parents; the commandment was extended to include all those in authority—employer, prince, and pastor alike.

The members of the Lutheran Church in America today are not so different in their attitudes. They claim that two major sources of learning about the meaning and purpose of life have been parents and listening to sermons (L–Q3). They seem to enjoy being in harmony with the traditional teachings and doctrine of the church rather than having to work out their own answers (table 3). They give no evidence of having a revolutionary agenda for society or, at least, of having any confidence that such an agenda would be realized.

We see this especially in the list of behaviors that they find most morally objectionable. Among the laity 93% agree that cheating on income tax is always or usually wrong, and 90% would say the same about showing disrespect to parents (table 15). Laws are helpful and ought to be enforced, even if this means putting business executives in jail, when, known to them, their companies break the law (table 16).[6]

Consensus in Personal Ethics

The Lutherans in this study have a rather large degree of consensus on certain issues in personal ethics. They are not in favor of behaviors that would seem to change or challenge the fabric of personal and family life. They overwhelmingly reject both homosexual relations and legalizing marijuana. They generally reject premarital sex, although a larger number are willing to be situational about this issue which probably has touched almost every family.

Yet, this consensus does not extend to detailed issues of public policy. Here, as the previous essays have shown, Lutherans tend to cover the political spectrum. This, too, does not seem surprising. Both family life and the role of government have changed dramatically since the sixteenth century. But in a basic sense, governmental patterns have changed more. No one can continue to teach Luther without some adaptation to a democratic society where people actively participate in decisions that would have been relegated to the prince in an earlier age.

On the other hand, issues of personal ethics may seem more continuous with traditional teachings. The Ten Commandments seem to give more direct guidance for the individual than for the organization of society. There have been changes here too, as, for example, in the majority of Lutheran laity who take a situational approach to the question of abortion (table 15). But it is not impossible to see how Lutherans could have more commonality on a cluster of family-related ethical issues than on issues of public policy for which there is no clear guidance in their tradition.

All of this suggests that Lutherans have not signed on to any new morality which was supposed to have emerged in the sixties, or, if they have, that it has been on a very selective basis. And increasingly this seems to be true of the society as a whole. Chapter 3 showed that premarital sex is a question with some seriously divisive possibilities for the church, but generally there is a wide consensus about matters of personal morality.

An Inclusive Church

Yet, beyond that consensus, there is great diversity in Lutheran social and ethical views. This is the point that I find reassuring, for, aside from the merits of each individual issue, the Lutheran church has hoped to be a church that might be inclusive of diverse people. There is a strong heritage of being a church-type rather than a sect-type church, able to accommodate deeply penultimate differences around a deeper ultimate core of faith.

And in my view this is something to celebrate. The church is what it says it wants to be—a church, including people of diverse views about social issues, with a full component of liberals, conservatives, and moderates. This is worth noting carefully—that the LCA is not mainstream or mainline in the sense of being composed almost entirely of people with either bland or middle-of-the-road views. Rather, on the various issues, and especially on the question of how active the church ought to be politically, there is great diversity.

We sense all of the potential tensions, as they have been spelled out in earlier chapters. The young and the old have somewhat different views of sex—or at least some young (and some old) have more permissive views than most of the rest. A number of people want the church directly involved in political action and a number want the church to deal only with spiritual matters. Yet, all these people are in the church together, and even the broad middle, which may be something of a buffer, is divided itself. On the last issue of political involvement, some want the church to make policy statements and some oppose policy statements. But the church imposes no political or social litmus test for membership—even indirectly.

I have been arguing that the portrait of Lutheran social and ethical opinions that emerges here is hardly surprising, because it is in large continuity with what one would expect from Lutheran theology and history. I am not prepared to argue a causal connection here. It may be that many of these continuities are accidental. I am only saying that the Lutherans in this study are what we would expect them to be from some of the classic portraits in modern theological literature—Niebuhr's in *Christ and Culture* or Althaus's in the *Ethics of Martin Luther*. But now it is time to look at the findings on some of the more specific issues.

SOME SPECIFIC ISSUES

Chapter 5 explored some of the social and ethical attitudes that emerged in the survey of lay attitudes. The laity were most enthusiastic about jailing business executives if, known to them, their companies break the law; about the ordination of women; and—to a somewhat lesser extent—about American leaders taking a tough stand in support of human rights in other countries. Most of them were opposed to legalizing marijuana, to spending more government money for people on welfare, and to more freedom for homosexuals (tables 15 and 16).

The support for a single standard of punishment that would include some forms of "white-collar crime" as well as violent crime is not completely surprising in a church that takes a strong view of the legitimate role of law, and that stresses responsibility in one's vocation as a way of living out Christian faith in the world. The opposition to the legalization of marijuana and greater freedom for homosexuals is also not surprising, given the strong sense of family that has characterized Lutheran piety. It is also quite possible that both marijuana and homosexuality seem like "remote" issues to a large segment of Lutherans, whether or not this is in fact the case, and that therefore somewhat more absolute responses are possible here than in the case of abortion and premarital sex, where respondents tended to take a more situational approach.

Two of the issues that received strong support have been prominent in recent years as the subjects of church action and much discussion. The LCA voted to ordain women in 1970, and the slow but steady increase in the number of LCA women pastors has rightly received a good deal of publicity. At its national convention in 1978 the church adopted a detailed statement on human rights. This means that at the time of the survey (winter 1978–79) many Lutherans would have been involved in the studies leading up to or resulting from this action, while an even greater number would have some minimal awareness that their church was "pro–human rights."

This leaves the question of the government spending more for people on welfare. The strength of the rejection of this suggestion deserves examination. It was supported by only 6% of the laity and by 22% of the clergy (table 16). Given recent developments in American politics, this shows, perhaps, that Lutherans share a general distaste for high levels of government spending and disillusionment with social programs that are said to have failed.

But I suspect that something about the wording of the question guaranteed a highly negative response.[7] The precise wording was whether one mostly favored or mostly opposed "spending more government money for people on welfare." I think there are three code words of phrases here—"more," "government money," and "people on welfare." These all tend to trigger certain resentments that many people have of high levels of welfare spending and, whether true or false, perceptions of high levels of fraud and endless cycles of dependency. We can assume that these members are overwhelmingly opposed to "spending more government money for people on welfare." But it would be fascinating to see how the responses might change if one had a question worded in a more sympathetic way —assuring adequate welfare benefits or even providing a decent standard of living for people who cannot help themselves.

I must admit that I have some of the same regrets about the wording of the item "more freedom for homosexuals" (table 16). We know that LCA members feel quite strongly that homosexual relations are always wrong (66% of laity; 50% of clergy) (table 15). We cannot be certain, however, about the triggering effect of the word "more" in this question concerning freedom for homosexuals. More freedom might suggest more visibility or support for activist gay-liberation groups, and we have good reason to doubt that LCA members would be very sympathetic to that. On the other hand, the church during the convention in 1970 adopted a statement on "Sex, Marriage, and Family" which rather firmly supports "understanding and justice in church and community" for homosexuals.[8] Would that be "more freedom," or do people take such understanding and basic civil rights for granted?

On other social issues Lutherans were divided and undecided. These included changes in form of government, the death penalty, more power to the police, active support for Soviet dissidents, special opportunities for blacks to go to college, and leaving South Africa alone to solve its own problems (table 16). These are complex issues on which the society itself seems divided or perplexed, and it isn't surprising to find the same degree of uncertainty among LCA members.

One wonders what bound together the quarter of laity and clergy who did support "major changes in our form of government" (table 16). This might be anything from socialism to states' rights to reform of the electoral-college system. In fact, the surprise to me is that so many would endorse such a vague proposal without a clearer sense of what was being offered. Further studies may want to see whether this represents a "dissatisfaction-with-government" factor, or whether there are trends among this significant minority who do favor major changes.

On four of the six issues on which opinion was divided there also emerged a difference in clergy and lay attitudes. The largest group of laity (49%) support the death penalty; the largest group of clergy (68%) oppose it. The largest group of laity (39%) support giving more power to the police; the largest group of clergy (62%) oppose it. Clergy favor support for Soviet dissidents (61%) and oppose "leaving South Africa alone to solve its own problems" (62%). The largest group of laity are undecided on these issues (38% in each case) suggesting that the issue may be unfamiliar or the wording of the question too difficult. "Leaving South Africa alone to solve its own problems" sounds neutral and fair unless you know something about how those problems would probably be solved. Only 33% of the laity and 19% of the clergy were willing to support this proposal (table 16).

Two areas where the LCA has made rather strong institutional commitments in recent years have been those of racial and sexual equality. A social statement on "Race Relations" (1964) was made much more concrete in 1978 by a convention action on Ministry to Minorities. Here, the church pledged itself to work for racial justice and racial inclusiveness at every level, and to recruit black clergy. Specific numerical goals were even included to try to give this document something more than token status.[9]

Chapter 5 has pointed out the lack of grass-roots enthusiasm for implementation of these goals, especially regarding the responsibility of congregations to "be doing more to increase the number of minorities holding membership." This lukewarm support for racial inclusiveness in the church deserves serious consideration. On the other hand, given the large patterns of residential segregation in our society, it may be that many LCA members do not live in those black and racially changing communities where substantial progress toward the meeting of these goals seems to be taking place, and, therefore, that the issue seems abstract or impossible to them.

More information is available concerning member attitudes toward sexual equality in our society. We have noted the strong support for the ordination of women (69% laity; 81% clergy), which seems substantial, given how recently this change has been made. Chapter 5 also notes strong support for "women becoming more involved in politics" and general support for "current societal efforts to strengthen or change women's status in society" (table 18).

But when it comes to a question regarding "current overall efforts of the various women's liberation groups," only 23% of the laity and 40% of the clergy are favorable (table 18). This does not seem surprising to me, nor does the strong evidence that these members lack enthusiasm for the changing status of men and women in society. Some resistance could be expected and is present. The passage of the Equal Rights Amendment is favored by laity by a slim 41% to 36% margin, with a full 20% undecided about an issue that has been widely discussed (table 17). But the lack of enthusiasm for "various women's liberation groups" is not surprising at all. Since no indication is given of which groups are meant, the respondent is left to fill in with her or his own imagination, and the groups that come to mind are likely to be those which have been strident or controversial, making frequent appearances on television talk shows and in the press.

The composite picture that emerges is not one of "conservative" Lutherans as in the title of this chapter, nor of "moderate" Lutherans who take the middle of the road on each issue, but of a group with truly diverse opinions about major issues that are before the American society today. Those who want the church to lead the campaign for social change are bound to be disappointed (although they can hardly be surprised). But it would be a mistake to see the church as generally and instinctively conservative. The portrait that emerges is one of people who are reasonably nonideological and who think through individual issues with some independence.

THE CHURCH'S SOCIAL STATEMENTS

If the social and ethical opinions of the members and clergy of the LCA are moderate, diverse, or even not "simply conservative," this may be a major victory in itself. Given the ethical heritage outlined above, and given the very conservative role of the church in Germany, it would not have been surprising for the Lutherans in North America to be depressingly predictable on all such issues.

That this has not happened is probably the result of many factors, including the length of time that this church (through its predecessor churches) has been in America, the effects of secularization, and the large influx of members from other backgrounds. Still, a general theological/confessional heritage has been maintained, and a conservative or quietist approach to ethics has not.

The institution itself has played a modest role in helping members rethink major social issues. In the past two decades this has been done largely through the adoption of sixteen social statements at national conventions. These statements have been occasions for the church, at this representative level, to wrestle with a large variety of the issues that were considered in this survey. The statements have included: "Prayer and Bible Reading in the Public Schools" (1964), "Race Relations" (1964), "Poverty" (1966), "Vietnam" (1966), "The Church and Social Welfare" (1968), "Conscientious Objection" (1968), "Religious Liberty" (1968), "Sex, Marriage, and Family" (1970), "World Community" (1970), "The Human Crisis in Ecology" (1972), and "The Offender and Systems of Correction" (1972). No new statements were adopted at the conventions in 1974 and 1976 (the church was busy with a new worship book, communion practices, and restructuring and was perhaps also a bit weary of the pace), but four additional statements have been added in recent years: "Aging and the Older Adult" (1978), "Human Rights" (1978), "Economic Justice" (1980), and "Death and Dying" (1982).

These statements, taken as a whole, represent a remarkable production. If they are somewhat less than an all-inclusive examination of social ethics (there is, for example, no comprehensive statement on war and peace) they nevertheless represent a serious attempt on the part of the church to speak to society and to its own members, and in the course of this to set certain priorities. Recent statements have been possibly less controversial, but supported by a long study process, careful theological formulations, and extensive debate on the floor of the convention before being adopted.[10]

What are the purposes of these statements? This cannot be answered easily, because the statements seem to play several different roles. They are a word from the church to the wider community, and they have been used to some extent by Lutheran advocacy and lobbying offices. Obviously, they are of even greater interest to church members, and they have a certain educational effect from their first formulation, through the convention action, to the rather extensive attempts at follow-up by way of the church's publications and adult-education series.

But, in another sense, they also set priorities for the church. Once the church has spoken or acted on an issue in this formal way, there is an attempt to study the implications of such a statement for church action. Leaders, including parish clergy, tend to be somewhat informed about these actions, which therefore also represent, even in an informal way, certain setting of priorities for the congregations.

Therefore, it is interesting to examine questionnaire responses for evidence of congruity with or rejection of the church's official positions. This is a rather speculative matter, since we cannot hope to establish any causal connection. It may even be that the church simply tends to act officially on what the traffic will bear. But these statements represent such a major effort of the church that we ought to look for possible correlations with the results of the social and ethical attitudes section of the study.

Human Rights

Mention has already been made of the church's 1978 statement on human rights. The statement, subtitled "Doing Justice in God's World," is designed to be something of an overview and theological foundation for other statements and actions. After a review of the current situation which brings the human-rights question into focus, the statement gives a theological foundation for understanding "the human" and relates specific rights to "the basic aspects of human relationship which undergird the Ten Commandments."

The statement was timely, given the tensions within U.S. foreign policy in the area of human rights and the opposition that policy was receiving from aspiring presidential candidates at the time the survey was taken. However, the statement is theoretical enough that it contains few specific policy suggestions; rather, these are treated in an appendix which is not published with the basic document.

We have already seen that there is support among survey respondents for "American leaders taking a tough stand in support of human rights in other countries." Lay members favor this by a mere majority of 51% (with 22% opposed and 25% undecided). Clergy support such action by a strong majority of 79%, with 10% opposed and 10% undecided (table 16). We have seen before that clergy are most likely to be influenced by the official stand of the church and are more likely than all but the most active laity to be aware of such stands.

It would be very interesting to see how opinion on this question has changed, given the different foreign policy of the current administration and the time that has passed since the survey was taken. Human rights, on the whole, seems a less popular issue now, although a nominee for assistant secretary of state recently failed to receive Senate confirmation (and actually withdrew his name) in part because of his strong opposition to a human-rights basis for foreign policy. This nominee was sharply criticized by various church bodies, including individual theologians of the LCA.

Abortion

The 1970 statement on "Sex, Marriage, and Family" contains a discussion of the question of abortion which has been both highly praised and sharply attacked. It is worth citing the exact language of the text to give a precise sense of the church's stand:

> In the consideration of induced abortion the key issue is the status of the unborn fetus. Since the fetus is the organic beginning of human life, the termination of its development is always a serious matter. Nevertheless, a qualitative distinction must be made between the claims and the rights of a responsible person made in God's image who is in living relationships with God and other human beings. . . . On the basis of the evangelical ethic, a woman or couple may decide responsibly to seek an abortion.[11]

The matter is always serious, but a contextual approach is developed in which individuals "may decide responsibly to seek an abortion."

This position is in basic harmony with the position taken by respondents in this study, although it is clear that not all would agree. In asking whether abortion is wrong, the survey found 53% of the laity and 55% of the clergy saying that it depends on the situation. In addition, 13% of the laity and 31% of the clergy chose the answer "usually wrong," which does not seem totally out of keeping with the sober permission given abortion in the LCA statement (table 15).

Our purpose here is not to claim that the statement in 1970 influenced the answers in 1979. We can only note that the answers given to the questions are at least in rough harmony with the position taken by the church, which has recently refused to ally itself with either pro-life or pro-choice groups. It is also interesting to note that clergy, who tend on many items to be more "liberal" than laity, were

RELIGIOUS BELIEFS AND SOCIAL-ETHICAL ATTITUDES

very reluctant to choose the answer "not at all wrong" (only 1% taking this option). A small but significant minority of laity (6%) was willing to argue that abortion is not at all wrong (table 15). It would be interesting to study this group more carefully to see what other views they might have in common.

Premarital Sex

Reference has been made several times in this chapter, and in earlier chapters, to the general disapproval of premarital sexual intercourse. Sixty-seven percent of the laity and 72% of the clergy identified this behavior as always or usually wrong. Only 20% of the clergy and 23% of the laity chose the more situational or contextual answer, "depends on the situation" (table 15).

Here again, the views found in the survey correspond rather well to the position taken by the church in its 1970 statement. It must be granted that there is a certain ambiguity in the statement. It develops a view of marriage that transcends the notion of "marriage as a legal contract." It speaks of coitus achieving its "full potential" within the context of "the permanent covenant of fidelity." But a clear line at the end warns the reader, and the church, of the continuing official disapproval of premarital sexual intercourse:

> Because the Lutheran Church in America holds that sexual intercourse outside the context of the marriage union is morally wrong, nothing in this statement on "Sex, Marriage, and Family" is to be interpreted as meaning that this church either condones or approves pre-marital or extra-marital sexual intercourse.[12]

Capital Punishment

We have spoken so far of issues in which there is at least rough congruence between church teaching and public opinion within the church. There are other issues, however, in which the church's official position is at odds with the results of the survey. The most striking of these is probably capital punishment.

Lutherans have traditionally upheld the right of the state to execute criminals. Luther himself felt that one could be a hangman to the glory of God, since this is a part of the secular sword which God has entrusted to the state. The LCA's 1966 statement, which opposes capital punishment, therefore had to acknowledge that it was going against its own ethical tradition. Once again, the language is interesting enough to cite directly:

134

The biblical and confessional witness asserts that the state is responsible under God for the protection of its citizens and the maintenance of justice and public order. For the exercise of its mandate, the state has been entrusted by God with the power to take human life when the failure to do so constitutes a clear danger to the civil community. The possession of this power is not, however, to be interpreted as a command from God that death shall necessarily be employed in punishment for crime. On the other hand, a decision on the part of civil government to abolish the death penalty is not to be construed as a repudiation of the inherent power of the state to take life in the exercise of its divine mandate.[13]

The statement goes on to argue that capital punishment, even if an inherent right of the state, ought to be abolished in this society because of its disproportionate use against those unable to defend themselves and because of the "invalidity of the deterrence theory."

LCA members have not accepted this new position, on the whole. When asked about the death penalty, 49% of the laity were in favor and 32% opposed, with a substantial 17% undecided. Clergy, here again, seeming to support the teachings and actions of the church, opposed the death penalty 68% to 24% (table 16).

Because we do not know much about members' views on specific Social Statements, we do not know here whether members realized that their opinions on the subject went against the official action of the church. It would be safe to guess that a great many were not aware of this. It is also possible, however, that the church's statement has a certain restraining influence, so that without the statement on capital punishment, the number favoring the death penalty might be even higher.

World Justice

The survey showed that laity did not favor "a more equitable distribution of wealth according to the demands of poorer nations in the world today." Only 6% strongly favored this and another 34% favored it. On the other hand, opinion was truly scattered on this issue, and the 34% favoring redistribution of wealth was actually the largest group responding. The finding was that 28% were opposed and 11% strongly opposed. Clergy, again, took a somewhat different attitude, with 25% strongly in favor and 50% in favor (table 17).

I have two reactions to this finding before we turn to the Social Statements. First, it is rather astonishing to find 40% of an American church favoring an action which would seem to be opposed to their immediate self-interest. I also wonder how much the terminology of the question—the word "demands" in relation to the poorer nations—may have elicited the negative response. We have seen plenty of evidence that Lutherans are not too comfortable with *demands* for rights.

My guess is that the greater interest of the clergy in this issue is not simply a result of a more liberal and internationalist stance generally, but that once again they are reflecting the formal actions of the church in its social statements. On three occasions the church has spoken to this issue:

> Any commitment to the elimination of domestic poverty must be accompanied by a commitment to seek justice in the reduction of the disparity between rich and poor nations by programs designed to assist the developing nations to raise their standard of living. ("Poverty," 1966, p. 2)

> It is the Christian community within the affluent countries that is, by virtue of its prophetic heritage, called to set forth the obligations of the wealthy and the rights of the poor. It is scandalous that the industrialized West uses so little of its great wealth for the economic and social development of the newer nations. ("World Community," 1970, p. 5)

> No person, business enterprise, government, or other human agency holds ultimate title to the resources it controls. Private property is not an absolute right. Goods and abilities are held in trust from God and are to be allocated and used for justice in community. ("Human Rights," 1978, p. 8)

The proposal for "more equitable distribution" is admittedly vague, and perhaps easy to support in principle. Yet I continue to marvel that as many as 40% of Lutheran laity, randomly selected, would endorse such an idea. We do not know the sources of such opinions, but if the church has been any influence, it may well have been through the educational efforts of the World Hunger Appeal which has raised the consciousness of a substantial minority on this point.

Prayer in the Public Schools

One of the earliest and most controversial of the social statements was that concerning "Prayer and Bible Reading in the Public Schools." Many Lutherans were surprised to find their church defending the 1963 Supreme Court decision concerning prayer and Bible reading. The statement defended the rights of non-Christians in a pluralistic society and expressed considerable theological skepticism about the content of such prayers as might be religiously neutral enough to be acceptable to all.

We do not have information in this survey about attitudes on this subject. This is a great shame, since the issue is quite heated again at this time and since the church has continued to oppose any constitutional amendment that would find a way to return prayer and Bible reading to the schools. It would be fascinating to know to what extent the members support this continuing stance of the LCA.

Church Statements and Political Affairs

These are some of the major correlations between the survey data and the official stances of the church. Before we leave this subject, however, it would be good to take a final look at the range of opinions in the church on the subject of the church's involvement in political affairs. The study found a range of lay opinions from activist to quietist (table 19). A minority of less than 10% found "direct political action" acceptable, while another minority of 13% would limit the church to purely "spiritual matters" (table 19). The clergy took a more activist stance. A full 33% favored direct political action, while 35% favored policy statements. On the other hand, 23% chose the option of relating spiritual principles to political issues and only 1% were willing to limit the church to "deal only with spiritual matters." The fear of a church selling too short its own right to speak and act is clearly a live one for clergy (table 19).

What does this mean for the status and the future of LCA Social Statements? It is clear that small but significant groups in the church want either nothing of the sort or much more direct action. But what of the division between those favoring policy statements and those wanting spiritual principles related to political issues?

My guess is that the earlier statements of the LCA were seen as "policy statements" and therefore opposed by a small majority of LCA members. I would guess that the most recent statements seem to meet better the need for relating spiritual principles to political issues and therefore are more acceptable, even if they disappoint some of the more activist members. This is not to say that recent statements are bland, or that spiritual principles have no punch. What the "Human Rights" statement says about private property not being an absolute right generated as much controversy as the earlier stands against prayer in the schools and capital punishment.

FUTURE STRATEGY

I cannot read the results of the present study without turning to some consideration of future action. Lenin's question "What is to be done?" haunts all modern ethics, including Christian ethics, with the challenge to go beyond opinions to action. And several of the findings strike me as worthy of careful consideration by those who plan for the life and ministry of the LCA.[14]

The Meaning of Justice

Great attention must be given in the preaching and teaching of the church to help members see what justice means in relation to Christian faith. We have seen some evidence of how the Social Statements themselves draw on the concept of justice as one of the key ethical norms in their reasoning. But when we look at how justice is understood within the church, we find a great disparity between clergy and lay views, a disparity that may be a key to many of the other differences. When asked the meaning of a "God of justice," less than one-quarter of the laity understood that to mean that "the church should work for justice, and support groups that are working to end inequality and oppression" (table 23). It is clear that something like this definition of justice is at work in the Social Statements of the LCA and in the whole thrust for justice worldwide that underlies so much of the church's national program. It is also clear that this concept is little understood or that it is resisted, at least among laity. Clergy give a strikingly different set of responses—one of the greatest disparities in the whole survey, with 71% choosing the answer involving working for justice and only 15% choosing the individual's responsibility to be "just and fair in all my dealings" (table 23).

A great teaching effort is needed to help interpret the concept of justice in relation to love, fairness, and other ethical concepts, as well as in relation to the core confessional faith discussed in chapters 2 and 3 of this volume. In many ways, Lutheran theology has made great progress in this respect in the last few decades, and new views are characteristic of clergy. But there is special need to show how one can think of God and Christ in relation to something more than individual actions and decisions. The strong preference for an individualized understanding of God's justice is strong (and depressing) evidence that the ethic of Lutherans still tends to be privatized.

The Meaning of Suffering

Thinking about justice will require a rethinking of how God relates to the world, and this must lead, eventually, to the question of suffering in the world. The survey asked an important question about the Holocaust. It was reassuring to find that very few Lutheran laity or clergy saw the murder of six million Jews as either punishment for sins or the work of the devil (C–Q12; L–Q13).[15]

Nevertheless, the answer chosen by large numbers of respondents is still far from happy, theologically. The favorite response about how God could allow such things to happen was: "we don't know why these things happen, but we know that God is able to use them for good." As an eschatological statement, I cannot quarrel with this, but I am still uneasy at how quickly the second clause seems to follow the first. Sobering tragedies in human existence—the Holocaust, slavery, concentration camps, the fate of native Americans, and the prospect of nuclear war—cannot be lightly or too quickly dismissed with the affirmation that "God is able to use them for good." This kind of statement has its greatest power in the biblical witness when it is used confessionally, as by Joseph in Gen. 50:20 or Paul in 2 Cor. 12:9. When used to "solve" the problem of the sufferings that others face, it runs the danger of being a "cheap theodicy," if not strictly a "discompassionate theodicy."

What can be done? Once again the church's teaching must be addressed with greater force and clarity to such issues. There is no easy or satisfactory theological solution to the problem of suffering and injustice in the world. But the Luthern church with its particular heritage of a theology of the cross has a way of affirming God's presence in and with suffering that does not move too quickly to the glib response, "God is able to use them for good."

The Meaning of Human Sexuality

The evidence about sexuality in this study shows, I think, a certain continuing confusion about the subject on the part of LCA members and clergy. We know that young single adults generally have a different view of the acceptability of premarital sex, and that this difference represents, or appears to be tied to, a wholly different (and more distant) relation to the core of Christian faith.

We also know that LCA members are strongly opposed to homosexual relations and to more freedom for homosexuals, that they take a generally very negative view of premarital sexual intercourse, and that they are somewhat more contextual about the question of abortion. We also surmise that they continue to struggle with the theological and practical questions of the roles of and relations between women and men.

This is an area in which there is also great need for teaching—and even for preaching. We know from the clergy sample that there is no sermon topic more regularly avoided (out of twenty-two possibilities) than sexual conduct (C–Q27). On the other hand, this is understandable, since these issues are delicate and controversial, and since many pastors today are eager to be gospel-centered rather than to preach law.

But the meaning of our human sexuality is something that cries out for fresh interpretation and for relation to the fundamentals of our faith. Lutherans are rarely willing to say that God's laws must be obeyed blindly and without understanding. Our hope rather is that one can come to see the reason for rules. In the Small Catechism Luther struggles in his explanations of the Ten Commandments to help Christians do just that.

I am not calling for preaching sexual advice from the pulpit, or even suggesting that there are certain ideas and attitudes about sexuality which ought to be propagandized among our members. Rather, the whole issue calls for a fresh biblical and theological interpretation. What is the meaning of human sexuality in relation to creation, to Christ, to our calling in the world? How do Christians understand the differences between men and women in society today? How do we think about those whose sexual behavior differs from ours or even shocks us? We have ample reason from the press and television to know that these issues are regularly put before LCA members. What is less clear is that any specifically Christian or even Lutheran response is being formulated to help persons deal with their own sexuality and with the issues that touch almost every family.

A Cheer for Youth Ministry

Every reader should take a careful look at table 22. The author of chapter 6 has already explained a certain fascinating correlation between participation in church youth groups and certain social attitudes which the church has declared to be highly desirable. These include openness to such things as racial integration of congregations, a concern for human rights internationally, an openness to changing social status and roles of women, and church support for certain advocacy programs to equalize resources and benefits in the world.

Even if the correlation is somewhat ambiguous, it is sufficient to warrant some rethinking of the high importance of youth ministry as an activity of the church. Youth ministry must not be seen as a direct programmatic way of building the future of individual congregations; in our mobile society it has to be seen rather as an investment in the future of the church as a whole. On the other hand, I think that national agencies and especially parish pastors may want to be more positive about youth ministry and to make it more central to their own priorities. Certainly it emerges in the present study as one of the clearly open doors to reinforcing and even changing the social attitudes of members, bringing them more in line with those of the official teachings of the church.[16]

Continue the Process

A church with a conservative heritage emerges as having diverse political and social views. A church with some historic tendencies toward quietism has been struggling to address the issues of the day and to help members wrestle with them. These are exciting developments in the long and slow history of the church, and something to rejoice about.

Therefore the church should continue its efforts in the direction of social statements, social ministry, and selected advocacy. This questionnaire study contains helpful reality testing for the effectiveness of some of those efforts and information about where future work might be done.

In the same way, the process of studying the views of members needs to be continued. This means more questionnaires, more money, more analytical volumes like this, more people involved in the formulating of the questions. In public life there is always a danger that opinion sampling will become a substitute for policy, with leaders bending to the latest notions of what the people want. At this time that isn't a great danger in the church. There are plenty of counterweights to public opinion in the theological heritage, in continuing biblical study, and in research of other sorts. The danger of the church is more that the members will not be heard, that clergy/laity differences will be ignored, or even that the results will be greeted with unwarranted impatience and even disappointment. But there is no substitute for knowing what people think and feel and hope, and the Lutheran Listening Post surveys now represent crucial and even indispensable material for the doing of ethics today.

Other Views on Belief and Attitudinal Responses

8
Continuity and Diversity Among Lutherans

JERALD BRAUER

Historians are reluctant to speculate concerning the way historical developments may or may not have influenced human opinions and attitudes. Narrative is the backbone of the historian's art, and historians are anxious to tell a good story on how things came to pass and to analyze the way past events shaped succeeding events. But historians usually find it difficult to discuss the way events have shaped the thoughts or spirit of human beings. Thus the assignment to relate the findings of the Lutheran Listening Post (LLP) to the historical context of Lutheranism in America presents special problems.

The assumption behind the assignment is that the historical past of Lutheranism in the American scene will help us better to understand the responses to questions concerning religious beliefs and experiences. Henry Ford once said, "History is bunk," and so made clear that he thought nothing could be learned from history. Supposedly, a knowledge of the past gives one a perspective on the present, and even on the future, that otherwise would be lacking. The present has not dropped out of the sky but is the consequence of past factors, actions, institutions, thoughts, and movements. Society and human life is an ongoing process that grows out of the past into the present as it prepares to move on into the future. Both a society and an individual are to a large part determined by their past. History presents the givenness, the very stuff of life itself, out of which humanity lives. Both individuals and institutions are interested in the roots from whence they spring, because they think they will then understand better who they are and even where they are going.

Undoubtedly this was the concern that prompted the invitation to a historian to comment on the LLP findings in light of the particular historical experience of Lutheranism in the American scene. In preparing the LLP questionnaire on religious beliefs and experiences, special attention was given to the doctrinal or confessional intent of the questions. Supposedly, Lutherans have a particular theological stance marked by their adherence to historic confessions which gives a special emphasis to such doctrines as justification by grace through faith alone apart from any works, a profound christological orientation, a radical distinction between law and gospel, a special emphasis on the sacraments as means of grace, a belief in the real Presence apart from transubstantiation, and a quietism in the area of public ethics.

Did the clergy and laity responses reflect this assumed Lutheran theological stance? If they did not, what did they reflect? What did the Lutheran experience in America have to do with these responses? Were Lutherans conditioned by the American experience and context so that they became different types of Lutherans, or so that they no longer reflected a traditional Lutheran confessional attitude? In short, did Lutheran historical experience in America in any way condition the way Lutherans now believe and act on the implications of their faith?

These are difficult, if not impossible, questions for a historian to answer. Among the numerous problems encountered in working on an answer, two predominate. First, there is the problem of the adequacy of the questionnaire as a means of properly analyzing a so-called confessional Lutheran response. Though great care was taken in preparation of the questions, through consultation with Lutheran theologians and a constant working and reworking of the questions, two highly peculiar Lutheran emphases do not seem adequately represented, explicitly or implicitly, in the questionnaire. One is Luther's and Lutheranism's constant emphasis on struggle—rather than peace with God—as the hallmark of the religious life.

Perhaps nothing has marked Luther and Lutheranism as clearly as the ongoing struggle between faith and doubt in the life of believers. To cast one's life on God's grace and forgiveness is not a once-and-for-all experience that brings serenity, peace, and enduring certainty. The life of faith remains a dialectic between belief and unbelief, faith and doubt, in which grace is required ever anew until the end of life. Luther and Lutheran confessions embodied this belief in the doctrine of *simul justus et peccator,* that one is simultaneously a saint and a sinner, a forgiven sinner. Were these two peculiar Lutheran emphases adequately reflected in the questionnaire?

Even if one answers that question satisfactorily, there remains an equally, if not more, serious problem for the historian. How does one correlate the responses of clergy and laity with their actual historical experience in the American context? It is always difficult for a historian to make explicit the relationship between belief and historical action. Normally, the method employed to do this is to make clear what a person or group believes by quoting from what they have said in their writings, particularly their public writings, and then to relate that to specific actions or occurrences within history. Behind that method lies an assumption that certain beliefs by an inner logic lead to certain actions; therefore, if one can further demonstrate that these individuals or groups act in logical consistency with those beliefs, then one has demonstrated the relation between beliefs and action. It is clear why historians are reluctant to make such claims. Any set of beliefs may have more than one possible logical consequence for action. Further, particular actions may be grounded in a variety of sources beyond, or other than, a pattern of belief.

These and other problems confront the historian in trying to make judgments concerning the impact of American historical experience on Lutherans as that is reflected in responses. However, this historian must admit that he was not surprised by most of the answers, but he feels constrained to move with great caution, both because of the problems outlined above and because of the fact that comparative data are lacking which would make easier the task of sketching out the impact of history on the given answers.

For example, if one had a similar set of questions given to clergy and laity in European Lutheran nations such as Germany, Sweden, Norway, Denmark, or Finland, then one might be in a position to comment on the impact of the American experience on Lutheranism with regard to confessional answers. Though reference was made to some of the questions given by previous analysts such as Gallup and Glock and Stark, there was no in-depth comparison between these Lutheran responses and other Protestant responses to similar questions in the American context. This makes it doubly difficult to analyze the data from a historical perspective. With great caution, a few generalizations can be offered for the purpose of discussion.

Historians have long noted that the most distinctive characteristic about the American experience is the radical separation of church and state, with its consequent rampant pluralism and the necessity of voluntarism. Sidney E. Mead has argued that this condition gave birth to a new form of the church, the denomination, which is quite different from the traditional church and sect-type church that dominated Western Christendom.[1] This is the context in which Lutheranism flourished in America. In Europe, Lutheranism was the established church throughout Scandinavia and Germany, and it tolerated other churches. Lutherans who emigrated to America came out of that background. What distinguished Lutheranism from other groups was a theological confession combined with a particular nationalistic tradition or group of people; that is, the language, customs, and history combined with a particular set of religious beliefs and practices to give definition both to a nation or people as well as to a religion. The two were indistinguishable. To be a Swede was to be a Lutheran, or to be a northern German was to be, in over 90% of the cases, a Lutheran. It is this attitude that was brought to the American scene.[2]

Particular national Lutheran groups tended to settle together and so predominated in a given locale or region, but at no point did they experience the luxury of being the established religion. Their confessions, which were once territorial, were now purely personal, or intended only for a voluntary group. One suspects, but can only hazard the guess, that there was far greater unanimity in confessional beliefs in eighteenth- and nineteenth-century American Lutheranism than in the twentieth century. At that time, Lutherans were more isolated from the rest of the population due to language and settlement patterns, and there were no mass media of communication to influence them. Pluralism has always been the mark of the American scene, but it is experienced in a far different way in contemporary life. Thanks to mobility and to mass communication, the homogenization of life has proceeded apace, so that earlier pluralism, which was experienced basically between groups, is now experienced even within groups.

One of the distinctive LLP findings involved what was thought to be a surprising diversity. Though there usually was a dominant view, or a large minority view, frequently there were several other views that did not correspond with the so-called confessional response. Ought one to be surprised at this diversity, even in the life of a confessional group? The surprise is the small degree of diversity. When one takes into account the American context, the fact that the Lutheran Church in America is a primarily middle-class church, the educational levels of the people questioned, and the geographical distribution, one could have anticipated far greater diversity.

There were two primary forms of diversity. One involved the variety of answers given to specific questions with the confessional orientation. The other was the considerable diversity between responses of clergy and laity at a number of key points. Because we do not have data, we cannot compare the degree of diversity with that of Lutherans from various European cultures; nevertheless, we can assert that diversity is to be anticipated in the American scene because of its own particular nature. It would be interesting to compare the degree of diversity within the LCA with that encountered in other mainline Protestant denominations such as the Presbyterians, the Methodists, or the Episcopalians.

It would also be enlightening to compare the degree of diversity within the LCA with that found in one of the more fundamentalist evangelical groups. Probably the degree of diversity in the latter would be far less than it is in the LCA, even though the LCA supposedly has strong historic confessional standards, whereas fundamentalist, evangelical groups claim not to be credal. Perhaps an unofficial creed, grounded in biblical literalism, provides a stronger guard against diversity than does a specific historical confession of faith. Further, diversity should be anticipated when one studies a group whose confession is dialectical and not literalistic. The nature of Lutheran theology is, in its essence, dialectical and nonsimplistic. On the surface, justification by grace through faith alone sounds simple enough, but when one affirms once and for all that this is fully a gift of God and is never held by any human, or that it cannot be manipulated by human beings, one is inviting a diversity of interpretation.

Granted the past history of Lutheranism in America, it was inevitable that diversity would mark the piety and belief of its people. Even a cursory glance at the history of Lutheranism in America reveals the inevitability of diversity in the patterns of belief and practice of both clergy and laity, while, at the same time, it also sheds light on the surprising degree of unanimity with regard to fundamental Lutheran beliefs and practices. The first thing that strikes one is the nature of the theological views of those Lutherans who came to the American scene. When Lutherans began to appear in sufficient numbers in America, they already presented a dual theological orientation.[3]

On the one hand, they represented a historic Lutheran confessional stance as embodied particularly in the Augsburg Confession and in Luther's Small Catechism, but also in the collection known as *The Book of Concord*. Confessionalists were always deeply concerned about Lutheran identity as it was specified in the historic confessions of faith made by Lutheran groups at various critical points in their history. The confessions were thought to be important because at a particularly crucial moment in history they lifted up clearly and logically what was believed to be the essence of scriptural revelation concerning the relation of God to humanity. They built on Scripture and on the historic catholic confessions of faith, and they made them relevant to a special moment in history. They were believed to be confessions of scriptural and historic Christian truth in the face of contemporary error and misinterpretation.

The responsibility of the church was to teach these beliefs correctly and to engage in proper Christian practice which flowed out of such beliefs. Therefore, there was an abiding concern with doctrinal clarity and truth as well as the correct practice which developed from it. Faith was personal, and personal experience was not to be denied or overlooked; but it was not central, it was derivative. Central was the objective grace of God, revealed in Scripture, confessed in historical ecumenical creeds, and reconfessed in the documents of the Lutheran churches.

Though personal faith was necessary, it was not the ground for Christian faith; and because it involved a high degree of subjectivity, ultimately it could not be trusted. At its best, confessionalism represented a balance between the objective grace of God, revealed in Scripture and creeds, and the profoundly existential response to that revelation. At its worst, it involved an overemphasis on the pure doctrine of the church, rationally and logically presented and held more as a series of intellectual propositions than as an existential faith.

On the other hand, at the same time that confessional Lutheranism came into America through emigration, another theological emphasis entered simultaneously. Pietism, advanced by two great Lutheran leaders, Philipp Jakob Spener and August Hermann Franke, at the turn of the seventeenth into the eighteenth century, made a profound impact on Lutheranism both in Germany and in Scandinavia. Though it did not deny or ignore the confessions, its emphasis was in a quite different direction. Pietism was concerned with the piety, or the personal response, to the call of the gospel. Though it is an oversimplification to state that pietism was concerned with the subjective side of religious faith primarily, while confessionalism was concerned with the objective side, there is considerable truth in that generalization.

Pietism stressed the personal, vital response of faith to the offer of forgiveness in the gospel. If one had not experienced and could not recount the experience of faith, then one was not a Christian. In a classic theological educational struggle, the pietists argued that nobody should be appointed to a theological faculty who did not demonstrate the personal dimension of true and genuine faith, whereas the confessionalists argued that fundamental to a professor was his knowledge and grasp of true doctrine as expressed in the historic confessions of faith.

Both confessionalism and pietism came hand in hand with Lutheran immigrants to the American scene. Muhlenberg embodied a rare combination of the two that was later to become distinctive of much of Lutheranism in America, but he was unusual. By the nineteenth century, it was clear that within Lutheranism all of the varieties of interpretation found in European Lutheranism were present in America, and the tension between the confessionalists and the pietists increased until it produced a split. Diversity was built into Lutheranism from its very beginnings, and it is not surprising to find it to this day.

The American context provided a religious scene quite different from the Lutheran confessional and even pietistic emphasis. Evangelical revivalism predominated throughout the nineteenth and twentieth centuries in American religious life. The centrality of conversion, biblical literalism, and millenarianism marked that tradition which predominated among the Baptists and Methodists, by far the two largest groups of Protestants. All was subordinated to the absolute necessity and centrality of conversion—to be born again was the essence of the Christian life. Worship, preaching, hymnology, ecclesiology—all were subordinate to the personal experience of rebirth. Without the experience of rebirth, there was no Christian faith. Local church services were aided and abetted by traveling itinerants who specialized in saving souls. Great revivals were held in every portion of the country in an effort to reap a harvest of souls.

Pietistic Lutheranism responded to the American emphasis on revivalism, and, under the leadership of S. S. Schmucker, developed a form of Lutheranism that closely paralleled the American revivalistic tradition.[4] It is a mistake to think that Schmucker gave up the Lutheran confessions, but he did seek to modify them in light of American revivalistic experience. It was that effort which brought about an open conflict with the confessionalists and ultimately led to the formation of the General Council which split away from the General Synod, the first large American Lutheran denomination. Revivalism also made vast inroads into the Norwegian and Swedish groups, which brought a similar tradition from their homelands. To a lesser degree, the Finnish and the Danish churches were also influenced by this movement.

One of the interesting facts apparent from this study is that revivalism today appears to have little influence in the life of LCA clergy or laity. It is notable that far more clergy than laity had a self-conscious personal experience; however, the question was so phrased that its implications went far beyond a revivalistic type of born-again experience. Its wording was: "in your own life, would you say that you had been 'born again' or had had a 'born-again' experience—that is, a turning point in your life when you committed yourself to Christ?" (C–Q19; L–Q16). Another question did not contain the qualification after the full dash, but the response was quite similar (C–Q5b; L–Q5b). Even in the question with the highly significant qualification, only a quarter of the lay members said that they had had such an experience, though 42% of the pastors indicated that they had had an experience (C–Q19; L–Q16).

In almost all polls taken, Lutherans, certainly LCA Lutherans, demonstrate that the born-again experience is not central or basic to their faith. It is not surprising that more clergy than laity responded positively to that question. In many cases, it can be assumed that the turning point in their lives came when they committed themselves to Christ through the decision to enter the ministry, which involves a special degree of commitment to Christ. In any case, the responses to these questions demonstrate that LCA Lutherans do not reflect the mainstream American revivalistic tradition as central to their faith.

A second thing that strikes one about Lutheran development in the American context is the fact that Lutheran immigration tended to cluster in certain geographical areas in America; in fact, in certain regions, such clusters were predominant in the culture. There are two areas in the United States where Lutherans predominate in a sufficient number of counties so that they represent the preeminent numerical religious tradition in a pluralistic society. In the East they have considerable strength in Pennsylvania, and in the Midwest they are the strongest denomination in Wisconsin, Iowa, Minnesota, and parts of the Dakotas and Illinois.[5] In the late twentieth century the Northeast region provides almost 40% of the membership of the LCA, and most of that is located in Pennsylvania. The central region provides a little over 30% of the LCA membership. Thus, these two regions between them represent 70% of the LCA membership. Only the LCA has considerable strength in the northeastern portion of the United States, just as the remaining Lutheran bodies have most of their strength in the Midwest.[6]

Lutherans were no different from other foreign-language groups that immigrated to America. Whether they went to the rural areas or settled in the cities, they tended to cluster together. This provided them with an opportunity to maintain their national customs, including their religious orientation. In the midwestern states where Lutherans predominated, their major contact with other religious traditions was with the Roman Catholics. It is safe to say that Lutherans in America had far more daily contact with Roman Catholics than did Lutherans in Europe until after World War II. In the Northeast, including Pennsylvania, where Lutherans had contact with a much more diverse group of denominations, it was a different story. In Pennsylvania the Quakers, German Reformed, and Presbyterians were considerably stronger than they were in the Midwest. The point is that in certain rural areas in America, the Lutherans were virtually an unofficial established religion, but even then they had contact with other religious groups with whom they were on equal footing under the law. It would have been interesting to discover if this questionnaire revealed any significant differences due to regionalism. Further, it is unfortunate that we do not have data from the past to compare with the present data, so as to ascertain if any major shifts have occurred in belief patterns within Lutheranism.

A further historical fact of interest concerning Lutheranism is the length of time it took it to become Americanized. It now appears to be fully Americanized and very similar to most other mainline American denominations; however, it does have certain distinctive emphases which will be discussed later. It is now largely a middle-class American denomination and appears to reflect most of the customs and mores and attitudes of middle-class America. That is not strange; the same could be said about Lutheranism in most European countries. Lutheranism hardly represents the laboring classes in Scandinavia and Germany and has not done so for generations; nor does it hold the allegiance of the intelligentsia and the upper classes in those nations. Again, we do not have data from the European Lutheran groups to make a meaningful comparison and contrast with Lutheranism in the American context.

The German roots of the LCA go back well into the eighteenth century; those of the other Lutheran groups, well before the Civil War; and the Scandinavian group, roughly to the mid–nineteenth century. One would have anticipated the Americanization of Lutherans by the turn of the twentieth century, but that was not the case. This fact was brought home to me by the late Henry Sloane Coffin, for many years president of Union Theological Seminary, when he pointed out that I was the first Lutheran not in the practical theological areas to be officially appointed to the faculty in 1948. When appointed to the faculty of the Divinity School of the University of Chicago in 1950, I was again the first Lutheran.

Lutherans were eager for Americanization, but they resisted assimilation. All denominations insisted on uniqueness and particularity in the American context, but there was something about Lutherans that made them stand out. Probably this was due to the fact that they were a foreign-language group and they retained the customs of their native lands. However eager Lutherans were for Americanization, they never had an opportunity to turn their backs on their foreign languages and customs because immigrants kept pouring in afresh throughout the nineteenth century, and even into the twentieth.

Each time Lutheran groups were on the edge of adapting to the American scene, a fresh wave of immigrants would arrive to maintain the language and traditions from the old country. Further, Lutheran groups tended to concentrate on theological arguments which were inherited from their native countries, rather than to participate in the arguments or movements that marked the remainder of the American scene. Even the insistence on Lutheran confessionalism was largely the consequence of fresh immigration from Germany, where the question was agitated anew in the nineteenth century.

Lutherans quickly developed a life style and religious pattern that made them somewhat peculiar in the American scene, and certain aspects of that continue to this day. The data of the present study reflect most of these peculiarities, which cannot be termed simply confessional. The confessions make clear a Lutheran theological stance, but they do not specify liturgical practice or the worship life of the Lutheran communities. It is the latter, as much as the former, that distinguishes Lutheranism in the American context; or better yet, it seems to be a combination of these two factors that has distinguished it. The questionnaire appears to present data to substantiate this point of view, but the data would have be compared with findings from other denominational groups in order to determine if this is uniquely Lutheran.

The questionnaire provides information at certain key points that demonstrate that however Americanized Lutherans have become, they still retain certain distinctive confessional emphases. At three points this is made quite clear. With regard to the nature of faith, Lutherans hardly fall into the pattern of emphasizing their own personal experience of rebirth or conversion as central to their faith. Though the proportions differ somewhat, both clergy and laity affirm the centrality of the forgiving merciful grace of God as the only basis for their salvation and their faith. Though a significant proportion of laity affirmed the importance of their own moral actions in relation to salvation, a clear majority of clergy and laity together affirmed the traditional Lutheran confessional understanding. When that is combined with the percentage who did not feel it necessary to be born again as central to their religious experience, Lutherans appear to reflect their historic interpretation of the Christian faith.

This is even more significant when one notes that the present membership of the LCA is composed "fully one-quarter (of those who) have been received as a result of adult baptism, affirmation of faith, reception from non-Lutheran congregations."[7] One would anticipate a far less consistent Lutheran view of faith or belief patterns. It would be enlightening to gather data from this group of individuals and compare it with data from people who are born and bred in the Lutheran tradition. If the sampling method was accurate, it can be assumed that the 25% of the members from non-Lutheran backgrounds were adequately represented in the overall findings.[8]

A second key point where Lutherans reflect their historic tradition, regardless of all that has happened to them in the American context, is in the area of the sacraments. Though Lutherans do not look on the sacraments as necessary to salvation, they find them indispensable and necessary as a means of grace in their lives. In that grace, rather than the sacraments, is central, this remains good Lutheran doctrine. Probably Roman Catholics, Orthodox, and High Anglicans would show a profile similar to the Lutherans with regard to their view of the sacraments. Forty percent of the lay people and 41% of the pastors believed that baptism was essential to salvation, though 51% of the pastors regarded baptism as a way of receiving forgiveness and new life (table 7). Sixty-two percent of the lay people and 72% of the pastors viewed the Eucharist as a way of receiving forgiveness and new life (table 7). All found both sacraments meaningful and necessary for their religious lives.

In similar fashion, 90% of clergy and laity held to a concept of real presence in the Eucharist, while only 10% viewed the Eucharist primarily as a memorial (table 6). Sixty-eight percent of the pastors and 45% of the lay people reflected the traditional Lutheran belief with regard to the real presence, and the remainder tended toward some sort of transubstantiation view. LCA members are not aligned either with the conservative evangelicals or the older mainline Protestant churches with regard to their view of the sacraments. They remain traditionally Lutheran.

Their view of Scripture reflects the traditional Lutheran dialectic as to the written word. They clearly affirm the authority and normative quality of written Scripture, but they do not hold an inerrant conception that marks so much of conservative evangelical American Protestantism. For LCA Lutherans, Scripture is important and authoritative because it contains the word of God, not because it *is* the word of God in every jot and tittle. Ninety-three percent of the pastors believed that the Bible is the inspired word of God, but not everything in it should be taken literally (table 11). Seventy-three percent of the laity took a similar view, which indicates that the traditional Lutheran view of Scripture, grounded in Luther himself, still holds the field within the LCA. It would be interesting to compare these statistics with those for other Lutheran groups, particularly the Missouri Synod. It can be assumed, until proven otherwise, that at this point the Missouri Synod reflects traditional conservative American evangelicalism, which would indicate that the Missouri Synod has been more Americanized than the other Lutheran groups.

With regard to Christology, none of the questions were framed so that a distinctive Lutheran emphasis could be detected. That which has marked Lutheranism as distinctive from the Reformed tradition, the cosmic Christ and the divine presence in, with, and under all the forms of nature, was not factored into the questionnaire. Rather, the questions centered on the traditional views of the divinity and humanity of Jesus Christ. Both pastors and laity gave answers typical of historical orthodox Christianity and shared by the vast majority of Roman Catholics, Orthodox, and conservative evangelicals (table 2).

One of the surprising findings was the attitude of the clergy toward political action, social and socioeconomic policies, and church advocacy efforts. One would have anticipated a much more quietistic and conservative stance on the part of the pastors, but that was not the case. It was not until the late 1940s and early 1950s that the first serious efforts to develop an American Lutheran social ethic occurred in the church bodies that merged into the LCA.

The laity reflect the older quietistic Lutheran position: only 9% of the laity feel that the church should take a direct role in political involvement, as over against 33% of the pastors (table 19). Seventy-one percent of the pastors thought that the church should work for justice, and support groups that seek to overcome inequality and oppression, whereas only 23% of the laity took that attitude (table 23). Forty-three percent of the laity thought that the church should relate spiritual principles to political issues but ought not to make policy statements in light of that (table 19). On the whole, both clergy and laity thought the church ought to stay out of direct involvement in political life (table 19). These responses demonstrate that pastors have moved with regard to the church's responsibilities in the political arena, but the laity appear largely unchanged. In short, LCA Lutherans overall are suspicious of direct ecclesiastical involvement in the political order. That is a traditional Lutheran point of view.

It is difficult to generalize concerning the historical experience of Lutheranism in America and these questionnaire findings. The Scandinavian emphasis on a rich liturgical and sacramental life seems to have won out in the LCA. The German confessional and theological concerns seem to have won out over the pietistic strain within the Lutherans who came to America. Though we lack data and statistics from earlier epochs, it appears that the contemporary LCA is more politically concerned, if not active, than the earlier Lutheran denominations that went into the LCA. In this respect, Lutheranism in America seems more akin to its fellow Protestant groups in America than it does to its European brethren. Lutheranism has learned to live with ease in a pluralistic and voluntaryistic situation, but it has been unable to work out the relationship between its faith and practice and its overall responsibilities for the public order. In that respect, it is similar to many of its sister denominations in the American context. These findings do not present anything astonishing with regard to the beliefs and the religious practices of LCA clergy and laity.

9

To Have and To Hold

KRISTER STENDAHL

God's love for us as sinners; trusting in God's grace; experiencing God's forgiveness—these are clearly the theological topics that dominate the preaching of LCA pastors, at least as pastors think about their sermons (C–Q27). It seems as if the message is consistent with the theological convictions of the clergy, and it also seems as if the message comes across. The questions designed to test the confessional core are mostly cast in that same language of forgiveness, grace, and love; and, lo and behold, on the whole the LCA gives the "right" answer, especially the clergy (tables 2, 4, and 1).

We shall take a more careful look at these answers later on, but for now my point is that the pastors' sermons and the members' perceptions seem to be mutually reinforcing of a religious life in which the faith functions primarily as consoling, comforting, and inspiring (that is, to feeling more than action). Both clergy and laity find the Bible to be twice as helpful for comfort and inspiration as for decision-making and moral questions (C–Q35; L–Q37). The code words grace, love, and forgiveness dominate to such an extent that when the question is asked about God as a "God of justice" only 23% of the laity think in terms of justice in the corporate, public realm, while 56% think the term refers to God's demands and punishments in private and spiritual terms (table 23). This is more striking since the question forms part of a section entitled "the Church's relation to social and political affairs." Among pastors the score is 71% who chose the public meaning of justice and 17% who selected the privatist and spiritual definition.

Conversely, the least chosen topics for sermons (of the choices given clergy) are: following the Ten Commandments; sexual conduct; the dual nature (divinity and humanity) of Christ.* It could be argued that these topics do not lend themselves to be *main* topics of sermons, and we note that some attention has been given to them. As to the Ten Commandments, the relatively recent reentry of the Old Testament in the lectionary has not yet affected the Lutheran habit of almost exclusive New Testament preaching. Even so, the tendency is clear and we should hence be less surprised that the Bible is primarily a source of comfort among us.

The lack of sermons on the Ten Commandments relates interestingly to the answers given to the question concerning rules: "Do you think that God has given us rules to live by?" Here 67% of the pastors, but 43% of the laypersons answer: "God has given us some general rules, but we have to decide how to apply them to our own situations," while 20% of the pastors and 49% of the lay respondents choose "God has given very clear, detailed rules that apply to everyone" (table 23). My concern here is not the pros and cons of situation ethics. My point is: how much help do we give in teaching the use of Law, of commandments? Or are those "general rules" of which this question speaks so general that we are of little help? The answers from lay members here show sound instinct, constitute a challenge, and call for more attention to wise teaching about Law. After all, 81% of the pastors and 78% of the lay people had found the Ten Commandments helpful many or several times in their decision making during the previous year (C–Q33; L–Q35). Thus, here is an area of common concern—yet not stressed in preaching.

Another discrepancy between preaching and confessed convictions: pastors (82% of them) tell us that the dual nature of Christ is "very important to them" (table 2); yet the topic is not prominent among themes for sermons. Only 11% of pastor respondents preached on that topic more than once during the previous year (C–Q27). Is it thought of as too "theological" for communication to lay people? Or is the lower percentage (58%) of laity who identify their belief in Christ's divine and human nature "very important" to them rather a sign that we have not found the right language for expressing the great things that happen when the divine and human (table 2) mix? And, as we shall see, there is a persistent tension be-

---

*I have not included "Making a definite decision for Christ" since the 17% "no" are balanced off by the 20% "yes, many." I would see that answer demonstrate the polarity and spectrum within the LCA clergy, the more so since the question made use of an evangelical idiom.

tween the dialectic of theologians and the straightforward mind-set of lay people.

As a teacher of ministers, pastors, and priests, I have, of course, a special interest in the gap between clergy and lay responses. When is the perception of lay people a corrective to the "in-the-club" attitudes of clergy? When is the gap an indicator of the theological insights that pastors take for granted as seminary graduates, but have not managed—or deigned—to communicate? On some issues lay people seem more "orthodox"; on others, the clergy seem so.

I seem to discern a difference in style and in mind-set between lay people and clergy. The lay responses have a tendency to leave more open, to claim a little less both for oneself and for the church, to have less need of producing precise answers. Let me give a few examples.

Eighty-six percent of the pastors have an answer to the question "What is the purpose of life?" Only 7% mark the response: "I somehow believe that there must be an answer, although I don't know what it is" (C–Q2). Lay respondents are more modest. Forty-one percent have an answer to the question, while 42% believe there must be an answer, but do not know what it is (L–Q2).

On a quite different level, 46% of pastors are "absolutely certain" that they are saved and will go to heaven when they die (C–Q7). Only 26% of the lay respondents share this certainty (L–Q9).

Similarly, pastors are more sure about their experience of God's forgiveness: "In your lifetime, have you ever felt God's forgiveness?" Seventy-nine percent of the pastors say, "yes, it has had a deep impact on my life," while only 8% are not sure (C–Q9). In contrast, only 32% of lay respondents are sure they have experienced God's forgiveness and that it has had a deep impact. Forty-nine percent are not sure (L–Q11).

Table 12 shows the same tendencies as to "your view about life after death." Eighteen percent of the pastors, but 43% of the laity, choose the answer: "I believe that there must be something beyond death, but I have no idea what it may be like." Apparently pastors "know" more than lay people. It is interesting, however, that exactly at this point many pastors (29%) are uneasy with choices given and offer their own formulations. It would also have been interesting to test the hope for reunion with loved ones, a hope that I would expect to be well represented among lay people (cf. clergy and lay, item 5i: 14% of the lay respondents, but only 7% of the clergy, report a specific experience of "a feeling of being in contact with someone who has died"). The "orthodox" answer, with rewards for some and punishment for others in life after death, was chosen by 45% of the clergy and 36% of the lay respondents.

The answers to "your view of prayer" have 76% of the clergy, but 47% of lay respondents, choosing "prayer is talking with God, and God always answers," while 19% of the clergy and 45% of the lay respondents choose "prayer is talking with God but God doesn't always answer" (C–Q38; L–Q40). My guess would be that here lay and clergy hear and use language differently. To the ears of many lay people, "answer prayer" means to get what one asks for; for many pastors, "answer prayer" means that God of course answers, although the "answer" may be quite different. Here, as so often, lay people have a sense for the plain meaning of words, while pastors and theologians often bend and theologize words.

On some subjects it is the clergy that takes the less assertive attitude, as for example in the question concerning proof of God's existence: "Do you feel that it is possible to prove that God exists?" Forty-six percent of the pastors, but only 22% of the laity answer, "no, we don't have the kind of evidence it would take" (table 9). Of those who answer yes or probably yes (42% of clergy and 68% of laity), only 33% of the clergy but 57% of the laity think that proof can be achieved "from evidence in the Bible." Later we shall observe how lay people have a substantially different attitude toward the uniqueness of Christianity and toward "foreign mission" than do pastors for whom the lines are more sharply drawn.

These examples add up to a pattern showing clergy answers to be more precise or more pointed than those of lay people. Perhaps this is just what we should expect. Even so, it is important to discern what I like to call different styles of answering and perhaps different mind-sets. The style of lay people often has a note of humility which is quite attractive. Thus, I would not interpret the variance between laity and clergy as signs of less or more conviction. As a matter of fact, on the question about "certainty of beliefs," there is no significant variance between clergy and laity (C–Q25; L–Q26).

This style of humility occurs in a different form in a set of questions where the variance between laity and clergy is often quite substantial. In the lay answers there is an allergy to "both-and," dialectical, or paradoxical language. This leads to answers that appear more straightforward and sometimes more "orthodox" than those of the clergy. But when we see how they stand over against the clergy's predilection for the dialectical, we may again be right in suggesting that we are here dealing with styles and mind-sets. We may well suspect that lay people have negative or eerie feelings about "both-and" answers.

One example is the question about how God influences events (table 10). The choice answer for pastors is dialectical: "God influences individuals, but also shapes events directly through nations and social affairs" (61% of clergy, 31% of laity). The answer "God influences individuals who then shape events" is not very popular with clergy (27%), but is preferred by lay people (36%). Here the preference for a nondialectical answer may be enforced by the personalistic cast of the lay responses in questions of society and politics (cf. table 23, concerning justice).

Clearer evidences come in the question exploring "the biblical view" and "the scientific view" of creation as alternatives (table 11). For clergy, the dialectical option is most attractive, with 78% of pastor respondents choosing *both* the biblical and scientific views, while 20% go for the biblical view alone. This differs significantly from the lay responses, which give 47% to the biblical view alone and 47% to the dialectical "Both (biblical and scientific) in their own ways."

A question concerning the Bible points in the same direction. Asked which statement comes closest to describing their feelings about the Bible, 93% of the pastors choose: "the Bible is the inspired word of God but not everything in it should be taken literally, word for word" (table 11). While this is the choice of the majority of the lay responses, it is less overwhelmingly so (73%). While only 2% of the clergy choose: "the Bible is the actual word of God and is to be taken literally, word for word," 16% of lay respondents prefer it; while none of the pastors see the Bible as "an ancient book of fables, legends, history, and moral precepts recorded by men," 5% of the lay respondents do. (I take it that the zero return for clergy is not due to the sexist use of "men.")

Dialectic, but of a different nature, is also involved in the question about Christ as "fully God and fully human during his life on earth" (table 2). It is surprising that this somewhat overstated orthodox formulation (at least from a biblical perspective) causes little doubt (no doubts: 86% of clergy and 75% of laity). There is, however, striking diversity in the estimate of the importance of the doctrine: "very important" to 82% of the clergy, but to only 58% of the lay people. As we noted above, the clergy's estimate of importance has not led to commensurate attention in sermons (C–Q27).

It also seems that theological education has prepared pastors to "smoke out" the proper answers on salient doctrinal questions. This is particularly striking in the question concerning faith (table 4). Here the pastors recognize *the* Lutheran question, and consequently 74% define faith as "my trust in God's grace," compared with only 40% of the laity. "A life of commitment to God that I demonstrate by trying to do what is right" has response support from only 10% of the clergy but 27% of the lay people. Zero percent of the clergy but 10% of the lay people choose "as long as people are truly sincere in their beliefs, they show faith."

This difference is also demonstrated in the question concerning response to one's relation to God (table 1). The majority of both clergy and laity choose, "I know that I am a sinner but God loves me and is giving me new life," but the density is widely different (86% of the clergy, 57% of the laity). Almost as many lay people (46%) but only 13% of the clergy choose "as long as I do the best I can, I feel that God cares for me and watches over me" as expressing very well their relation to God; and while only 2% of the clergy prefer this among the six choices, 29% of the laity say that this is the *best* of the choices given, while 84% of the clergy and 52% of the laity prefer the "sinners loved by God" option (table 5). I would read such data as an indication that pastors here respond with more confessional awareness than do lay people. They "understand" what the questionnaire seeks to attain.

Finally, there is an unrelated yet delightful question with divergent responses. When asked about two kinds of situations in which God's presence was experienced, 68% of the clergy but only 29% of the laity say that they have "experienced God's presence or activity" while having fun (27% of the clergy compared with 8% of the laity say, "yes, many times"; table 14). This is a nonconventional question, and it comes more naturally to pastors.

Another area of striking divergence between clergy and laity is in the church's relation to social and political affairs. We noticed how differently clergy and laity "hear" the expression "a God of justice" (table 23). Clergy responses to this whole section conform to the common perception of today's clergy being convinced of the church's direct responsibility in social and political matters, as opposed to an indirect responsibility through the lives of its members. Sixty-one percent of the clergy consider it proper to "discuss political issues from the pulpit," while only 25% of the lay people think so (table 19). It is also worth noting that the "unsure" responses are higher in those sections of the questionnaire dealing with the church's relation to social and political affairs and are relatively higher for laity than for clergy. However, most of the specific social or political issues pursued in table 16 indicate rather similar attitudes among laity and clergy, with the clergy somewhat to "the left" of the lay people—an old tradition in American church life, distinctly different from the European mother churches.

This section may well be the most dated of the study, since the change from privatism toward virulent political action in large segments of evangelical circles can be expected to change both positive and negative answers. As the study stands, however, it does suggest that lay people see the church as centered in a spiritual mission to and for its individual members while clergy envision a more outgoing and risky mission in society at large.

The questions relating to ecumenism show some interesting variations (table 24). The vast majority of both clergy and laity approve of joint worship with Presbyterians, Roman Catholics, and Baptists. With Baptists, the laity are more eager than the clergy (72% versus 66%). In addition, when asked about differences of beliefs, 25% of the clergy found many differences with the Baptists, while only 9% of the laity did. Jehovah's Witnesses are far more objectionable to clergy (88%) than to lay people (59%). Actually, the clergy think that there are more important differences between their religious beliefs and the beliefs of Jehovah's Witnesses (93%) than between those of Lutherans and Zen Buddhists (91%). That strikes me as an overstatement and leads me to think that we experience the ancient feeling that Christian "heresy" is worse than other faiths. And by the early 1980s in the U.S. neither Calvinists, Baptists, nor Roman Catholics are looked at as "heretics." Thus, difference in doctrine does not rule out joint worship.

The answer about Jews is interesting since the lay response to "joint worship" is more positive (44% for, 30% against) than that of the clergy (32% for, 48% against). The clergy discerns more "differences" of belief (70%) than did laity (60%) when comparing themselves with Jews.

The answer of clergy could be seen as due to their awareness of the serious questions that the Jewish community may have with "joint worship," especially in churches with crosses and prayers in Jesus' name. But if we look at the question that deals with attitudes toward Jews, the clergy has a more missionary attitude than do the laity (table 13). Twenty-four percent of the clergy favor special efforts to preach Christ to the Jews, versus 17% of the laity; 61% of the clergy favor mission without "special efforts toward Jews," versus 40% of the laity; and 7% of the clergy favor no efforts to convert Jews, while 20% of the lay people do favor such an attitude. Twenty-one percent of laity versus 6% of the clergy are not sure, which may indicate that lay people have given less attention to this aspect of our relation to people of other faiths, a topic to which we shall finally turn.

It is clear that "other world religions" have contributed very little to the respondents' understanding of "the meaning and purpose of life," and there is little difference between clergy and laity in this respect (C–Q3; L–Q3). But there are marked differences in attitudes toward other religions. Here the pastors are more hard-line than the lay people. For example, 60% of the clergy (45% of the laity) hold that "Christianity is the one true religion"; 30% of clergy (46% of laity) choose "most religions have some handle on the truth" (C–Q50d; L–Q52d). Pastors seem to have underestimated the lay views on this matter. When asked if most of the laity in their congregations "believe that most religions have some handle on the truth," only 29% agreed (C–Q31). In fact, a few more laity did choose this option—"Most religions have some handle on the truth"—than its opposite (L–Q52d). On the question of "relative" peace and joy, the clergy is more affirmative (C–Q50e).

The same tendencies are clear in the question concerning attitudes toward people of other faiths in foreign lands (table 13). Even with the beautiful language, "a desire to share the love of Christ with them," the "foreign mission" option gathers only 61% of the lay response, compared with 89% of the clergy; and only 4% of the clergy chooses "a feeling that we should respect their religions and stop trying to impose Christianity on them," while 16% of the lay people identify with that option.

These observations could perhaps be best evaluated by raising the question: is the LCA well prepared for a lively future? That is not the perspective from which the questionnaire was constructed—it probes the present. Apart from witness to non-Christians in foreign lands, the focus is on "to have and to hold"—both beliefs and members. The church that speaks out of the questions and answers given in this study is a congregation which appreciates forgiveness, grace, and love as meaningful in their lives. But where are we going? How does our mission fit into God's meaning of the creation, what Jesus spoke of as the kingdom with justice and peace?

The answers give *some* pointers. The perception of lay people is worth taking seriously. Their answers were less conditioned by "saying the right thing." At two points they pose questions to the clergy which deserve attention: the necessity of clear commandments as over against the preachers' shyness about Law, and the greater willingness to see value in other traditions and faiths. These are perceptions that should be taken seriously. While clergy display the capacity of dialectics in the traditional topics of theological inquiry, these two points are where lay people *practice* the dialectic of life. Thereby, they also point to two areas in which traditional confessional Lutheran theology shows weakness. In a world like ours it is hard to believe that God's main problem with the world is too many good deeds. In a world like ours it is mandatory that communities of faith learn to live—rather than fight—with each other. Lay people know that.

One of the sharpest divergencies between lay and clergy were found in the perception of social and political strategies. The tension between the privatism of the lay responses and the more systemic understanding of clergy calls for this question: is not the perception of the church centered in forgiveness, grace, and love—which both clergy and lay people affirm so strongly—leading more naturally into the privatist model? If the central issues to which the church addresses itself are matters of consoling and comforting, rather than matters of decision making and justice, how can it be otherwise? Yes, the theologian can change and manipulate the meaning of words, but lay people are not impressed. They are the common-sense voice within God's people.

So, when all is said and done, the final issue is whether the church understands itself as an agent for God's kingdom, or as the club for those who enjoy the comfort and consolation of spiritual warmth. The second part of the Lord's Prayer—the community part with forgiveness, protection, and assurance of help—is well in focus. But what about the first part—Hallowed be Thy name, Thy kingdom come, Thy will be done on earth as in heaven? What about the salt and the light in the midst of the world? What about the actions that make people look up and praise God?

10
Social Research and the Church

CHARLES GLOCK

The question addressed in this final chapter is: "how can social research be of benefit to the church?" An answer is implicit in much that has gone before. Giving the matter explicit attention now can serve to highlight the contributions of the research reported on earlier in this book. It can also serve, hopefully, to further the potential for future collaboration between social scientists and those concerned with the nourishment, sustenance, and vitality of the church.

Essentially, there are three kinds of questions which social research can help to answer about any social phenomenon: it can describe it; it can contribute to understanding what brought the phenomenon about; and it can afford an assessment of what consequences may follow or have followed from the phenomenon. Or, to put it more simply, social research allows inquiry into the nature of social phenomena, into their causes, and into their consequences. Sometimes the functions of social research are specified as description, explanation, and prediction. The term "prediction" is used somewhat idiosyncratically, as will be seen. Still it will be useful to organize the discussion around these three rubrics.

DESCRIPTION

Description involves specifying the characteristics of a phenomenon which distinguish it from other phenomena. Or, if more than one phenomenon is the subject of inquiry, description calls for specifying how the phenomena are alike or different from one another. In effect, description involves setting forth the ways in which phenomena vary.

This would not seem to be the case where a single phenomenon is to be described; for example, a single congregation, or the organizational structure of a denomination, or the content of a sermon. Description of a single phenomenon is made possible and useful, however, only when it is compared, implicitly or explicitly, with other similar phenomena. Thus, to describe a congregation as large, or as heterogeneous in membership, or as a member of the Lutheran Church in America is to compare it in size, hetereogeneity of membership, and denominational affiliation with other congregations irrespective of whether other congregations are explicitly mentioned. In effect, what is being said is that without variation—as would be the case if, for example, there were only one color in the world—there would not be anything to describe.

Once the focus of description becomes two or more units, it is more obvious that comparison and variation are essential ingredients of description. The describer will almost inevitably include observations about how the units resemble or are different from each other.

Much social-science description is based on so-called qualitative procedures. Functioning as an observer or as open-ended interviewer, the investigator seeks to accumulate information which will allow him or her to judge and then to describe the characteristics of a phenomenon. Thus, through participation alone or in combination with interviewing of informants, a skilled investigator can arrive at a description of a congregation which transcends what individual members of the congregation or even the pastor can provide.

Social-science description can also be quantitative in nature and is the more likely to take this form the more units there are to describe. Two congregations or three or four can be compared fairly easily in a qualitative fashion. When the number of units gets larger than that and is in the hundreds, thousands, or even millions, it is no longer practical to compare each unit with every other one. Instead uniform data are collected on each unit, as in a census, or on a sample of the units, as in a survey, and the units are described in terms of how different characteristics are distributed in the total population or in the sample population. Thus, the congregations of the church may be described according to how they are distributed in geographic location, in the size of their memberships, in the amount of their annual budgets and benevolence contributions to synods, and so on.

In quantitative social research, surveys are employed much more frequently than censuses simply because surveys are much less expensive and therefore more practical. With all its resources, the U.S.

Government can only afford a census of the U.S. population every ten years. In between, the Bureau of the Census relies on sample surveys to measure changes between the decennial censuses. The beauty of a survey is that it allows for collecting data from only a relatively small sample of units in a population and, where the survey has been conducted properly, projecting the results accurately to the larger population from which the sample was drawn. It behooves the user of surveys to know what standards need to be met to assure the survey's reliability. Properly used, however, surveys are a highly efficient means to obtain information about large populations of persons or of larger units such as congregations, Sunday schools, Lutheran women's groups, and so forth.

Social research pursued for descriptive purposes can be illustrated by reference to several of the chapters of this book. Chapter 2 by Wuthnow, for example, is given largely to describing the distribution of lay and clergy responses to a wide range of survey questions asked about religious beliefs and religious experiences. Chapter 5 by Weber is, in turn, devoted to describing the distribution of the opinions of clergy and laity on a wide range of social, moral, and political issues. Both of these chapters are written by social scientists. Chapter 9, written by a theologian but utilizing data collected by social scientists, also contains considerable descriptive information about the attitudes and opinions, beliefs and experiences of Lutheran clergy and laity.

Before commenting further on these illustrations, it is necessary to note that they all constitute "differentiated" rather than "pure" description. The distinction is based simply on whether one population is being described ("pure") or two or more populations are being compared ("differentiated"). In chapters 2, 5, and 9 attitudes of laity are compared with attitudes of clergy. Differentiated description is usually richer and more informative in content than pure description.

Now, what use is such descriptive information about lay and clerical beliefs, experiences, attitudes, and opinions? How can it benefit the church? Some insight into answers is obtained by making reference to what the theologians have to say in the chapters they have written for this book. Lundeen, in chapter 4, is inspired by the description of lay and clerical religious beliefs and experiences in chapter 2 to comment extensively on their theological significance. They provide him with, to this observer, new and fresh insights into the nature of faith and to important distinctions between faith and belief. The same insights are unlikely to have been arrived at without the stimulus of the empirical materials. In this instance, then, the important function served by descriptive social research was to stimulate theological reflection which otherwise might not have occurred.

A quite different function of such research is illustrated by Lull's comments in chapter 7 about the description of lay and clerical social and political attitudes contained in chapter 5. For Lull, the information affords a measure of the extent to which attitudes are in accord with those developed in the church's social statements. In effect, the data on social attitudes afford a measure of the success which the church has achieved in winning lay and clerical acceptance of its social positions. It would also have been possible—although for the most part Lundeen doesn't act on the option—to use the data on religious beliefs and experience in chapter 2 in a similar fashion, namely, to assess the extent to which clergy and laity accept central tenets of the faith as promulgated by the church.

The potential for utilizing descriptive social research to evaluate the effectiveness of the church's effort to educate, to inform, and to win commitment from its constituency extends to a considerably wider range of subjects than are illustrated in the chapters of this book. Clearly, it is possible to measure clerical and lay knowledge, attitudes, and opinion on virtually any topic of concern to the church. Sunday-school students can be surveyed to assess how much they are learning from parish educational materials. Parishioners can be surveyed to learn how much they know about and support the efforts of the church at large to deal with problems of world hunger. Pastors and members of mission congregations can be surveyed to obtain information to assess the strengths and weaknesses of American missions. Nonmembers in communities where Lutheran churches are located can be surveyed to discover just who they are and what the potential is for winning them to church affiliation. In sum, descriptive social research can be a highly effective tool in evaluating the degree to which the church's efforts to reach its goals are, in fact, achieved.

Still another, albeit more subtle, function of descriptive social research is illustrated in Stendahl's commentary in chapter 9 on similarities and differences between Lutheran laity and clergy as revealed in their responses to the questionnaires reproduced in appendix 1. Adroitly, Stendahl examines the patterning of responses to sets of questions to arrive at insights unobtainable from viewing responses to individual questions singly. Thus, for example, he notes as a pattern that the laity respond more to the comfort than to the challenges to be derived from religion. Comparing responses of clergy and laity, Stendahl sees the former as more disposed to want closure on theological issues, the latter as more open to the often-times inherent ambiguities. In these and other ways, Stendahl draws from the material a portrait of laity and clergy not derivable from casual observation.

The value of descriptive social research is enhanced when it is re-peated. Repetition produces information about trends, and about change and stability in phenomena. Unfortunately, except for a nar-row range of demographic-type statistics, there are few data about the church that have been collected repeatedly over time. Missing entirely are any extended periodic data about the religious beliefs and experiences of clergy and laity or about their attitudes on social and moral issues. The absence of such data makes it difficult to judge what has taken place historically in such realms. As is illus-trated in Brauer's chapter 8, there are no past surveys, certainly none going back to early Lutheran history in America, on which he can draw to facilitate comparison of the past with the present. He ably utilizes other data to make inferences about the status of Lu-theran beliefs and religious experiences in the past. It is evident, however, that his task would have been considerably more simple if repeated data on the matters addressed in this volume had been available.

In this regard, contemporary efforts of the LCA and of some other denominations, notably the United Presbyterian Church, to collect data periodically about their constituencies is worthy of note. The Lutheran effort—called the Lutheran Listening Post and the source of virtually all of the data presented in this book—provides for a sample of pastors and lay people being surveyed repeatedly on matters of importance to the church. Some of the data being col-lected is of topical importance only and is not repeated. On subjects such as those addressed in this book, however, there has already been some repetition and, resources allowing, it is planned that the repetition will be continued. If it is, a body of data will gradually be accumulated that promises to establish, more clearly than ever be-fore, where the church has been, where it is now, and what the most likely prospects are for its future.

Descriptive social research is useful generally in helping to make clear where things stand. It is not an appropriate tool for learning how things got to be the way they are. Thus, it can be of genuine help to the church in identifying the extent to which church goals have been met. Once this has been established, however, the results of descriptive research don't help very much to explain how success was achieved or how failure came about. To help answer such accounting-type questions, explanatory rather than descriptive social research is called for.

EXPLANATION

Description, as has been seen, is concerned with how phenomena vary. Explanation in social research deals with how the variation came about. Description has to do with the *what* of social phenomena, and explanation deals with the *why*.

The results of descriptive research can be an important source of explanatory-type questions. The descriptive information presented in chapters 2, 5, and 9, for example, to which we have just referred, gives rise to a whole host of such questions. Indeed, explanatory-type questions may be raised about every descriptive distribution reported in these chapters. Why, for instance, do some parishioners believe in the devil, while others do not? What leads people to different interpretations of the meaning of faith? How do the quite different views which Lutheran laity hold about Holy Communion come about? What accounts for there being relative consensus on some matters of faith, and relative dissensus on others? Why are clergy more liberal than laity in their social attitudes? Why do some parishioners oppose legalizing marijuana, giving more freedom to homosexuals, ordaining women, and spending more government money for people on welfare, while others support these proposals?

An underlying assumption of explanatory social research is that variation, such as is illustrated in the above questions, comes about through a process of cause and effect. The task of explanatory research is to discover what that process is and how it works. The procedure followed is to formulate first one or more hypotheses in this regard and then to proceed to collect data which will allow testing the hypotheses in order to see which one or combination of them best represents the process that is producing the effect. In actual practice it is rare that a specified variation can be wholly accounted for. In most instances the best that can be hoped for and achieved is a partial explanation, that is, research which is successful in establishing some, but not all, of the things that are operative in producing an effect. In part, this gap is a result of social-science research still not being far enough advanced. It is also a result of the processes at work being so complex as to make impractical the mounting of a study large enough in scope to disentangle them entirely. It is not necessary, however, for an explanation to be complete for it to be useful. To learn, for example, that parishioners in congregations in which pastors were all trained at the same seminary are more likely to take a highly unorthodox view of Holy Communion than parishioners in congregations where pastors were not trained at that seminary affords a partial, but nevertheless useful, explanation of how the unorthodox view came about.

In the present volume the principal examples of research pursued for explanatory purposes are contained in chapter 3. (It might seem, offhand, that chapter 6 is also devoted to explanation; however, for reasons that will be given shortly, the results of that chapter will be discussed under the rubric "prediction.") In chapter 3, it will be recalled, Wuthnow tries first to account for variation in the extent to which parishioners find a set of confessional beliefs salient in their lives. Following an analysis undertaken to address that task, he then attempts to identify the sources of doctrinal diversity among laity on questions bearing on the meaning of faith, the nature of one's relation to God, the role of Communion as a means of forgiveness, the necessity of baptism for salvation, and the nature of Christ's presence in Communion.

The two analyses are not grounded in any elaborate theory about the sources of saliency variation or doctrinal diversity. In both instances, however, Wuthnow proceeds to test a series of hypotheses in an effort to account for the variation in the two phenomena. As regards the saliency of confessional beliefs, his hypotheses are that saliency will be dependent upon the content of pastors' sermons, on the frequency of worship attendance, on the amount and character of early religious training, on the degree to which questions of meaning and purpose in life have been thought about, and on such demographic factors as age, sex, and education, which in other studies have been found to be associated with differences in religious commitments. On doctrinal diversity, he also tests for the effects of demographic characteristics, for religious background, for the amount of exposure to popular religious culture, and for religious participation.

His results are relevant to denominational policy in that they reveal that the content of pastors' sermons is an important element in determining the saliency of confessional beliefs, and that this effect is produced irrespective of differences in early religious training and such background characteristics as parishioners' sex, age, and level of education. Also of relevance for church policy is that salience of belief is highly influenced by whether or not parishioners are more generally concerned with meaning and purpose in life. The research on doctrinal diversity, it will be recalled, also produced results which have implications for church policy; most importantly, perhaps, the results suggest that a consequence of a theological emphasis on "grace and faith alone" is a high tolerance among Lutherans for doctrinal diversity.

It is to be noted that the data utilized by Wuthnow were collected originally for descriptive rather than explanatory purposes. The plan of analysis he pursues in chapter 3 was developed after, rather than before, the data were collected. Ordinarily, in explanatory research, the hypotheses to be tested are formulated prior to the collection of data. The hypotheses function, in effect, as instructions to show what data to collect. In this respect, then, Wuthnow's chapter falls short of exemplifying what is possible when explanatory analysis is conducted under ideal conditions. The chapter does, however, illustrate the logic governing the pursuit of explanation in social research and also the potential for fruitful secondary analysis of data collected for other purposes.

Wuthnow's analysis only hints at the wide range of applications to which explanatory social research may be put in service of the church. Actually, virtually any problem church executives face that requires an understanding of why people act the way they do is subject to being illuminated through such research. Deciding how to communicate the gospel more effectively, for example, would be illuminated by knowledge of why some people reject, while others accept, its message. Recruiting talented young people into Christian ministry would be made the easier through knowledge of why young people are attracted, or are indifferent, to the profession. Parish education could be made the stronger if knowledge about the learning process in Sunday-school settings were more advanced.

Despite these and other possibilities, churches have shied away from engaging in or contracting for explanatory social research to be done on their behalf. This is probably due, in part, to church executives not being familiar enough with the possibilities. Cost is also undoubtedly a factor. Explanatory research tends to be expensive. Such research also tends to take time; and when decisions have to be made quickly, a delay to await the results of research is simply not possible. Still, similar obstacles seem not to have prevented churches from engaging in and sponsoring extensive descriptive research.

A possible additional factor inhibiting churches from employing explanatory research is that church people may be made uneasy by the underlying deterministic assumptions of such research. Such assumptions seem to make robots of people, to deny their ability to act out of their own free will. In addition, they do not ordinarily countenance the possibility of divine intervention in individual lives or in the affairs of the world.

It is true that explanatory social research is grounded in deterministic assumptions about the way the world works. Social scientists use no alternative assumption, really, on which to base explanatory hypotheses, nor do they have methodologies that would allow them to test hypotheses other than those based on deterministic assumptions. There is no way, for example, for social scientists to establish that individuals are acting out of free will in any situation. Strictly speaking, there is no way for them to demonstrate *absolutely* the operation of deterministic forces either. Even under the strictest experimental conditions, a casual hypothesis cannot be proven absolutely. However, in many instances social scientists are able to make a highly plausible case for their deterministic hypotheses simply because the likelihood of alternative explanations is so slim.

While the deterministic assumptions underlying explanatory research are acknowledged, it is to be recognized that the determinism is of the soft rather than the hard variety. That is to say, the factors found to be determinative in particular instances are ordinarily not immutable. They are subject to being changed, and as a consequence to being made no longer determinate.

To illustrate, racial prejudice is a human characteristic which is uniformly deplored, yet remains widespread. Recent research has suggested that racial prejudice, rather than being a personality deficiency as has long been thought, is more accurately understood as the result of cognitive failure on the part of those who practice it. That is to say, prejudice comes about because people are not educated and sophisticated enough to understand the true causes of the group differences they perceive. While the adequacy of this explanation has still to be validated fully, the determinism underlying it is not fixed. If it is established that cognitive failure is a principal source of prejudice, then there is something to be done about it. It is not as if racial prejudice is immutable and something that human beings have to live with inevitably.

174

To take another example closer to home, many congregations are currently facing the problem that youth in their neighborhoods appear to be falling away from the church. Indeed in many congregations the average age of adult members is far in excess of the average age of the adult population in the community. Research on this subject could help to identify the sources of youth's disaffection with the church. Learning how disaffection comes about, however, would in no way warrant a conclusion that nothing can be done to change the situation. On the contrary, if church officials were better informed about why youth are discontented, they would be in a stronger position to do something about it. Disaffection, like prejudice, is not immutable.

The soft character of the determinism informing social research of an explanatory kind is often not recognized by those critical of such inquiry. Such recognition, however, can undermine much of the uneasiness that is grounded in the deterministic assumptions of such research. Indeed, for those whose opposition is on humanistic grounds, there is a case to be made for these people to embrace rather than to reject explanatory research.

The case can be simply made. It rests on the premise that the more that can be learned about the now unrecognized forces governing human behavior, the freer one becomes of the control of those forces. In the Middle Ages, the belief that life was subject to the control of evil spirits exercised a considerable degree of control over human behavior. Being free of that belief, through the findings of science, has made human beings more, not less, in control of their own destinies.

If we really knew about the forces producing greed, suffering, war, corruption, prejudice, and racism in the world, the chances of becoming free of these evils would be greater, not less. Social science is far from providing satisfactory explanations of such phenomena, of course. Yet, among human activities, it is virtually unique in offering a potential for doing so.

This is not to imply that there is more hope for the world in social science than in religion. Rather, the implication is that religious institutions stand to be strengthened rather than weakened by the findings of social-science research. Social science has the potential to teach us ever more about the way that the world works. Given that knowledge, however, social science has no innate capacity to inform us about how the world should work. Religious institutions, which

175

claim that capacity, can do a better job in this respect the more that their guidance is informed by an advanced knowledge of human and social behavior.

This book was conceived as a step in this direction. From this observer's viewpoint, however, it seems more likely to be a force in legitimizing for church application the use of descriptive rather than explanatory social research. In the chapters written by social scientists descriptive social research is more effectively exemplified than explanatory social research. And in the chapters written by theologians it is the descriptive social-science material rather than the explanatory work which dominates their observations.

Lundeen, in his comments on the Wuthnow chapters, makes considerably more reference to the descriptive material of chapter 2 than to the explanatory findings of chapter 3. Moreover, his remarks about the contents of chapter 3 deal only conceptually with Wuthnow's distinction between conformity and diversity. Peculiarly, no attention is given to the causal issues addressed in the chapter. The chapters which Lull reviews do not provide explanatory material parallel to that contributed by Wuthnow. It is noteworthy, nevertheless, that Lull devotes virtually all of his attention to the descriptive material which Weber presents in chapter 5 on the social attitudes of the laity. The more analytic material in chapter 6, where Weber addresses the question of whether or not religious factors have any consequence for the social, moral, and political positions of Lutherans, is not commented upon.

In his chapter, Stendahl presents only descriptive data, so it is perhaps not to be expected of him that he address explanatory matters. Still, in reading his chapter, one is struck by the virtual absence of explanatory questions being raised, much less speculated about, especially so since the sometimes startling differences in the attitudes of clergy and laity almost cry out for explanation. Whatever the reasons for the theologians' neglect of explanatory issues, the net effect of their posture will hardly encourage church personnel to invest in explanatory research. There remains, of course, this chapter to turn the tide.

PREDICTION

Ordinarily the term "prediction" is associated with future rather than current events, with forecasting what is likely to follow from an informed knowledge of what is and has been. The term is certainly used in this way in the social sciences; the presumption being that descriptive and explanatory understandings of past events can provide a basis for prediction of future events. The term "prediction" has also come to be used in the narrower sense of trying to establish whether, or how much, an effect is the consequence of a particular cause. In contrast to explanatory research with its focus on the sources of a given variation, predictive research in this special sense is directed to trying to establish the consequences of that variation. Thus, doctrinal diversity among Lutherans may be made the subject of both explanatory and predictive research. An attempt can be made to explain how doctrinal diversity comes about. In turn, given doctrinal diversity, the consequences which follow from it can be investigated.

The classic method of predictive research of this narrower variety is, of course, the experiment. Experiments are concerned ordinarily with trying to establish the consequences that follow from variation in some stimulus. Will people be more persuaded to change their minds about an issue by hearing arguments on both sides of the issue or by being given an argument opposing what they now believe? Will church people donate more to benevolences if they are besieged with requests from their local congregation, from the synod, and from the binational church, or if requests for support are restricted to benevolences going through the local congregation?

Surveys are also suited to predictive research. They are not as rigorous as experiments for this purpose. It is more difficult in surveys than in experiments to raise the odds that it is the stimulus, rather than something else, which has produced a consequence. Surveys have the advantage over experiments, however, of being applicable in natural settings. For example, the consequences for race relations which follow from whether people are prejudiced or unprejudiced are not a topic suitable for experimental study simply because it is not possible to assign subjects randomly to a prejudiced experimental group and an unprejudiced control group. Surveys, because they substitute statistical for experimental controls, can be used in such study.

The present volume affords no example of experimental research pursued for predictive purposes. The use of surveys for such purposes, however, is illustrated in chapter 6. In that chapter, Weber examines the consequences of different ways in which Lutherans express their religion for their attitudes on a range of social, moral, and political issues. In effect, she asks, does a person's reli-

177

gion make a difference to the way he or she responds to contemporary social, moral, and political problems?

To this end, the procedure Weber follows is to specify first how she proposes to measure religious variation. Rather than settle on a single method for doing this, she opts for a variety of measures so as to capture the different dimensions on which religiosity may be expressed. In the end, she adopts fifteen different means for measuring religious commitment: eight having to do with religious beliefs, four with religious participation, and three with organizational participation.

She then examines the statistical relationship between each of these measures of religious commitment and parishioners' positions on a variety of social, moral, and political issues about which they have been asked. In taking this step, her purpose is to discover the differences, if any, that variation in religious commitment makes to the way in which the attitude questions are answered. She then introduces a series of statistical controls to make sure that the differences are not a result of factors other than religious commitment. (For readers who may wish to refresh their memory about how this latter step is done, the discussion is in the endnotes to chapter 6 rather than in the text.)

The material Weber presents in short compass is so extensive as to make it difficult to digest, even for someone familiar with the procedures. There is consequently a danger that her chapter may not communicate to the uninitiated reader just how the kind of research she has pursued may be useful to the church.

As noted earlier, Lull restricts his comments on Weber to her descriptive material. Consequently, his remarks do not help to elucidate the utility of her predictive analysis. Its value, of course, depends on whether or not the church cares about the consequences of religious commitment for the kinds of attitudes Weber examines. If there is concern, then the results suggest the need for serious churchly reflection—first about the expectations harbored as to how religious commitment ought to be expressed, and secondly about what should follow from that expression. Weber's results indicate that the influence of religious commitment on secular attitudes is greatest (and in a conservative direction) in the area of individual moral behavior—on such contemporary issues as homosexual relations, the use of marijuana, premarital sexual intercourse, and honesty in paying taxes. On matters having to do with social inequality in society, racial prejudice, and the status of women, religious com-

mitment is found to have no effect or, in some instances, a reaction-
ary one. The question posed for the church is whether or not this is
the way that the church wants it to be.

More generally, predictive social research is likely to be most useful to the church where there are new ideas to be tested before they
are adopted full scale. Such research, especially in its experimental
format, is especially suited to testing the effects of communications'
materials including, of course, the church's vast product in parish
education. It can also be employed to assess the impact of various
pedagogical techniques, the content of sermons, alternative ap-
proaches to fund raising, and the like. Mention should also be made
of its use as an evaluative tool, although evaluation is best pursued
making use of all of the functions that social research can provide.

CONCLUSIONS

The central theme of this chapter has been that the churches have
something to gain from becoming more familiar with and making
greater use of the social sciences. The emphasis has been on the use
of social-science research as a tool of church administration. It needs
also to be pointed out that there has been accumulated, by now, a
considerable amount of social-science knowledge about the functioning of society and about religion's place in it which is of relevance and of potential use to churches. Churches are to be encour-
aged, then, not only to commission new research on their problems,
but also to make more effective use of the knowledge that is already
available. Except to a limited extent, churches are not doing these
things now, and even if they wanted to it is not entirely self-evident
just how they might best proceed.

Generally speaking, churches have neglected to make provision in
their organizational structures for research and development. By
now, the importance of research and development to planning and
growth in business organizations, educational institutions, and government agencies is widely recognized. The record affords strong
evidence that the effective performance of these functions goes
hand in hand with corporate success, governmental efficiency, and
educational excellence. Central to the success of research and development is the opportunity afforded people to get away from day-to-
day pressures and to research and reflect about the nature of an organization, its past and current performance and its plans for the
future.

In a period of tight budgets, the prospect of individual religious denominations making research and development an integral part of their corporate structures seems remote. The possibility of something being done collectively along this line, however, may be more feasible and worthy of consideration. The image of a church-sponsored "think tank" comes to mind, or more appropriately perhaps, an institute organized for research and reflection about the institutional church. Something of this nature is called for if the promise of this chapter is to be fulfilled. Such an institute would fill a need, now largely unmet, as a fitting vehicle not only for undertaking or sponsoring research on behalf of churches but also for digesting and disseminating the knowledge already available. Most importantly, such an institute could provide a setting in which the church's role and performance in the world—past, present, and future—might be contemplated critically and constructively, and without the inevitable pressures of the "in" basket.

Appendixes

Appendix 1

Religious Beliefs and Experiences Questionnaire

LAY RESPONSES

First, here are some questions about the meaning and purpose of life.

1. How much, if at all, do you think about each of the following kinds of questions? *(For each of the questions listed, please circle the one number indicating whether you think about it a lot, some, only a little, have thought about it in the past but don't now, or have never thought much about it)*

N.R.*		A lot	Some	Only a little	Don't now but have in the past	Never thought about it
1	What the purpose of life is	42	41	11	4	1
2	How the world came into being	23	42	23	10	1
2	The existence of God	58	29	6	5	1
2	How to live a worthwhile life	64	29	4	1	0
1	What happens after death	31	44	18	4	1
1	Why there is suffering in the world	36	41	18	3	1

2. Going back to the question, "What is the purpose of life?" which of the following statements comes closest to expressing your view about answering this question? *(Please circle the one number that best expresses your view)*

7 I don't think the question can be answered, and it doesn't bother me that it can't

4 I don't think that the question can be answered, but I wish there were an answer

42 I somehow believe that there must be an answer, although I don't know what it is

41 I believe there is an answer. For me that answer is:

_____

_____

3 I haven't thought about it very much, so I really can't say

3 N.R.

†
*N.R. = No Response

3. As you think about your life, how much have you learned about the meaning and purpose of life from each of the following? *(For each of the items listed, please circle the one number that best expresses your answer)*

N.R.	I have learned:	A lot	A fair amount	A little	Almost nothing	Nothing
3	From going to school	22	38	26	9	2
4	From watching television	3	15	37	30	11
2	From listening to sermons	33	43	19	3	0
3	From being out in nature	34	37	23	2	1
3	From my parents	40	36	16	5	1
2	From reading the Bible	35	35	24	3	1
3	From other Christian books	17	30	34	11	4
4	From private meditation	23	35	28	8	2
4	From religious TV programs	6	18	36	24	11
5	From books about other world religions	3	12	32	28	20
5	From psychology	5	15	28	22	25

4. Do you ever spend quiet time reflecting about your life? *(Circle one number)*
    9 No *(If not, please skip to question 5)*
    89 Yes *(If yes, please answer the questions in the box, 4a and 4b)*
    2 N.R.

4a. How often, on the average, have you done this within the past year? *(Circle one number)*
    27 Nearly every day
    26 At least once a week
    20 Several times a month
    17 Several times during the year   10 Not applicable

4b. Please say whether these times of quiet reflection usually, sometimes, or never involve each of the following:

	Usually	Sometimes	Never	NA*
Sitting or breathing techniques	3	17	63	18
Prayer	41	43	4	12
Clearing your mind of all thoughts	17	42	25	16
A church service	26	55	5	14
Being outdoors	29	54	5	13
Bible reading	20	51	15	14

*NA = Not Applicable

5. Below is a list of some of the experiences that people have described as having been deeply meaningful in their lives. *(For each one, please circle the appropriate number indicating whether or not you have had this experience)*

N.R.			Yes, at a specific time I can remember	Yes, but not at any time I can remember	No, but I'd like to	No	Not sure
2	a.	A deep sense of awe and wonder at the beauty of nature	72	25	1	0	0
4	b.	An experience of being "born again"	14	15	19	40	8
3	c.	A sense of God's love	53	34	6	2	3
4	d.	A feeling of being filled with the Holy Spirit	28	24	21	12	10
6	e.	A feeling of being in harmony with the universe	19	32	17	16	11
4	f.	A feeling of being tempted by the devil	32	30	1	23	11
3	g.	A feeling of close fellowship with Christians (other than your own family)	57	28	5	5	3
4	h.	A feeling that God was telling you something	42	28	10	9	7
4	i.	A feeling of being in contact with someone who has died	14	6	9	61	7
5	j.	A sense of closeness to the holy or sacred	23	30	12	20	11
4	k.	A feeling of intense happiness or ecstasy	54	26	7	6	4

5a. If any of the above experiences have had a *lasting impact* on your life, please indicate this by circling below the letters that correspond to these experiences. *(Circle as many as apply)*

    48 a.   13 b.   45 c.   18 d.   8 e.   11 f.   32 g.   28 h.   9 i.   12 j.   26 k.

6. Has there ever been a time in your life when you have experienced deep grief, suffering, or even tragedy? *(Circle one number)*

    25 No *(If not, please skip to question 7)*

    71 Yes *(Please say briefly what happened. If you have had more than one such experience, please describe the one that is most vivid in your memory)*

    5 N.R.

_____

_____

If yes, please answer the question in the box:

6a. Did you have the following experiences during this time?
(Circle one number for each item)

	Yes	No	Don't recall	NA
Came to be more concerned about others	50	8	10	32
Felt that God was especially close to you	48	12	8	31
Gained new insights about yourself	49	10	8	33
Wondered how God could let this happen to you	31	33	4	32
Felt support from church members	39	21	7	33
Felt that God was punishing you	9	55	3	33
Grew in your understanding of God's love	48	10	10	32

Next are some questions about your religious faith and what your faith means to you.

7. "Faith" has meant many different things to people. Which one of the following statements *comes closest* to describing your own view of faith? *(Circle one number only)*

   27 A life of commitment to God that I demonstrate by trying to do what is right

   9 My decision to accept Christ instead of going on in my own sinful ways

   40 My trust in God's grace

   3 My belief in all that the Bible says

   10 In my view, as long as people are truly sincere in their beliefs, they show faith

   2 I am not sure what "faith" means, although I am convinced that it is important

   1 To be honest about it, the idea of faith doesn't seem very meaningful to me

   7 None of these; what faith means to me is: _____

   _____

   1 N.R.

8. As you think about the various beliefs and activities that make up your life, how important a part do religious beliefs and activities play in your life? *(Circle one number only)*

   20 My religious beliefs and activities are the most important part of my life *(Please answer the question in the box)*

   64 My religious beliefs and activities are important to me, but other things are important to me too *(Please answer the question in the box)*

   9 Religious beliefs and activities play a minor role in my life, but I do consider them important *(Please answer the question in the box)*

   1 Religious beliefs and activities used to be important to me, but they no longer are *(Go on to question 9)*

185

1 Religious beliefs and activities have never played an important role in my life *(Go on to question 9)*
2 I am uncertain about the role of religious beliefs and activities in my life *(Go on to question 9)*
2 N.R.

If religious beliefs and activities are important to you, please answer the question in the box:

8a. Here are some of the benefits people say they experience from their religious commitments. For each one, please indicate whether or not you have experienced it in your own life during the past year. *(Circle one number for each)*

	Yes, all the time	Yes, many times	Yes, a few times	No, but I'd like to	No, and it's not important to me	Not sure	NA
Not worrying as much	10	38	26	12	2	4	9
A better sense of who I am	13	36	24	9	3	5	9
Guidance in making decisions	16	43	26	4	1	2	9
Better family relations	21	42	20	5	1	3	9
Friendship	18	45	22	3	1	2	9
Knowing I'll go to heaven when I die	27	19	15	14	3	11	10
Comfort when I'm feeling low	21	41	22	4	0	2	9
Freedom in Christ	24	25	16	6	1	14	12
More concern for others	21	51	16	1	0	1	9
Success in my work	11	34	25	6	4	9	11
Joy and excitement about being alive	24	40	19	4	1	3	9
More meaning in life	28	38	17	5	0	3	9
Feeling at peace with God	32	36	17	5	0	3	8

Next are some questions about God and God's activities.

9. Some of the ways in which people describe their relation to God are listed next. As far as you are concerned personally, how well does each description express your feelings about your own relation to God? *(Circle only one number for each)*

N.R.	Expresses my feelings:	Very well	Fairly well	Not very well	Not at all	Unsure
9 a.	I am a helpless sinner under the wrath and judgment of God	13	15	21	37	5
4 b.	I know that I am a sinner but God loves me and is giving me new life	57	29	4	2	3
7 c.	I am absolutely certain that I am saved and that I will go to heaven when I die	26	29	16	10	13
5 d.	As long as I do the best I can, I feel that God cares for me and watches over me	46	30	10	7	2
11 e.	I am not sure what my relation to God is	7	14	14	48	7
13 f.	I don't think of myself as having any relation to God	3	5	6	70	4

9a. Now look back over your answers to the previous question. Suppose you had to choose one of these statements as the *best* description of your relation to God. Which one would that be? *(Circle the number beside the letter that corresponds to the letter of the statement you chose)*

  3 a.   52 b.   5 c.   29 d.   3 e.   0 f.   2 Just can't choose

  2 None of the above; I think: _____

  _____

  4 N.R.

10. Has there been any time during the past year when you personally experienced God's presence or activity in your life? *(Circle one)*

  14 No   34 Not sure   47 Yes   5 N.R.

  If yes, answer the question in the box:

10a. Have you experienced God's presence or activity in each of the following kinds of situations during the past year? *(Circle one number for each)*

NA		Yes, many times	Yes, a few times	Yes, once	No	Not sure
49	While reading the Bible	13	18	2	13	6
47	During private prayer	26	19	2	3	4
49	While working	11	23	2	10	6

51	While having fun	8	21	1	10	8
47	While attending church	28	20	1	2	2
48	In nature	25	19	1	3	3
50	During a baptism	10	14	5	13	7
49	During Holy Communion	31	15	2	3	2
48	While meditating	21	19	2	5	4
48	While among friends	12	22	2	9	7

11. In your lifetime, have you ever felt God's forgiveness? *(Circle one)*

   49 I'm not sure   4 No   7 No, but I'd like to

   4 Yes, but it hasn't been very important to me

   32 Yes, it has had a deep impact on my life. *(Please describe briefly what happened. If this has happened more than once, give at least one example):*

   _____

   4 N.R.

12. Which one of the following comes closest to your view of the way in which God influences the things that happen in the world? *(Circle only one)*

   3 God sets history in motion but really doesn't interfere with it anymore

   36 God influences individuals, who then shape events

   31 God influences individuals, but also shapes events directly through nations and social affairs

   13 I don't think of God as "influencing" the things that happen

   9 Not sure because I haven't thought about it much before

   6 None of these; my view is: _____

   3 N.R.

13. People often wonder how a merciful God can allow terrible things to happen, such as the killing of of six million Jews during World War II. Which statement *comes closest* to your view of why God lets these things happen? *(Circle only one)*

   1 God allows terrible things to happen in order to punish people for their sins

   49 We don't know why these things happen, but we know that God is able to use them for good

   2 God doesn't have anything to do with these things; the devil causes them

   31 People cause these things to happen; not God

   6 Frankly, I don't know how God can allow these things to happen; it doesn't seem right to me

   4 I don't have a view on this topic

   5 None of the above; my view is: _____

   2 N.R.

188

14.   Do you feel that it is possible to prove that God exists? *(Circle only one)*

    22   No, we don't have the kind of evidence it would take *(Skip to question 15)*

    6   No, it would be wrong even to try *(Skip to question 15)*

    34   Yes, I think it probably is

    34   Yes, I know it is   4 N.R.

If yes, please answer the question in the box:

14a.   Please indicate whether or not you think it is possible to prove that God exists in each of the following ways: *(Circle one for each)*

	Yes	No	Don't know	N.R.
From evidence in the Bible	57	4	5	35
By means of a logical argument	20	25	17	39
Through personal experience	50	5	9	36
Through the actions of the Holy Spirit	51	2	11	36

---

15.   Which of the following statements comes closest to expressing what you believe about God? *(Circle only one)*

    68   I know God really exists, and I have no doubts about it

    25   While I have doubts, I feel that I do believe in God

    2   I find myself believing in God some of the time, but not at other times

    2   I don't believe in a personal God, but I do believe in a higher power of some kind

    0   I don't know whether there is a God, and I don't believe there is any way to find out

    0   I don't believe in God

    2   None of the above represents what I believe. What I believe about God is: _____

_____

    1 N.R.

The next set of questions is about Christ.

16.   In your own life, would you say that you have been "born again" or had a "born-again" experience—that is, a turning point in your life when you committed yourself to Christ? *(Circle one)*

    50 No   23 Not sure   25 Yes   2 N.R.

17.   Traditionally, a central belief of the church has been that Christ was fully God *and* fully human during his life on earth. Is this a belief about which you have no doubts, some doubts, or serious doubts? *(Circle only one)*

    75 No doubts   22 Some doubts   2 Serious doubts   1 N.R.

17a. In your own life, how important is this belief to you? *(Circle only one)*
    58 Very important   2 Not at all important
    23 Fairly important   7 I'm not sure
     9 Not very important   1 N.R.

18. The church has also held that Christ was crucified on the cross. Is the crucifixion meaningful to you? *(Circle only one)*
    2 No   7 Not sure   91 Yes   * N.R.

18a. In your opinion, which one of the following statements best expresses the main reason why Christ was crucified? *(Circle only one)*
    88 To forgive our sins
     1 As a protest against social injustice
     2 To show us how to love our neighbor
     2 The main reason was the disbelief of the Jews
     1 I'm not sure that Christ was crucified
     5 Other: _____
     1 N.R.

19. Which of the following comes closest to your attitude toward people in other countries who have never heard about Christ *(Circle only one)*
    61 A desire to share the love of Christ with them
     2 A feeling that if we do not preach Christ to them, they will be damned forever
     1 A feeling that we shouldn't worry about them because there are so many people in this country who haven't heard about Christ
    16 A feeling that we should respect their religions and stop trying to impose Christianity on them
     6 Frankly, I haven't thought about it
    13 Can't choose   1 N.R.

20. As far as Jews are concerned, do you feel Christians should *(Circle only one)*:
    17 Make special efforts to preach Christ to Jews
    40 Tell people about Christ, but direct no special efforts toward Jews
    20 Not try to convert Jews to Christianity
    21 Not sure   1 N.R.

Next are several questions about some other kinds of belief.

21. What about the belief that the devil actually exists? *(Circle only one)*
    33 I'm absolutely sure there is a devil   4 I'm absolutely sure there is no devil
    32 I'm pretty sure there is a devil   22 Don't know
     7 I'm pretty sure there is no devil   2 N.R.

* = Less than 1%

22. Which one of the following statements comes closest to expressing your view of life after death? *(Circle only one)*

1 I don't believe that there is life after death

7 I am unsure whether or not there is life after death

43 I believe that there must be something beyond death, but I have no idea what it may be like

4 There is life after death, but no punishment

36 There is life after death, with rewards for some people and punishment for others

2 The notion of reincarnation expresses my view of what happens to people when they die

6 None of these expresses my view. What I think about life after death is: _____

_____

1 N.R.

23. Have you ever known anyone who came very close to dying, but revived and was able to tell what the experience of dying was like?

87 No, not personally *(Go on to question 24)*

9 Yes, I've known someone who had an experience like this

2 Yes, I've had such an experience myself   1 N.R.

If yes, please describe this experience in the box:

9 R.
91 N.R.

24. Which one of these statements comes closest to describing your feelings about the Bible? *(Circle only one)*

16 The Bible is the actual word of God and is to be taken literally, word for word

73 The Bible is the inspired word of God but not everything in it should be taken literally, word for word

5 The Bible is an ancient book of fables, legends, history and moral precepts recorded by men

1 None of these

3 Can't say   1 N.R.

25. The Bible says that humanity was created by God. Science says that humanity evolved from other forms of animal life. In your opinion, which of these views is correct? *(Circle only one)*

47 The biblical view   0 Neither

2 The scientific view   4 Not sure

47 Both, in their own ways   1 N.R.

26. Think now for a moment about your religious beliefs as a whole. How certain are you about your beliefs? *(Circle only one)*

51 I'm quite certain about what I believe

44 I'm pretty certain even though I have some doubts

5 I have some fairly serious doubts about what I believe
1 I have very serious doubts about what I believe   1 N.R.

Your church activities and what they mean to you are the focus of the next several questions.

27. Do you feel that God speaks to you through the church service on Sunday mornings? *(Circle only one)*

47 Yes, most of the time   1 No, and it doesn't matter to me
35 Yes, once in awhile   2 No, because I don't attend church
11 No, but I wish I did feel that way 3 Not sure
                                    1 N.R.

If yes, please answer the question in the box:

> 27a. How, in your opinion, does this most often happen? *(Circle only one)*
>
> 18 God speaks to me through the sermon   10 It's just a quiet time for my own reflections
> 41 God speaks to me, but not necessarily through the sermon   13 I'm not sure how, but I know it happens
>   17 NA

28. Which one of these statements comes closest to your feelings when you say the Apostles' Creed? *(Circle only one)*

1 I'm not sure what the Apostles' Creed is
5 Saying the Apostles' Creed is pretty much a meaningless ritual for me
7 I do not believe in everything it says, but saying it is still meaningful to me
2 I haven't said the Apostles' Creed recently
85 I believe in what it says and regard it as a meaningful confession of my faith
1 N.R.

29. In the column on the *left*, please *circle* the statement that best fits your feelings about *Holy Communion*. Then in the column on the right, *circle* the statement that best fits your feelings about *baptism*.

(A) Communion		(B) Baptism
24	It is essential in order to receive salvation and everlasting life	47
62	It is not essential for salvation, but it is a way of receiving forgiveness and new life	30
8	It is only one of the "traditions" of the church, but it is still meaningful to me	11
1	It is a tradition that has no meaning to me personally	1
1	None of these	2
3	N.R.	9

30. In your view, how is Christ present when you take Holy Communion? *(Circle only one)*
    - 24 The bread and wine actually become the body and blood of Christ and are no longer bread and wine
    - 45 Christ himself is present in the administration of the bread and wine but they remain bread and wine
    - 17 Christ is present in some mysterious way that can't be defined
    - 10 Holy Communion is a memorial service that helps us remember Christ's life and death, but Christ himself is not present
    - 3 I don't think about Communion in any of these ways
    - 2 N.R.

31. All in all, which of the following statements best summarizes the role of the church in your life? *(Circle only one)*
    - 42 The church is absolutely essential for my spiritual growth
    - 47 Although the church is not essential, I would find it difficult to grow spiritually without being involved in a church
    - 7 It is just as easy for me to live a Christian life without going to church as it is with going to church
    - 3 None of these; the statement that best expresses my view is: _____

       _____

    - 1 N.R.

32. In thinking about the kind of church member you are, which one of these descriptions fits you the best? *(Circle only one)*
    - 25 Very active in the church and committed to it
    - 45 Fairly active in the church and committed to it
    - 23 Not very active in the church, but committed to it
    - 4 Not very committed to the church
    - 3 Uncertain about my commitment to the church
    - 1 N.R.

33. In general, how satisfied or dissatisfied have you been with your local church in the past few years? *(Circle only one)*
    - 41 Quite satisfied overall
    - 48 Mostly satisfied, but dissatisfied about some things
    - 10 Dissatisfied about many things
    - 2 N.R.

The next set of questions deals with your views about what it means to live a Christian life.

34. Is it possible, in your opinion, to be certain that one is living a Christian life? *(Please circle the statement that most closely expresses your opinion)*
    - 46 Yes, there are clear marks of Christian living that can be seen in people's lives
    - 22 You can't be certain, but you can tell if you're on the "right track"
    - 2 There is just no way to know

27 You shouldn't worry about being certain; trust God and do the best you can

3 None of these; I think _____

_____

2 N.R.

35. Can you think of times during the past year when you have been guided by the following in making decisions about your life?
(Circle one number for each)

N.R.		Yes, many times	Yes, several times	No	Unsure
6	The "golden rule"	42	39	7	7
3	Your conscience	66	28	1	2
5	The Ten Commandments	37	41	8	9
6	The example of other people in your church	11	38	31	15
5	What your pastor preaches in sermons	23	46	15	11
4	The teachings of Jesus	47	36	3	9

36. Do you feel that God has given us rules to live by? (Circle only one)

49 God has given very clear, detailed rules that apply to everyone

43 God has given us some general rules, but we have to decide how to apply them to our own situations

3 God gives rules, but the rules may be different for different people

2 I don't think that God has given us rules

2 I'm not really sure   1 N.R.

37. Has reading the Bible ever been of help to you for each of the following?
(Circle one number for each item)

N.R.		Yes, many times	Yes, several times	Yes, once	No	Not sure
5	In making decisions	16	37	3	23	16
3	As a source of comfort	36	42	4	9	7
4	For inspiration	34	41	3	9	9
6	On moral questions	19	38	3	18	16

38. Please indicate whether or not you personally consider each of the following to be wrong. (Circle one number for each)

N.R.		Always wrong	Usually wrong	Depends on the situation	Not at all wrong	Can't decide
2	Telling a small lie	26	31	40	0	1
1	Showing disrespect to parents	60	30	8	0	0
6	Not trying to discover who I really am	20	24	16	15	20

#						
2	Missing an appointment and not calling to apologize	52	31	15	0	1
2	Disobeying the teachings of the Bible	56	31	8	1	3
2	Working to overthrow the government	48	18	29	1	3
2	Homosexual relations	66	10	8	4	11
3	Smoking marijuana	64	16	7	4	7
2	Receiving support from public welfare	4	7	74	12	1
3	Taking part in political protests	7	11	61	16	3
1	Cheating on your income tax	75	18	4	1	1
2	Premarital sexual intercourse	46	21	20	5	6
2	Abortion	22	13	53	6	4

39. Imagine the following situation. Suppose you had been offered two equally good jobs and were trying to decide which one to take. Which *one* of the following do you think you would probably do? *(Circle only one)*

    23 I'd probably pray that God would give me a sign about which job he wanted me to take

    57 I'd probably pray about it, and then I'd use my own judgment to make the best decision I could

    15 I'd probably try hard to make the best decision I could; it wouldn't occur to me to pray about something like this

    4 Just can't say

    1 N.R.

40. Which one of the following statements comes closest to your view of prayer? *(Circle only one)*

    0 I don't believe in prayer

    2 Prayer is talking to yourself, but that is sometimes helpful

    45 Prayer is talking with God, but God doesn't always answer

    47 Prayer is talking with God, and God always answers

    5 I'm not sure what to think about prayer

    1 N.R.

41. Were there any times during the past year when you found it helpful to pray? *(Circle only one)*

    2 No, I didn't pray

    3 No, I prayed, but it really wasn't helpful

    26 Yes, a few times

    69 Yes, a number of times

    1 N.R.

If yes, please answer the questions in the box:

41a. For each of the following, was prayer helpful to you in this way during the past year?

	Yes	No	Unsure	NA
God showed me clearly what I should do	25	27	27	11
Prayer was a source of comfort	89	1	2	8
It helped me think more clearly	77	3	11	9
It drew me closer to other people	53	15	21	11
I felt that my sins were forgiven	61	10	20	10
I felt closer to God	82	2	7	8

41b. How often, during the past year, has your own praying—that is, prayer outside of church services—involved each of the following?

	Frequently	Occasionally	Never	NA
A special quiet time when you pray for at least several minutes	46	39	8	8
Short sentences to God in the midst of your daily activities	55	35	3	7
Just thinking things through, but not really praying formally to God	39	46	4	11
Praying aloud with family members (other than saying grace)	9	29	52	10

One aspect of Christian living that is often discussed has to do with loving your neighbor. Please answer frankly the following questions:

42. Christ said that we should love our neighbor. Have you done anything within the past year that you felt was really an example of "loving your neighbor"? *(Circle one)*

    5 No

    37 I'm not sure

    57 Yes. What was it? _____

    2 N.R.

43. You have probably heard reports on the news from time to time about people who have been the victims of floods, earthquakes, or other disasters. When you hear about such people, what is your response? *(Circle only one)*

    24 I feel sorry for them, but I feel that there are governmental agencies and other organizations which have been established to help out in these situations

    20 I feel that I should personally do something to help, but I usually never get around to doing anything

27 If there is a clear need, I try to send some money or do something else to help out

22 My own feeling is that the best thing I can do in these situations is to pray that God will be of comfort to the people involved

5 None of these; my tendency is to _____

2 N.R.

44. Thinking back over the past year, have you ever felt guilty about not loving your neighbor as much as you should? *(Circle only one)*

43 Yes, there have been times when I have felt very guilty because I knew I should be doing more

7 No, I really feel that I've done about as much as I could

43 I haven't felt guilty or not guilty; I've just enjoyed helping people whenever I could

3 Frankly, I haven't thought much about "loving my neighbor"

2 I really don't remember

1 N.R.

The following questions ask your views about the church's relation to social and political affairs.

45. As far as political affairs are concerned, do you feel that: *(Circle only one)*

9 It is OK for the church to take direct political action as an organization

31 The church should stay out of politics as an organization, but it is OK for the church to make policy statements

43 The church should relate spiritual principles to political issues, but not make policy statements

13 The church should deal only with spiritual matters

3 None of these; my view is: _____

2 N.R.

46. Christians sometimes describe God as a "God of justice" or a God who commands us to bring about justice. Which *one* of these statements comes closest to your own ideas about what this means?

23 It means that the church should work for justice and support groups that are working to end inequality and oppression

43 I think of it at a more personal level. It means I should try to be just and fair in all my dealings

13 I think this is actually a spiritual term that refers to God punishing evil, rather than activities of the church or individuals

1 Frankly, the concept of God's justice doesn't have any particular meaning to me

14 I'm really not sure what it refers to

3 None of these; its meaning to me is _____

3 N.R.

47. In your opinion, it is all right for pastors in their leadership roles to *(Circle one response for each statement):*

N.R.		Yes	No	Unsure
2	Speak out against political corruption	71	12	14
4	Discuss political issues from the pulpit	25	54	17
4	Endorse candidates for office	11	69	16
4	Participate in protest marches or demonstrations	23	49	24
4	Criticize the actions of other countries	30	35	31

48. As far as more specific social issues are concerned, do you mostly favor or mostly oppose each of the following? *(Circle one for each)*

N.R.		Mostly favor	Mostly oppose	Don't know
1	Legalizing marijuana	10	80	9
2	The death penalty	49	32	17
3	Ordination of women	69	16	12
5	Actively supporting Soviet dissidents	27	30	38
3	More freedom for homosexuals	12	66	20
3	Leaving South Africa alone to solve its own problems	33	26	38
3	American leaders taking a tough stand in support of human rights in other countries	51	22	25
3	Giving more power to the police	39	31	27
4	Major changes in our form of government	27	43	27
3	Putting business executives in jail if, known to them, their companies break the law	64	10	24
2	Providing special opportunities so that more black people can go to college	41	28	29
2	Spending more government money for people on welfare	6	75	17

Another issue that comes up frequently is the idea of promoting cooperation and greater understanding among different kinds of religious groups.

49. In this regard, please indicate whether you would tend to approve or tend to disapprove of having common worship services between Lutherans and each of the following *(Circle one number for each):*

	Tend to approve	Tend to disapprove	Unsure	N.R.
Roman Catholics	75	13	11	2
Baptists	72	12	14	2
Jews	44	30	24	2
Presbyterians	80	7	11	2
Jehovah's Witnesses	18	59	21	2

50. In your opinion, are there any important differences between your religious beliefs and the beliefs of each of these groups? *(Circle one number for each)*

198

	Yes, many	Yes, some	Yes, a few	No, none	Not sure	N.R.
Roman Catholics	16	49	28	3	3	1
Baptists	9	40	32	6	12	2
Jews	60	22	8	1	8	2
Zen Buddhists	67	5	2	1	23	3
Presbyterians	3	32	38	15	11	2
Jehovah's Witnesses	66	14	5	1	13	2

51. How do you feel about people who "speak in tongues"? *(Circle one)*

47 I'm not sure what "speaking in tongues" means

12 I disapprove of speaking in tongues

25 Speaking in tongues is OK for some people, but it's not for me

12 I approve of speaking in tongues, but I haven't done it myself

2 I approve and have spoken in tongues myself

2 N.R.

51a. How much do you know about speaking in tongues? *(Circle one)*

5 A lot   22 Some   36 Only a little   36 Nothing   2 N.R.

52. The final question in this section involves several pairs of statements that reflect different views on various Christian issues. Neither statement is likely fully to reflect your own views, but what we'd like you to do is to say which one *comes closest* to your views. *(Circle only one number for each item)*

   a. 42 Meaning in life comes mostly from one's day-to-day experiences
      50 Meaning in life comes mostly from having a clear and consistent doctrine or philosophy to live by
      6 Just can't choose   2 N.R.

   b. 41 My religious views are very personal and private
      51 I like to discuss my religious views with others
      7 Just can't choose   1 N.R.

   c. 11 Becoming a Christian is a once-and-for-all decision
      84 Becoming a Christian is an on-going spiritual journey
      4 Just can't choose   1 N.R.

   d. 45 Christianity is the one true religion
      46 Most religions have some handle on the truth
      7 Just can't choose   2 N.R.

   e. 59 Christians have a sense of peace and joy that other people don't experience
      25 Basically Christians have no more peace and joy than other people
      15 Just can't choose   1 N.R.

   f. 66 Christians are generally more concerned about the needs of others than other people are
      18 Christians usually aren't any more concerned about the needs of others than anyone else
      14 Just can't choose   2 N.R.

Thank you very much! Please return the completed questionnaire to:
Office for Research and Planning
Lutheran Church in America
231 Madison Avenue, New York, NY 10016

In the cover letter we raised the possibility of sending you an evaluation questionnaire about *The Lutheran* magazine in 1979 or 1980. Would you be willing to receive such a questionnaire? *(Circle one)*

    41 Yes   45 No   14 N.R.

CLERGY RESPONSES

First, here are some questions about the meaning and purpose of life.

1.   In your own personal life, how much do you think about each of the following kinds of questions? *(For each of the questions listed, please circle the one number indicating whether you think about it a lot, some, only a little, have thought about it in the past but don't now, or have never thought much about it)*

N.R.		A lot	Some	Only a little	Don't now but have in the past	Never thought about it
0	What the purpose of life is	56	31	6	7	0
*	How the world came into being	12	34	32	20	1
1	The existence of God	48	22	13	15	1
1	How to live a worthwhile life	69	22	4	3	0
*	What happens after death	24	46	23	8	0
*	Why there is suffering in the world	28	45	18	9	0

2.   Going back to the question, "What is the purpose of life?" which of the following statements comes closest to expressing your view about answering this question? *(Please circle the one number that best expresses your view)*

    4 I don't think the question can be answered, and it doesn't bother me that it can't

    2 I don't think that the question can be answered, but I wish there were an answer

    7 I somehow believe that there must be an answer, although I don't know what it is

    86 I believe there is an answer. For me that answer is:

_____

_____

    0 I haven't thought about it very much, so I really can't say

    1 N.R.

3. As you think about your personal life, how much have you learned about the meaning and purpose of life from each of the following? *(For each of the items listed, please circle the* one *number that best expresses your answer)*

N.R.	I have learned:	A lot	A fair amount	A little	Almost nothing	Nothing
*	From going to school	33	40	22	4	1
2	From watching television	2	12	43	35	8
1	From listening to sermons	25	48	22	3	1
1	From being out in nature	10	33	44	10	3
1	From my parents	38	39	19	4	0
*	From reading the Bible	70	25	3	1	0
*	From other Christian books	41	46	11	1	0
1	From private meditation	32	41	23	3	0
2	From religious TV programs	2	9	34	40	13
1	From books about other world religions	2	13	41	30	13
*	From psychology	8	33	36	17	6

4. Do you ever spend quiet time reflecting about your life? *(Circle one number)*

    4 No *(If not , please skip to question 5)*

    96 Yes *(If yes, please answer the questions in the box, 4a and 4b)*

    1 N.R.

4a. How often, on the average, have you done this within the past year? *(Circle one number)*

    38 Nearly every day

    29 At least once a week

    17 Several times a month

    11 Several times during the year

    4 N.R.

4b. Please say whether these times of quiet reflection usually, sometimes, or never involve each of the following:

	Usually	Sometimes	Never	N.R.
Sitting or breathing techniques	3	16	73	8
Prayer	51	43	2	4
Clearing your mind of all thoughts	18	51	24	7
Being in a church service	22	63	10	5
Being outdoors	13	75	6	5
Bible reading	34	60	2	4

---

* = Less than 1%

5. Below is a list of some of the experiences that people have described as having been deeply meaningful in their lives. *(For each one, please circle the appropriate number indicating whether or not you have had this experience)*

N.R.			Yes, at a specific time I can remember	Yes, but not at any time I can remember	No, but I'd like to	No	Not sure
1	a.	A deep sense of awe and wonder at the beauty of nature	71	26	1	1	1
1	b.	An experience of being "born again"	16	29	2	47	5
1	c.	A sense of God's love	70	28	1	1	1
1	d.	A feeling of being filled with the Holy Spirit	40	41	2	11	5
2	e.	A feeling of being in harmony with the universe	23	43	6	19	8
1	f.	A feeling of being tempted by the devil	38	30	1	25	6
1	g.	A feeling of close fellowship with Christians (other than your own family)	75	23	1	1	0
1	h.	A feeling that God was telling you something	60	30	2	5	2
1	i.	A feeling of being in contact with someone who has died	7	4	4	76	7
1	j.	A sense of closeness to the holy or sacred	50	39	1	4	4
1	k.	A feeling of intense happiness or ecstasy	57	30	3	7	3

5a. If any of the above experiences have had a *lasting impact* on your life, please indicate this by circling below the letters that correspond to these experiences. *(Circle as many as apply)*

38 a. 23 b. 67 c. 32 d. 12 e. 11 f. 58 g. 45 h. 4 i. 32 j. 25 k.

6. Has there ever been a time in your life when you have experienced deep grief, suffering, or even tragedy? *(Circle one number)*

26 No *(If not, please skip to question 7)*

67 Yes *(Please say briefly what happened. If you have had more than one such experience, please describe the one that is most vivid in your memory)*

7 N.R.

_____

_____

If yes, please answer the question in the box:

6a. Did you have the following experiences during this time?
(Circle one number for each item)

	Yes	No	Don't recall	NA
Came to be more concerned about others	53	9	8	30
Felt that God was especially close to you	54	10	6	30
Gained new insights about yourself	63	3	4	30
Wondered how God could let this happen to you	20	47	3	31
Felt support from church members	51	14	5	30
Felt that God was punishing you	2	66	1	31
Grew in your understanding of God's love	59	5	5	30

Next are some questions about God and God's activities.

7. Some of the ways in which people describe their relation to God are listed next. As far as you are concerned personally, how well does each description express your feelings about your own relation to God?

N.R.		Very well	Fairly well	Not very well	Not at all	Unsure
2	a. I am a helpless sinner under the wrath and judgment of God	7	7	29	53	1
1	*b. I know that I am a sinner but God loves me and is giving me new life	86	12	1	1	0
1	c. I am absolutely certain that I am saved and that I will go to heaven when I die	46	35	10	5	2
2	d. As long as I do the best I can, I feel that God cares for me and watches over me	13	13	25	45	2
3	e. I am not sure what my relation to God is	2	2	10	82	2
3	f. I don't think of myself as having any relation to God	0	0	1	95	1

7a. Now look back over your answers to the previous question. Suppose you had to choose one of these statements as the *best* description of your relation to God. Which one would it be? *(Circle the number beside the letter that corresponds to the letter of the statement you chose)*

  a. 2   b. 84   c. 6   d. 2   e. 1   f. 0   1 Just can't choose

  2 None of those; I think: _____

_____

  2 N.R.

8. Has there been any time during the past year when you personally experienced God's presence or activity in your life? *(Circle one)*

    3 No   88 Yes   6 Not sure   3 N.R.

    If yes, please answer the question in the box:

8a. Have you experienced God's presence or activity in each of the following kinds of situation during the past year?

NA		Yes, many times	Yes, a few times	Yes, once	No	Not sure
10	While reading the Bible	40	38	2	6	3
9	During private prayer	42	39	1	6	2
9	While working	46	38	1	4	2
12	While having fun	27	41	3	10	7
9	While attending church	56	29	1	3	2
11	In nature	23	42	6	11	7
11	During a baptism	35	30	5	12	7
9	During Holy Communion	63	22	2	3	2
10	While meditating	41	40	2	5	3
10	While among friends	33	45	2	6	4

9. In your lifetime, have you ever felt God's forgiveness?

    8 I'm not sure   1 No   1 No, but I'd like to

    8 Yes, but it hasn't been very important to me

    79 Yes, it has had a deep impact on my life. *(Please describe briefly what happened. If this has happened more than once, give at least one example):*

    _____

    3 N.R.

*10. "Faith" has meant many different things to people. Which one of the following statements *comes closest* to describing your own view of faith? *(Circle only one)*

    10 A life of commitment to God that I demonstrate by trying to do what is right

    4 My decision to accept Christ instead of going on in my own sinful ways

    74 My trust in God's grace

    0 My belief in all that the Bible says

    0 In my view, as long as people are truly sincere in their beliefs, they show faith

    0 I am not sure what "faith" means, although I am convinced that it is important

    0 To be honest about it, the idea of faith doesn't seem very meaningful to me

    11 None of these; what faith means to me is: _____

    _____

    1 N.R.

*Confessional Lutheran item

204

11. Which one of the following comes closest to your view of the way in which God influences the things that happen in the world? *(Circle only* one)

    1 God set history in motion but really doesn't interfere with it anymore

   27 God influences individuals, who then shape events

   61 God influences individuals, but also shapes events directly through nations and social affairs

    2 I don't think of God as "influencing" the things that happen

    0 Not sure because I haven't thought about it much before

    7 None of these; my view is: _____

_____

    1 N.R.

12. People often wonder how a merciful God can allow terrible things to happen, such as the killing of six million Jews during World War II. Which statement *comes closest* to your view of why God lets these things happen? *(Circle only* one)

    0 God allows terrible things to happen in order to punish people for their sins

   42 We don't know why these things happen, but we know that God is able to use them for good

    3 God doesn't have anything to do with these things; the devil causes them

   35 People cause these things to happen; not God

    1 Frankly, I don't know how God can allow these things to happen; it doesn't seem right to me

    0 I don't have a view on this topic

   18 None of the above; my view is: _____

_____

    1 N.R.

13. Do you feel that it is possible to prove that God exists? *(Circle only* one)

   46 No, we don't have the kind of evidence it would take *(Skip to question 14)*

   10 No, it would be wrong even to try *(Skip to question 14)*

   17 Yes, I think it probably is

   25 Yes, I know it is

    2 N.R.

If yes, please answer the question in the box:

13a. Please indicate whether or not you think it is possible to prove that God exists in each of the following ways:

	Yes	No	Don't know	NA
From evidence in the Bible	33	7	2	58
By means of a logical argument	11	23	4	62
Through personal experience	38	3	2	58
Through the actions of the Holy Spirit	39	2	2	58

14. Which of the following statements comes closest to expressing what you believe about God? *(Circle only one)*

    61 I know God really exists, and I have no doubts about it

    28 While I have doubts, I feel that I do believe in God

    2 I find myself believing in God some of the time, but not at other times

    0 I don't believe in a personal God, but I do believe in a higher power of some kind

    0 I don't know whether there is a God, and I don't believe there is any way to find out

    0 I don't believe in God

    8 None of the above represents what I believe. What I believe about God is: _____

    _____

    2 N.R.

The next set of questions is about Christ.

15. Traditionally, a central belief of the church has been that Christ was fully God *and* fully human during his life on earth. Is this a belief about which you have no doubts, some doubts, or serious doubts? *(Circle one)*

    86 No doubts   13 Some doubts   1 Serious doubts   1 N.R.

*15a. In your own life, how important is this belief to you? *(Circle one)*

    82 Very important   2 Not very important   1 I'm not sure

    14 Fairly important   0 Not at all important   ** N.R.

*16. The church has also held that Christ was crucified on the cross. Is the crucifixion meaningful to you? *(Circle one)*

    1 No   1 Not sure   98 Yes   ** N.R.

*16a. In your opinion, which one of the following statements best expresses the main reason why Christ was crucified? *(Circle only one)*

    79 To forgive our sins

    0 As a protest against social injustice

    2 To show us how to love our neighbor

    2 The main reason was the disbelief of the Jews

    0 I'm not sure that Christ was crucified

    17 Other: _____

    ** N.R.

17. Which of the following comes closest to your attitude toward people in other countries who have never heard about Christ? *(Circle only one)*

    89 A desire to share the love of Christ with them

    1 A feeling that if we do not preach Christ to them, they will be damned forever

*Confessional Lutheran item
** = Less than 1%

206

0 A feeling that we shouldn't worry about them because there are so many people in this country who haven't heard about Christ

4 A feeling that we should respect their religions and stop trying to impose Christianity on them

1 Frankly, I haven't thought about it

4 Can't choose   1 N.R.

18. As far as Jews are concerned, do you feel Christians should *(Circle only one):*
   24 Make special efforts to preach Christ to Jews
   61 Tell people about Christ, but direct no special efforts toward Jews
   7 Not try to convert Jews to Christianity
   6 Not sure   2 N.R.

19. In your own life, would you say that you have been "born again" or have had a "born-again" experience—that is, a turning point in your life when you committed yourself to Christ?
   42 Yes   48 No   9 Not sure   1 N.R.

Next are several questions about some other kinds of belief.

20. What about the belief that the devil actually exists? *(Circle one)*
   44 I'm absolutely sure there is a devil   7 I'm absolutely sure there is no devil
   20 I'm pretty sure there is a devil   14 Don't know
   10 I'm pretty sure there is no devil   3 N.R.

21. Which one of the following statements comes closest to expressing your view of life after death? *(Circle only one)*
   1 I don't believe that there is life after death
   1 I am unsure whether or not there is life after death
   18 I believe that there must be something beyond death, but I have no idea what it may be like
   6 There is life after death, but no punishment
   45 There is life after death, with rewards for some people and punishment for others
   0 The notion of reincarnation expresses my view of what happens to people when they die
   29 None of these expresses my view. What I think about life after death is: _____

   _____

   * N.R.

22. Have you ever known anyone who came very close to dying, but revived and was able to tell what the experience of dying was like? *(Circle only one)*
   69 No, not personally *(Go on to question 23)*
   28 Yes, I've known someone who had an experience like this
   2 Yes, I've had such an experience myself   1 N.R.

* = Less than 1%

If yes, please describe this experience:

> 25 R.
> 75 N.R.

23. Which one of these statements comes closest to describing your feelings about the Bible? *(Circle only one)*
    - 2 The Bible is the actual word of God and is to be taken literally, word for word
    - 93 The Bible is the inspired word of God but not everything in it should be taken literally, word for word
    - 0 The Bible is an ancient book of fables, legends, history and moral precepts recorded by men
    - 3 None of these
    - 0 Can't say   2 N.R.

24. The Bible says that humanity was created by God. Science says that humanity evolved from other forms of animal life. In your opinion, which of these views is correct? *(Circle only one)*

20 The biblical view	0 Neither
1 The scientific view	1 Not sure
78 Both in their own ways	1 N.R.

25. Think now for a moment about your religious beliefs as a whole. How certain are you about your beliefs? *(Circle only one)*
    - 58 I'm quite certain about what I believe
    - 40 I'm pretty certain even though I have some doubts
    - 1 I have some fairly serious doubts about what I believe
    - 0 I have very serious doubts about what I believe   1 N.R.

26. The past decade has often been described as a period of theological ferment and change. In thinking about your own theological orientations, how much would you say they've changed in the past ten years (or since beginning your ministry, if that was more recent)? *(Circle one)*

20 A lot	19 Only a little	2 Not sure
43 Some	15 None or hardly any	2 N.R.

    If any change, please answer the question in the box:

> Please describe some of the important changes in your theological orientation that have occurred within the past decade.
> 63 R.
> 37 N.R.

27. During the past year, did you preach a sermon that dealt mainly with each of the following topics? *(Circle all that apply)*

N.R.		Yes, many	Yes, at least one	No, but touched on it often	No, but touched on it some	No	Not sure
3	Becoming more involved in the programs of the church	19	37	21	16	4	1
2	Christ's crucifixion	46	44	6	2	0	0
3	Coping with day-to-day problems	59	21	14	3	0	0
2	Current political issues	8	24	23	33	9	0
4	Discovering who one really is	28	28	22	11	4	2
2	Experiencing God's forgiveness	65	23	8	2	0	0
2	Finding inner peace	29	32	24	10	1	2
3	Following the Ten Commandments	7	21	28	29	11	1
3	Fostering Christian fellowship	36	30	23	7	0	0
2	God's love for us as sinners	74	15	8	0	0	0
3	Human rights	11	21	33	25	6	1
3	Issues of social justice	10	20	32	29	5	1
3	Making a definite decision for Christ	20	22	18	19	17	1
3	Prayer	20	42	18	13	3	1
2	Receiving God's forgiveness through Holy Communion	53	29	11	4	1	0
3	Serving others the way Christ did	52	27	15	3	0	0
2	Sexual conduct	2	13	16	43	23	1
2	Stewardship	20	48	20	9	1	0
2	The dual nature (divinity and humanity) of Christ	11	28	21	24	13	1
2	The family	17	43	24	11	1	1
1	Trusting in God's grace	67	19	11	1	0	0
2	What faith means	50	31	15	2	0	0

28. Which one of these statements comes closest to your feelings when you say the Apostles' Creed? *(Circle only one)*

83 I believe in what it says and regard the entire Creed as a meaningful confession of my faith

11 I do not believe in everything it says, but confessing it is still meaningful to me

2 Saying the Apostles' Creed is only meaningful to me as a liturgical act

3 Other _____

1 N.R.

*29. In the column on the *left*, please circle *one* statement that best fits your feelings about *Holy Communion*. Then in the column on the *right*, circle *one* statement that best fits your feelings about *baptism*.

(A) Communion		(B) Baptism
23	It is essential in order to receive salvation and everlasting life	41
72	It is not essential for salvation, but it is a way of receiving forgiveness and new life	51
1	It is only one of the "traditions" of the church, but it is meaningful to me	1
0	It is a tradition that has no meaning to me personally	0
3	None of these	3
2	N.R.	4

*30. In your view, how is Christ present when you take Holy Communion? *(Circle only one)*

3 The bread and wine actually become the Body and Blood of Christ and are no longer bread and wine

68 Christ himself is present in the administration of the bread and wine but they remain bread and wine

26 Christ is present in some mysterious way that can't be defined

0 Holy Communion is a memorial service that helps us remember Christ's life and death, but Christ himself is not present

1 I don't think about Communion in any of these ways   2 N.R.

31. In thinking about the members of your congregation, would you say that each of the following statements describes most of them, some of them, only a few of them, or none of them? *(Circle one number for each statement)*

N.R.		Most of them	Some of them	Only a few of them	None of them	Don't know
1	Consider the church absolutely essential for their spiritual growth	28	58	12	0	1
2	Are quite satisfied overall with their local church	64	30	4	0	1
2	Have serious questions about some of their religious beliefs	6	52	37	1	2
2	Feel they have experienced God's forgiveness in their lives	43	46	6	0	2
2	Have some doubts about the existence of God	3	31	46	8	10
3	Pray nearly every day	21	51	19	0	7
2	Would say they have had a "born-again" experience	1	17	65	7	8
1	Disapprove of speaking in tongues	60	18	9	1	11

*Confessional Lutheran item

1	Feel that political issues should be left out of the pulpit	38	44	13	1	3
2	Believe that most religions have some handle on the truth	29	40	20	1	9
2	Have had a deeply meaningful religious experience at some point in their lives	14	55	24	0	5
1	Frequently turn to the Bible when making decisions	4	43	44	1	7

The next set of questions deals with your views about what it means to live a Christian life.

32. Is it possible, in your opinion, to be certain that one is living a Christian life?
    (Please circle the statement that most closely expresses your opinion)
    - 51 Yes, there are clear marks of Christian living that can be seen in people's lives
    - 19 You can't be certain, but you can tell if you're on the "right track"
    - 1 There is just no way to know
    - 23 You shouldn't worry about being certain; trust God and do the best you can
    - 5 None of these; I think _____

    _____

    1 N.R.

33. Can you think of times during the past year when you have been guided by the following in making decisions about your life?

	Yes, many times	Yes, several times	No	Unsure	N.R.
The "golden rule"	27	42	20	8	3
Your conscience	61	35	2	1	1
The Ten Commandments	35	46	11	6	2
The example of other people in your church	28	53	11	6	2
What you have prepared in your own sermons	55	40	1	1	3
The teachings of Jesus	81	17	0	0	1

34. Do you feel that God has given us rules to live by?
    (Circle one number only)
    - 20 God has given very clear, detailed rules that apply to everyone
    - 67 God has given us some general rules, but we have to decide how to apply them to our own situations
    - 3 God gives rules, but the rules may be different for different people
    - 4 I don't think that God has given us rules
    - 2 I'm not really sure   4 N.R.

35. Has reading the Bible ever been of help to you for each of the following?

	Yes, many times	Yes, several times	Yes, once	No	Unsure	N.R.
In making decisions	36	49	2	6	6	1
As a source of comfort	62	35	0	1	1	1
For inspiration	77	21	0	1	1	1
On moral questions	39	50	2	4	4	1

36. Please indicate whether or not you personally consider each of the following to be wrong. *(Circle one number for each)*

	Always wrong	Usually wrong	Depends on the situation	Not at all wrong	Can't decide	N.R.
Telling a small lie	22	37	40	0	0	1
Showing disrespect to parents	44	42	14	0	0	1
Not trying to discover who I really am	32	31	16	10	8	3
Missing an appointment and not calling to apologize	40	40	17	1	0	1
Disobeying the teachings of the Bible	43	33	21	0	2	2
Working to overthrow the government	12	31	55	1	0	2
Homosexual relations	50	22	18	3	6	1
Smoking marijuana	39	33	16	5	6	2
Receiving support from public welfare	0	2	70	27	0	1
Taking part in political protests	1	3	66	29	1	1
Cheating on your income tax	75	20	4	0	1	1
Premarital sexual intercourse	36	36	23	2	2	1
Abortion	11	31	55	1	1	1

37. Imagine the following situation. Suppose you had been offered two equally good jobs and were trying to decide which one to take. Which *one* of the following do you think you would probably do? *(Circle only one)*

　　15 I'd probably pray that God would give me a sign about which job he wanted me to take

　　82 I'd probably pray about it, and then I'd use my own judgment to make the best decision I could

2 I'd probably try hard to make the best decision I could; it wouldn't occur to me to pray about something like this

0 Just can't say   2 N.R.

38. Which one of the following statements comes closest to your view of prayer? *(Circle only one)*

     0 I don't believe in prayer

     1 Prayer is talking to yourself, but that is sometimes helpful

     19 Prayer is talking with God, but God doesn't always answer

     76 Prayer is talking with God, and God always answers

     3 I'm not sure what to think about prayer   2 N.R.

39. Were there any times during the past year when you found it helpful to pray? *(Circle one)*

     0 No, I didn't pray   11 Yes, a few times

     0 No, I prayed, but it really wasn't helpful   88 Yes, a number of times

                                               1 N.R.

If yes, please answer the questions in the box:

39a. For each of the following, please indicate whether or not prayer was helpful to you in this way during the past year.

	Yes	No	Unsure	NA
God showed me clearly what I should do	33	36	28	3
Prayer was a source of comfort	95	1	2	2
It helped me think more clearly	91	3	4	2
It drew me closer to other people	84	4	10	2
I felt that my sins were forgiven	87	6	5	2
I felt closer to God	93	1	4	1

39b. How often during the past year has your own praying—that is, prayer outside of church services—involved each of the following?

	Frequently	Occasionally	Never	NA
A special quiet time when you pray for at least several minutes	59	36	3	1
Short sentences to God in the midst of your daily activities	79	19	1	1
Just thinking things through, but not really praying formally to God	59	35	3	2
Praying aloud with family members (other than saying grace)	27	54	12	2

One aspect of Christian living that is often discussed has to do with loving your neighbor. Please answer frankly the following questions:

40. Christ said that we should love our neighbor. Have you done anything within the past year that you felt was really an example of "loving your neighbor"? *(Circle one)*

    1 No   11 I'm not sure   87 Yes. What was it? *(Indicate below)*
    2 N.R.

    _____

41. Thinking back over the past year, have you ever felt guilty about not loving your neighbor as much as you should? *(Circle only one)*

    61 Yes, there have been times when I have felt very guilty because I knew I should be doing more

    5 No, I really feel that I've done about as much as I could

    31 I haven't felt guilty or not guilty; I've just enjoyed helping people whenever I could

    1 Frankly, I haven't thought much about "loving my neighbor"

    1 I really don't remember   2 N.R.

42. You have probably heard reports on the news from time to time about people who have been the victims of floods, earthquakes, or other disasters. When you hear about such people, what is your response? *(Circle only one)*

    20 I feel sorry for them, but I feel that there are government agencies and other organizations which have been established to help out in these situations

    18 I feel that I should personally do something to help, but I usually don't get around to doing anything

    44 If there is a clear need, I try to send some money or do something else to help out

    5 My own feeling is that the best thing I can do in these situations is to pray that God will be of comfort to the people involved

    13 None of these; my tendency is to _____

    1 N.R.

The following questions ask your views about the church's relation to social and political affairs.

43. As far as political affairs are concerned, do you feel that *(Circle only one):*

    33 It is OK for the church to take direct political action as an organization

    35 The church should stay out of politics as an organization, but it is OK for the church to make policy statements

    23 The church should relate spiritual principles to political issues, but not make policy statements

    1 The church should deal only with spiritual matters

    8 None of these; my view is: _____

    1 N.R.

44. Christians sometimes describe God as a "God of justice" or a God who commands us to bring about justice. Which *one* of these following statements comes closest to your own ideas about what this means?

   71 It means that the church should work for justice and support groups that are working to end inequality and oppression

   15 I think of it at a more personal level. It means I should try to be just and fair in all my dealings

    2 I think this is actually a spiritual term that refers to God punishing evil, rather than activities of the church or individuals

    0 Frankly, the concept of God's justice doesn't have any particular meaning to me

    1 I'm really not sure what it refers to

   10 None of these; its meaning to me is: _____

    1 N.R.

45. In your opinion, is it all right for pastors in their leadership roles to *(Circle one response for each statement):*

	Yes	No	Unsure	N.R.
Speak out against political corruption	95	1	3	1
Discuss political issues from the pulpit	61	23	15	2
Endorse candidates for office	17	64	16	3
Participate in protest marches or demonstrations	66	15	17	2
Criticize the actions of other countries	67	13	18	2

46. As far as more specific social issues are concerned, do you mostly favor or mostly oppose each of the following? *(Circle one number for each)*

	Mostly favor	Mostly oppose	Don't know	N.R.
Legalizing marijuana	24	66	9	2
The death penalty	24	68	6	2
Ordination of women	81	12	5	2
Actively supporting Soviet dissidents	61	11	26	2
More freedom for homosexuals	35	46	16	2
Leaving South Africa alone to solve its own problems	19	62	17	2
American leaders taking a tough stand in support of human rights in other countries	79	10	10	1
Giving more power to the police	16	62	20	2
Major changes in our form of government	23	56	18	2
Putting business executives in jail if, known to them, their companies break the law	67	11	20	2
Providing special opportunities so that more black people can go to college	69	9	20	1
Spending more government money for people on welfare	22	54	23	2

Another issue that comes up frequently is the idea of promoting cooperation and greater understanding among different kinds of religious groups.

47. In this regard, please indicate whether you would tend to approve or tend to disapprove of having common worship services between Lutherans and each of the following *(Circle* one *number for each):*

	Tend to approve	Tend to disapprove	Unsure	N.R.
Roman Catholics	89	7	2	1
Baptists	66	24	8	2
Jews	32	48	19	1
Presbyterians	89	7	2	2
Jehovah's Witnesses	4	88	6	2

48. In your opinion, are there any important differences between your religious beliefs and the beliefs of each of these groups? *(Circle* one *number for each)*

	Yes, many	Yes, some	Yes, a few	No, none	Not sure	N.R.
Roman Catholics	16	51	29	2	0	1
Baptists	25	55	19	0	0	1
Jews	70	24	3	0	1	1
Zen Buddhists	91	4	1	0	2	2
Presbyterians	5	36	50	6	1	2
Jehovah's Witnesses	93	4	1	0	0	1

49. How do you feel about people who "speak in tongues"? *(Circle only one)*

16 I disapprove of speaking in tongues

6 I approve and have spoken in tongues myself

49 Speaking in tongues is OK for some people, but it's not for me

8 I'm not sure what I think about "speaking in tongues"

20 I approve of speaking in tongues, but I haven't done it myself

2 N.R.

49a. How much do you know about speaking in tongues? *(Circle only one)*

26 A lot   55 Some   16 Only a little   1 Nothing   1 N.R.

50. The final question in this section involves several pairs of statements that reflect different views on various Christian issues. Neither statement is likely fully to reflect your own views, but what we'd like you to do is to say which one *comes closest* to your views. *(Circle* one *number for each item)*

a. 34 Meaning in life comes mostly from one's day-to-day experiences

60 Meaning in life comes mostly from having a clear and consistent doctrine or philosophy to live by

6 Just can't choose   * N.R.

* = Less than 1%

216

b.   4 My religious views are very personal and private
     94 I like to discuss my religious views with others
     1 Just can't choose   1 N.R.

c.   3 Becoming a Christian is a once-and-for-all decision
     96 Becoming a Christian is an ongoing spiritual journey
     1 Just can't choose   * N.R.

d.   60 Christianity is the one true religion
     30 Most religions have some handle on the truth
     9 Just can't choose   1 N.R.

e.   72 Christians have a sense of peace and joy that other people don't experience
     17 Basically Christians have no more peace and joy than other people
     10 Just can't choose   1 N.R.

f.   72 Christians are generally more concerned about the needs of others than other people are
     19 Christians usually aren't any more concerned about the needs of others than anyone else
     8 Just can't choose   1 N.R.

Thank you very much! Please return the completed questionnaire to:
Office for Research and Planning
Lutheran Church in America
231 Madison Avenue, New York, NY 10016

In the cover letter we raised the possibility of sending you an evaluation questionnaire about *The Lutheran* magazine in 1979 or 1980. Would you be willing to receive such a questionnaire? *(Circle one)*
    69 Yes   17 No   15 N.R.

Please write any additional comments you may have in the space below.

* = Less than 1%

Appendix 2

Religious Experience Tables

TABLE A
RELIGIOUS EXPERIENCE AMONG LAITY

(Weighted N = 1,472)

	Yes, at a specific time I can remember (%)	Yes, but not at any specific time I can remember (%)	No, but I'd like to (%)	No (%)	Not sure (%)	Had a lasting impact (%)
A sense of God's love	53	34	6	2	3	45
A feeling that God was telling you something	42	28	10	9	7	28
A sense of closeness to the holy or sacred	23	30	12	20	11	12
An experience of being "born again"	14	15	19	40	8	13
A feeling of close fellowship with Christians (other than your family)	57	28	5	5	3	32
A feeling of being filled with the Holy Spirit	28	24	21	12	10	18
A feeling of being tempted by the devil	32	30	1	23	11	11
A feeling of being in contact with someone who has died	14	6	9	61	7	9
A deep sense of awe and wonder at the beauty of nature	72	25	1	0	0	48
A feeling of intense happiness or ecstasy	54	26	7	6	4	26
A feeling of being in harmony with the universe	19	32	17	16	11	8

TABLE B
RELIGIOUS EXPERIENCE AMONG CLERGY

(Weighted N = 549)

	Yes, at a specific time I can remember (%)	Yes, but not at any specific time I can remember (%)	No, but I'd like to (%)	No (%)	Not sure (%)	Had a lasting impact (%)
A sense of God's love	70	28	1	1	0	67
A feeling that God was telling you something	60	30	2	5	2	45
A sense of closeness to the holy or sacred	50	39	1	4	4	32
An experience of being "born again"	16	29	2	47	5	23
A feeling of close fellowship with Christians (other than your family)	75	23	1	1	0	58
A feeling of being filled with the Holy Spirit	40	41	2	11	5	32
A feeling of being tempted by the devil	38	30	1	25	6	11
A feeling of being in contact with someone who has died	7	4	4	76	7	4
A deep sense of awe and wonder at the beauty of nature	71	26	1	1	1	38
A feeling of intense happiness or ecstasy	57	30	3	7	3	25
A feeling of being in harmony with the universe	23	43	6	19	8	12

219

Tables 1–24

TABLE 1
Description of Relationship to God

(Total N = 1,472 laypersons + 549 pastors)

Percentage of Laypersons and Pastors Who Indicated that Each of the Statements Listed Below Described Their Relationship to God "Very Well" or "Fairly Well"

	Laypersons (%)	Pastors (%)
Question: "Some of the ways in which people describe their relation to God are listed below. As far as you are concerned personally, how well does each description express your feelings about your own relation to God?"		
I am a helpless sinner under the wrath and judgment of God	28	14
I know that I am a sinner, but God loves me and is giving me new life	86	98
I am absolutely certain that I am saved and that I will go to heaven when I die	55	81
As long as I do the best I can, I feel that God cares for me and watches over me	76	26
I am not sure what my relation to God is	21	4
I don't think of myself as having any relation to God	8	0

NOTE: For *each* of the above statements, respondents were asked to indicate whether it expressed their feelings "very well," "fairly well," "not very well," "not at all," or whether they were "unsure." The percentages shown represent the percentage of all respondents in each sample who circled either "very well" or "fairly well" for each statement.

TABLE 2

Responses to Questions About Christ

(Total N = 1,472 laypersons + 549 pastors)

Percentage of Laypersons and Pastors Who Gave Each of the Responses
Shown to Each of the Four Questions About Christ Listed Below

	Laypersons (%)	Pastors (%)
Question: "Traditionally, a central belief of the church has been that Christ was fully God *and* fully human during his life on earth. Is this a belief about which you have no doubts, some doubts, or serious doubts?"		
No doubts	75	86
Some doubts	22	13
Serious doubts	2	1
(No answer)	1	0
Total	100	100
Question: "In your own life, how important is this belief to you?" (refers to the above question)		
Very important	58	82
Fairly important	23	14
Subtotal	81	96
Not very important	9	2
Not at all important	2	0
I'm not sure	7	1
(No answer)	1	1
Total	100	100
Question: "The church has also held that Christ was crucified on the cross. Is the crucifixion meaningful to you?"		
Yes	91	98
No	2	1
Not sure	7	1
Total	100	100
Question: "In your opinion, which one of the following statements best expresses the main reason why Christ was crucified?"		
To forgive our sins	88	79
As a protest against social injustice	1	0
To show us how to love our neighbor	2	2
The main reason was the disbelief of the Jews	2	2
I'm not sure that Christ was crucified	1	0
Other	5	17
Total	99*	100

*Error due to rounding

TABLE 3

Feelings About the Apostles' Creed

(Total N = 1,472 laypersons + 549 pastors)

Percentage of Laypersons and Pastors Who Selected Each of the Responses Listed Below to the Question Shown

	Laypersons (%)	Pastors (%)
Question: "Which one of these statements comes closest to your feelings when you say the Apostles' Creed?"		
I'm not sure what the Apostles' Creed is	1	NA
I do not believe in everything it says, but saying (confessing) it is still meaningful to me	7	11
I believe in what it says and regard it (the entire Creed) as a meaningful confession of my faith	85	83
Saying the Apostles' Creed is pretty much a meaningless ritual for me (only meaningful to me as a liturgical act)	5	2
I haven't said the Apostles' Creed recently	2	NA
Other	NA	3
Total	100	99*

*Error due to rounding

NA = Not asked (variant wording for pastors shown in parentheses)

TABLE 4

Definitions of Faith

(Total N = 1,472 laypersons + 549 pastors)

Percentage of Laypersons and Pastors Who Selected Each of the Responses Listed Below to the Question Shown

	Laypersons (%)	Pastors (%)
Question: "Faith has meant many different things to people. Which one of the following statements *comes closest* to describing your own view of faith?"		
A life of commitment to God that I demonstrate by trying to do what is right	27	10
My decision to accept Christ instead of going on in my own sinful ways	9	4
My trust in God's grace	40	74
My belief in all that the Bible says	3	0
In my view, as long as people are truly sincere in their beliefs, they show faith	10	0
I am not sure what "faith" means, although I am convinced that it is important	2	0
To be honest about it, the idea of faith doesn't seem very meaningful to me	1	0
None of these	7	11
Total	99*	99*

*Error due to rounding

TABLE 5
Statement Best Describing
Relationship to God

(Total N = 1,472 laypersons + 549 pastors)

Percentage of Laypersons and Pastors Selecting Each of the Statements
Listed Below as the Best Description of Their Relation to God

	Laypersons (%)	Pastors (%)
Question: "Suppose you had to choose one of these statements as the *best* description of your relation to God. Which one would that be?"		
I am a helpless sinner under the wrath and judgment of God	3	2
I know that I am a sinner, but God loves me and is giving me new life	52	84
I am absolutely certain that I am saved and that I will go to heaven when I die	5	6
As long as I do the best I can, I feel God cares for me and watches over me	29	2
I am not sure what my relation to God is	3	1
I don't think of myself as having any relation to God	0	0
Just can't choose	2	1
None of these	2	2
(No answer)	4	2
Total	100	100

NOTE: This question followed the question shown in Table 1 in which respondents were asked to say how well each statement described their relation to God. This question asked for a single statement to be selected as their best description.

TABLE 6
Views of How Christ Is Present
in Communion

(Total N = 1,472 laypersons + 549 pastors)

Percentage of Laypersons and Pastors Who Selected Each of the Responses Listed Below to the Question Shown

	Laypersons (%)	Pastors (%)
Question: "In your view, how is Christ present when you take Holy Communion?"		
The bread and wine actually become the Body and Blood of Christ and are no longer bread and wine	24	3
Christ himself is present in the administration of the bread and wine but they remain bread and wine	45	68
Christ is present in some mysterious way that can't be defined	17	26
Holy Communion is a memorial service that helps us remember Christ's life and death, but Christ himself is not present	10	0
I don't think about Communion in any of these ways	3	1
(No answer)	1	2
Total	100	100

TABLE 7

Beliefs About the Nature of
the Sacraments

(Total N = 1,472 laypersons + 549 pastors)

Percentage of Laypersons and Pastors Who Selected Each of the
Responses Listed Below to Describe Their Views of Communion and
Baptism

Communion			*Baptism*	
Laypersons (%)	*Pastors (%)*		*Laypersons (%)*	*Pastors (%)*

Question: "In the column on the left, please circle the
statement that best fits your feelings about *Holy
Communion*. Then in the column on the right, circle the
statement that best fits your feelings about *Baptism*."

Communion Laypersons (%)	Pastors (%)		Baptism Laypersons (%)	Pastors (%)
24	23	It is essential in order to receive salvation and everlasting life	47	41
62	72	It is not essential for salvation, but it is a way of receiving forgiveness and new life	30	51
8	1	It is only one of the "traditions" of the church, but it is still meaningful to me	11	1
1	0	It is a tradition that has no meaning to me personally	1	0
1	3	None of these	2	3
4	1	(No answer)	9	4
100	100	Total	100	100

227

TABLE 8
Beliefs About God

(Total N = 1,472 laypersons + 549 pastors)

Percentage of Laypersons and Pastors Who Selected Each of the Responses Listed Below to the Question Shown

	Laypersons (%)	Pastors (%)
Question: "Which of the following statements comes closest to expressing what you believe about God?		
I know God really exists and I have no doubts about it	68	61
While I have doubts, I feel that I do believe in God	25	28
I find myself believing in God some of the time but not at other times	2	2
I don't believe in a personal God, but I do believe in a higher power of some kind	2	0
I don't know whether there is a God, and I don't believe there is any way to find out	0	0
I don't believe in God	0	0
None of the above represents what I believe	2	8
Total	99*	99*

*Error due to rounding

TABLE 9

The Possibility of Proving God's Existence

(Total N = 1,472 laypersons + 549 pastors)

Percentage of Lay Persons and Pastors Who Selected Each of the Responses Listed Below to the Questions Shown

	Laypersons (%)	Pastors (%)
Question: "Do you feel that it is possible to prove that God exists?"		
No, we don't have the kind of evidence it would take	22	46
No, it would be wrong even to try	6	10
Subtotal	28	56
Yes, I think it probably is	34	17
Yes, I know it is	34	25
Subtotal	68	42
(No answer)	4	2
Total	100	100

(Total N^{**} = 1,001 laypersons + 231 pastors)

Question: "Please indicate whether or not you think it is possible to prove that God exists in each of the following ways": (ASKED ONLY OF RESPONDENTS WHO SAID "YES" TO THE ABOVE QUESTION)

	Laypersons (%)	Pastors (%)
From evidence in the Bible		
Yes	86	79
No	5	17
Don't know	8	4
	99*	100
By means of a logical argument		
Yes	33	29
No	41	61
Don't know	28	10
	102*	100
Through personal experience		
Yes	78	90
No	8	7
Don't know	14	3
	100	100
Through the actions of the Holy Spirit		
Yes	80	93
No	3	4
Don't know	17	3
	100**	100**

*Error due to rounding
**Numbers represent only respondents who asnwered "yes" to the initial question; percentages are based on these numbers, not on the total sample.

229

TABLE 10

Images of God's Influence

(Total N = 1,472 laypersons + 549 pastors)

Percentage of Laypersons and Pastors Selecting Each of the Responses
Listed Below to the Question Shown

	Laypersons (%)	Pastors (%)
Question: "Which one of the following comes closest to your view of the way in which God influences the things that happen in the world?"		
God set history in motion but really doesn't interfere with it anymore	3	1
God influences individuals, who then shape events	36	27
God influences individuals but also shapes events directly through national and social affairs	31	61
I don't think of God as "influencing" the things that happen	13	2
Not sure because I haven't thought about it much before	9	0
None of these	6	7
(No answer)	2	2
Total	100	100

TABLE 11

Beliefs About the Bible

(Total N = 1,472 laypersons + 549 pastors)

Percentage of Laypersons and Pastors Who Selected Each of the Responses Listed Below to the Questions Shown

	Laypersons (%)	Pastors (%)
Question: "Which one of these statements comes closest to describing your feelings about the Bible?"		
The Bible is the actual word of God and is to be taken literally, word for word	16	2
The Bible is the inspired word of God, but not everything in it should be taken literally, word for word	73	93
The Bible is an ancient book of fables, legends, history, and moral precepts recorded by men	5	0
None of these	1	3
Can't say	3	0
(No answer)	2	2
Total	100	100
Question: "The Bible says that humanity was created by God. Science says that humanity evolved from other forms of animal life. In your opinion, which of these views is correct?"		
The biblical view	47	20
The scientific view	2	1
Both in their own ways	47	78
Neither	0	0
Not sure	4	1
Total	100	100

TABLE 12
Beliefs About Life After Death
and the Devil

(Total N = 1,472 laypersons + 549 pastors)

Percentage of Laypersons and Pastors Who Selected Each of the Responses Listed Below to the Questions Shown

	Laypersons (%)	Pastors (%)
Question: "Which one of the following statements comes closest to expressing your view of life after death?"		
I don't believe that there is life after death	1	1
I am unsure whether or not there is life after death	7	1
I believe that there must be something beyond death, but I have no idea what it may be like	43	18
There is life after death, but no punishment	4	6
There is life after death, with rewards for some people and punishment for others	36	45
The notion of reincarnation expresses my view of what happens to people when they die	2	0
None of these expresses my view	6	29
Total	99*	100
Question: "What about the belief that the devil actually exists?"		
I'm absolutely sure there is a devil	33	44
I'm pretty sure there is a devil	32	20
Subtotal	65	64
I'm pretty sure there is no devil	7	10
I'm absolutely sure there is no devil	4	7
Subtotal	11	17
Don't know	22	14
(No answer)	2	5
Total	100	100

*Error due to rounding

TABLE 13

Attitudes Toward Non-Christians

(Total N = 1,472 laypersons + 549 pastors)

Percentage of Laypersons and Pastors Who Selected Each of the Responses Listed Below to the Questions Shown

	Laypersons (%)	Pastors (%)
Question: "Which of the following comes closest to your attitude toward people in other countries who have never heard about Christ?"		
A desire to share the love of Christ with them	61	89
A feeling that if we do not preach Christ to them, they will be damned forever	2	1
A feeling that we shouldn't worry about them because there are so many people in this country who haven't heard about Christ	1	0
A feeling that we should respect their religions and stop trying to impose Christianity on them	16	4
Frankly, I haven't thought about it	6	1
Can't choose	13	4
Total	99*	99*
Question: "As far as Jews are concerned, do you feel that Christians should":		
Make special efforts to preach Christ to Jews	17	24
Tell people about Christ, but direct no special effort toward Jews	40	61
Not try to convert Jews to Christianity	20	7
Not sure	21	6
(No answer)	2	2
Total	100	100

*Error due to rounding

TABLE 14

Settings for Experiences of God's Presence

(Total N^* = 721–80 laypersons + 483–500 pastors)
(Only respondents reporting having experienced
God's presence during the past year)

Percentage of Laypersons and Pastors Having Experienced God's Presence "Many Times" in Each Setting Listed Below:

	Laypersons (%)	Rank (%)	Pastors (%)	Rank (%)
During Holy Communion	58	(1)	69	(1)
While attending church	53	(2)	62	(2)
During private prayer	49	(3)	46	(4)
In nature	48	(4)	26	(10)
While meditating	40	(5)	46	(5)
While reading the Bible	25	(6)	44	(6)
While among friends	23	(7)	37	(8)
While working	22	(8)	51	(3)
During a baptism	20	(9)	39	(7)
While having fun	16	(10)	31	(9)

*Numbers vary due to different numbers of respondents answering each item

TABLE 15

Reactions to the Morality of Individual Behaviors

(Total N = 1,472 laypersons + 549 pastors)

Percentage of Laypersons and Pastors Who Selected Each of the Following Responses with Respect to Individual Morality

	Always wrong (%)	Usually wrong (%)	Depends on the situation (%)	Not at all wrong (%)	Can't decide (%)	N.R. (%)
Question: "Please indicate whether or not you personally consider each of the following to be wrong."*						
Cheating on your income tax	75/75**	18/20	4/ 4	1/ 0	1/1	1/1
Homosexual relations	66/50	10/22	8/18	4/ 3	11/6	2/1
Smoking marijuana	64/39	16/33	7/16	4/ 5	7/6	3/2
Showing disrespect to parents	60/44	30/42	8/14	0/ 0	0/0	1/1
Disobeying the teaching of the Bible	56/43	31/33	8/21	1/ 0	3/2	2/2
Missing an appointment and not calling to apologize	52/40	31/40	15/17	0/ 1	1/0	2/1
Working to overthrow the government	48/12	18/31	29/55	1/ 1	3/0	2/2
Premarital sexual intercourse	46/36	21/36	20/23	5/ 2	6/2	2/1
Telling a small lie	26/22	31/37	40/40	0/ 0	1/0	2/1
Abortion	22/11	13/31	53/55	6/ 1	4/1	2/1
Not trying to discover who I really am	20/32	24/31	16/16	15/10	20/8	6/3
Taking part in political protests	7/ 1	11/ 3	61/66	16/29	3/1	3/1
Receiving support from public welfare	4/ 0	7/ 2	74/70	12/27	1/0	2/1

*Responses have been reordered to reflect the relative numbers of laypersons who indicated that each was "always wrong."

**Throughout these tables, the percentages before the slash(/) refer to the lay sample and those after the slash to the pastors' sample.

TABLE 16

Support/Opposition with Respect to Social Issues

(Total N = 1,472 laypersons + 549 pastors)

Percentage of Laypersons and Pastors Who Indicated that They "Mostly Favor" ("Mostly Oppose") Each of the Following

	Mostly favor (%)	Mostly oppose (%)	Don't know (%)	N.R. (%)
Question: "As far as more specific social issues are concerned, do you mostly favor or mostly oppose each of the following?"*				
Legalizing marijuana	10/24	80/66	9/ 9	1/2
Spending more government money for people on welfare	6/22	75/54	17/23	2/2
More freedom for homosexuals	12/35	66/46	20/16	3/2
Major changes in our form of government	27/23	43/56	27/18	4/2
The death penalty	49/24	32/68	17/ 6	2/2
Giving more power to the police	39/16	31/62	27/20	3/2
Actively supporting Soviet dissidents	27/61	30/11	38/26	5/2
Providing special opportunities so that more black people can go to college	41/69	28/ 9	29/20	2/1
Leaving South Africa alone to solve its own problems	33/19	26/62	38/17	3/2
American leaders taking a tough stand in support of human rights in other countries	51/79	22/10	25/10	3/1
Ordination of women	69/81	16/12	12/ 5	3/2
Putting business executives in jail if, known to them, their companies break the law	64/67	10/11	24/20	3/2

*Responses have been reordered to reflect the relative numbers of laypersons who indicated that they "mostly oppose" each.

TABLE 17

Reactions to Public Policy Issues

(Total N = 1,539 laypersons + 590 pastors)

Percentage of Laypersons and Pastors Who Selected Each of the Following Responses with Respect to National Issues

	Strongly favor (%)	Favor (%)	Oppose (%)	Strongly oppose (%)	No opinion (%)	N.R. (%)
Question: "Circle one response for each item to indicate how strongly you favor or oppose each policy statement."*						
The quality of education in the United States should be a top priority social concern, in light of a recent U.S. Office of Education report which indicates that "less than half of the nation's adults possess the basic skills to function well in today's society."	50/51	38/41	2/ 2	1/ 1	5/ 3	4/2
There should be a national program to improve health-care services and curtail rising health-care costs.	34/46	39/39	10/ 6	8/ 4	5/ 4	4/2
Social programs (for example, welfare, education) should be given a higher priority in government spending than military programs.	17/40	37/42	21/11	10/ 1	11/ 4	5/3
The government should exercise wage and price controls (that would affect major industries) as a means to curtail inflation and unemployment.	14/14	35/39	21/27	17/ 8	9/10	4/2
The Equal Rights Amendment (ERA) should become part of the U.S. Constitution.	14/31	27/27	22/16	14/13	20/11	4/3
There should be a more equitable distribution of wealth according to the demands of poorer nations in the world today.	6/25	34/50	28/14	11/ 2	15/ 6	6/4
There should be a moratorium on oil exploration in Canada and Alaska until studies have been completed on the impact on native peoples and their environment.	8/11	24/30	23/27	9/ 6	31/23	5/2

*Responses have been reordered to reflect the relative numbers of laypersons who indicated that they favored each.

237

TABLE 18

Reactions to Issues of Women's Roles and Status

(Total N = 1,519 laypersons + 567 pastors)

Percentage of Laypersons and Pastors Who Selected Each of the Following Responses with Respect to Societal and Church Efforts

	Very favorable (%)	Favorable (%)	Neutral (%)	Unfavorable (%)	Very unfavorable (%)	No opinion (%)	N.R. (%)
Question: "What is your reaction to each of the following?"*							
Women becoming more involved in politics	15/33	44/48	25/13	7/ 2	2/1	5/1	4/2
The ordination of women	18/36	37/39	23/12	8/ 6	6/5	5/1	3/2
Current societal efforts to strengthen or change women's status in society	13/27	37/44	29/17	9/ 7	2/2	6/1	4/2
Current church efforts to strengthen or change women's status in society	11/25	38/47	30/17	7/ 5	2/3	8/1	4/2
Current overall efforts of the various women's liberation groups	4/ 9	19/31	33/26	24/23	9/8	7/1	4/2

Question: "Granted that various sections of the Bible present different and sometimes opposing portraits of a woman, taking the Bible as a whole, which of the following statements comes closest to your understanding of the biblical witness on the role of women in the church today?"*

63/75   Women and men are both called to identical discipleship and leadership in the mission of the church.

24/12   Generally speaking, the role of women is subordinate to that of men, although in some circumstances a woman may undertake a leadership position in the church.

3/ 1   The role of women is subordinate to that of men and under no circumstances should a woman undertake a leadership position in the church.

5/11   Other (write in) _____

5/ 3   N.R.

*Responses have been reordered to reflect the relative numbers of laypersons who indicated that they favored each.

TABLE 19

Reactions to Church Political Actions and Pastoral Advocacy

(Total N = 1,472 laypersons + 549 pastors)

Percentage of Laypersons and Pastors Who Indicated that Each of the Following Is (Is Not) "All Right"

	Yes (%)	No (%)	Unsure (%)	N.R. (%)
Question: "In your opinion, is it all right for pastors in their leadership roles to . . ."*				
Endorse candidates for office	11/17	69/64	16/16	4/3
Discuss political issues from the pulpit	25/61	54/23	17/15	4/2
Participate in protest marches or demonstrations	23/66	49/15	24/17	4/2
Criticize the actions of other countries	30/67	35/13	31/18	4/2
Speak out against political corruption	71/95	12/ 1	14/ 3	2/1

Question: "As far as political affairs are concerned, do you feel that . . ."

It is OK for the church to take direct political action as an organization	9/33
The church should stay out of politics as an organization, but it is OK for the church to make policy statements	31/35
The church should relate spiritual principles to political issues, but not make policy statements	43/23
The church should deal only with spiritual matters	13/ 1
None of these	3/ 8

*Responses have been reordered to reflect the relative numbers of laypersons who indicated that each was *not* "all right."

TABLE 20

Reactions to LCA Advocacy of Public Policies

(Total N = 1,539 laypersons + 590 pastors)

Percentage of Laypersons and Pastors Who Selected Each of the Following Responses with Respect to LCA Support of Policies

	Yes (%)	No (%)	Undecided (%)	No Opinion (%)	N.R. (%)
Question: "Circle one response for your opinion about whether or not the *LCA* should publicly support the policy as stated here."*					
The quality of education in the U.S. should be a top priority social concern, in light of a recent U.S. Office of Education report which indicates that "less than half of the nation's adults possess the basic skills to function well in today's society"	62/76	16/ 9	9/ 9	6/ 3	8/3
There should be a national program to improve health-care services and curtail rising health-care costs	51/70	27/16	10/ 8	6/ 2	7/4
Social programs (for example, welfare, education) should be given a higher priority in government spending than military programs	41/75	20/13	12/ 5	9/ 3	8/4
The government should exercise wage and price controls (that would affect major industries) as a means to curtail inflation and unemployment	18/25	54/44	12/21	8/ 7	7/4
The Equal Rights Amendment (ERA) should become part of the U.S. Constitution	24/45	41/33	13/11	15/ 8	7/4
There should be a more equitable distribution of wealth according to the demands of poorer nations in the world today	30/65	37/17	15/10	10/ 4	8/4
There should be a moratorium on oil exploration in Canada and Alaska until studies have been completed on the impact on native peoples and their environment	14/24	42/35	12/19	24/19	8/3

*Responses have been reordered to achieve comparability with table 17.

TABLE 21
Reactions to LCA World Hunger Advocacy

(Total N = 1,701 laypersons + 636 pastors)

Percentage of Laypersons and Pastors Who Selected Each of the Following Responses with Respect to LCA Advocacy Emphases

	Very much (%)	Quite a lot (%)	Some (%)	Little (%)	None (%)	Not sure (%)	No response (%)
Question: "One component of the Lutheran Church's World Hunger Appeal is its efforts as an advocate for the hungry poor of the world. How much emphasis do you feel the church ought to place in each of the following areas of its advocacy work?"*							
Assisting church members to take an active role in promoting just policies toward food production and distribution	22/40	30/40	32/17	6/ 2	3/**	5/**	2/1
Testifying before government committees and agencies about the problems of hunger at home and abroad	22/39	28/38	29/19	6/ 2	6/1	6/**	3/**
Assisting hungry people to form action groups so that they have a voice in programs that affect them	18/27	25/34	31/29	11/ 6	8/2	6/2	3/1
Participating in lawsuits against the government if public funds authorized for the poor and hungry are misused	22/25	17/23	22/31	9/10	17/7	10/4	2/1
Speaking to corporations about their ethical and moral responsibilities in pursuing policies which affect hungry people	16/32	20/36	33/26	12/ 4	9/2	7/1	3/**
Participating in lawsuits and proxy actions, when appropriate, which urge corporations to face their ethical and moral responsibilities toward hungry people	11/21	11/23	26/32	17/13	22/7	12/4	3/1

*Responses have been reordered to reflect the relative numbers of laypersons who indicated that each should receive "very much" or "quite a lot" of emphasis.
** = Less than 1%

241

TABLE 22

Summary of Research Findings Showing Positive, Negative and Nonexistent Relationships Between Religion and Conservatism (Part A)

Conservatism Regarding:	Orthodox Beliefs			Orientation Toward Salvation				
	Salience Index	Biblical Literalism/Creation	Other Orthodox Beliefs	"Saved"	"Works"	"Sincere"	Discompassionate Theodicy	God's Influence
Individual Behaviors								
Authority	+	+	+	+	+	−	+	+
New Morality	+	+	+	+	+	−	+	+
Political Actions								
Political Change	+	+			+	−		
Human Rights		+				−		
Social, Socio-economic Policies								
Corrective Policies		+			+		+	
Economic Equalization								
Congregational								
Minority Inclusion		+			+			
Women's Equality		+	+	+	+			
Church Advocacy Efforts								
Clergy Political		+			+			−
Church Advocacy/ Economic Equalization								
Church Advocacy/ World Hunger								
Church Advocacy/ Women's Equality		+	+	+				

Key: + Positive Relationship, $p(x^2) < .01$ − Negative Relationship, $p(x^2) < .01$

TABLE 22

Summary of Research Findings Showing Positive, Negative and Nonexistent Relationships Between Religion and Conservatism (Part B)

Conservatism Regarding:	Religious Practices				Religious Organizational Participation		
					Congregational Leadership		Membership in Church Youth Groups
	Frequent Church Attendance	Active in Church/ Congregation	Church Essential/ Important	Private/ Family Devotions	Elected Position	Voluntary Position	
Individual Behaviors							
Authority	*	+	+	+			
New Morality	*	+	+	+	+		
Political Actions							
Political Change			+	+			
Human Rights	–				–		–
Social, Socio-economic Policies							
Corrective Policies					+	–	
Economic Equalization	–					–	
Congregational							
Minority Inclusion		*				–	–
Women's Equality	*	*		+		–	–
Church Advocacy Efforts							
Clergy Political					+	–	
Church Advocacy/ Economic Equalization	–					–	–
Church Advocacy/ World Hunger							
Church Advocacy/ Women's Equality					+	–	–

* Curvilinear Relationship, $p(x^2) < .01$ Empty Cell   No Relationship, $p(x^2) > .01$

TABLE 23

Views of God's Justice and Law

Percentage of Laypersons and Pastors Who Selected Each of the Responses Listed Below to the Questions Shown

	Laypersons (%)	Pastors (%)
Question: "Christians sometimes describe God as a God of Justice or a God who commands us to bring about justice. Which one of these following statements comes closest to your own idea about what this means?"		
It means that the church should work for justice and support groups that are working to end inequality and oppression	23	71
I think of it at a more personal level. It means I should try to be fair and just in all my dealings	43	15
I think this is actually a spiritual term that refers to God punishing evil, rather than activities of the church or individuals	13	2
Frankly, the concept of God's justice doesn't have any particular meaning to me	1	0
I'm really not sure what it refers to	14	1
None of these; its meaning to me is: _____	3	10
No Response	3	1
	100	100
Question: "Do you think God has given us rules to live by?"		
God has given very clear, detailed rules that apply to everyone	49	20
God has given us some general rules, but we have to decide how to apply them to our own situations	43	67
God gives rules, but the rules may be different for different people	3	3
I don't think God has given us rules	2	4
I'm not really sure	2	2
No Response	1	4
	100	100

TABLE 24

Ecumenical Attitudes

Percentage of Laypersons and Pastors Who Selected Each of the Following Responses to the Questions Shown

	Laypersons			Pastors		
	Approve (%)	Disapprove (%)	Unsure (%)	Approve (%)	Disapprove (%)	Unsure (%)
Question: "In this regard, please indicate whether you would tend to approve or tend to disapprove of having common worship services between Lutherans and each of the following:"*						
Presbyterians	80	7	11	89	7	2
Roman Catholics	75	13	11	89	7	2
Baptists	72	12	14	66	24	8
Jews	44	30	24	32	48	19
Jehovah's Witnesses	18	59	21	4	88	6

	Laypersons					Pastors				
	Yes, many (%)	Yes, some (%)	Yes, a few (%)	No, none (%)	Not sure (%)	Yes, many (%)	Yes, some (%)	Yes, a few (%)	No, none (%)	Not sure (%)
Question: "In your opinion, are there any important differences between your religious beliefs and the beliefs of each of these groups?"**										
Presbyterians	3	32	38	15	11	5	36	50	6	1
Roman Catholics	16	49	28	3	3	16	51	29	2	0
Baptists	9	40	32	6	12	25	55	19	0	0
Jews	60	22	8	1	8	70	24	3	0	1
Jehovah's Witnesses	66	14	5	1	13	93	4	1	0	0
Zen Buddhists	67	5	2	1	23	91	4	1	0	2

*Responses have been reordered to reflect the approval of common worship services.
**Responses have been reordered to correspond with those in the first question in this table.

Notes and References

Notes

CHAPTER 1

1. John Gager, *Kingdom and Community* (Englewood Cliffs, N.J.: Prentice-Hall, 1975) is an early and prominent example of the appropriation of social theory for the historical reconstruction of the early Christian church; Howard C. Kee, *Christian Origins in a Sociological Perspective* (Philadelphia: Westminster Press, 1980) is a more recent example of a similar endeavor.

2. The Lutheran Church in America has, for the past several years, regularly surveyed the opinions of a scientifically selected sample of lay and clergy members through the Lutheran Listening Post (LLP). The questionnaire on Religious Beliefs and Experiences, which provides the focus for all the essays in this book and is reprinted in both lay and clergy versions in appendix 1, was the seventh questionnaire of a series. In addition to responses to this questionnaire, most chapters will also draw on information concerning the same respondents reported in prior questionnaires of the same series, for example, information on social background, habits of church participation, and so forth.

3. Robert Wuthnow was responsible for the design of the questionnaire. A large number of "confessional" questions was initially developed by Wuthnow through consultation with a small group of church theologians (including Lyman Lundeen and Timothy Lull). These questions were then reviewed as to their centrality and the adequacy of confessional responses by a larger number of theologians representing the several different seminaries of the LCA. The whole questionnaire was then field-tested with a sample of fifty laity and clergy attending a binational church convention and a similar sample of laity from Pennsylvania and New Jersey congregations. In light of these results, the original set of "confessional" questions was reduced to the ten identified on the questionnaire in appendix 1 by an asterisk, and the full questionnaire was reviewed and revised by Wuthnow, meeting with the research staff of the LCA, then including Albert L. Haversat, director, and Ray Nyce, William Erickson, and Mary Cahill Weber, and in consultation with Charles Glock and Roger A. Johnson.

4. After Robert Wuthnow and Lyman Lundeen had completed initial drafts of their responses to the data, theologians from each of the LCA's seminaries met with the authors of this volume and denominational research staff for a two-day consultation. The papers by Krister Stendahl and Jerald Brauer were initially shared as oral presentations at this conference. (The chapters by Mary Weber and Timothy Lull were not available at the time of this conference.)

The initial development of the questionnaire, the gathering of theologians and social researchers for a two-day consultation, and the publication of this volume were supported, in part, by a series of grants from the Aid Association for Lutherans to the Department of Planning, Research, and Evaluation, Office of the Bishop, Lutheran Church in America.

5. Charles Glock is preeminently qualified to write this chapter, not only because he is a pioneer in the development of survey methods for research in the study of religion, but also because of the direct contribution of his work to several major religious bodies in America. Indeed, more than any of the other participants in this research project, Glock is responsible for its original conception. As editor, I hope I may give credit where it is due, without imputing to Professor Glock any of the shortcomings of a project which he supported for so long and to which he gave so generously of his own time.

6. These responses to the questionnaire were gathered in the winter of 1978–79. Stendhal also suggests in chapter 9 that this sort of privatism might be significantly diminished by the entrance of conservative Christian movements into an active role in American political life. Some available evidence, however, suggests that such a turn in basic direction of American religious life has not occurred. For example, the first two questions discussed in the above paragraph were posed to a different, but similarly selected, constituency of this same denomination in the winter of 1982. For both questions, responses to the privatistic options declined by only 5 percentage points, while there was no increase in the percentage selecting the more public or corporate options.

7. In notes to his chapters, Wuthnow explains how the distinction between church-generated beliefs and the beliefs of popular religious culture was established. The former were specified by theologians involved in this research project; the latter were derived from other questionnaires measuring religiosity in American society in general. One of the contributions of this project to social research was the discovery that beliefs engendered by the church tended to be associated most closely with church activities, while many beliefs communicated through the popular media tended to be associated with the particularities of a person's social biography, not congregational participation.

8. For further discussion of the implications of this study's findings for ministry, see Roger A. Johnson, "Learnings for Ministry from Social Survey Data," *Partners* 3:1 (Winter 1981): 22–25.

9. The role of biblical literalism as a reliable indicator of social and political conservatism has been identified in a series of earlier studies, for example Jeffrey Hadden, *The Gathering Storm in the Churches* (Garden City, N.Y.: Doubleday & Co., 1969).

CHAPTER 2

1. The questionnaire was developed during the summer of 1978 and administered to the lay and clergy samples the following winter. The interviews with theologians were conducted by Roger A. Johnson and Robert Wuthnow. Simultaneously, a series of in-depth interviews was conducted among lay volunteers under the supervision of Ray Nyce. Initial drafts of questions were prepared by Robert

Wuthnow. Subsequent drafts were prepared collectively by staff of the Office for Research and Planning (now Office of the Bishop, Department of Planning, Research, and Evaluation), Albert L. Haversat, Mary Cahill Weber, William Erickson, and Ray Nyce in consultation with Roger A. Johnson, Charles Glock, and Robert Wuthnow.

It may be worth noting that the present study is unusual in comparison with most earlier studies of religious commitment. Previous studies have generally been designed by social scientists for the purpose of relating religious variables to other social or psychological factors. The measures of religious commitment employed have usually been restricted to rather simple, popular, or fundamentalistic orientations developed by the social scientists themselves. The attempt here to develop questions in conjunction with theologians, denominational planning staff, and social-science consultants goes considerably beyond previous studies both in the nature of the questions that were eventually asked and in the kinds of issues and orientations that informed the analysis. We hope that this experiment will generate other collaborative ventures in the future.

2. The order in which questions are here discussed does not necessarily correspond to the order in which they were presented in the questionnaires. The questionnaires (both lay and clergy versions) began with questions about meaning and purpose in life (see chapter 3, pp. 43–44) and then included questions on religious experience before turning to questions of religious beliefs. In preparing tables, we have tried to present the *response options* to individual questions in the order in which they were presented in the questionnaires.

All the percentages in this chapter are based on the total number of respondents in each of the samples who replied to the particular question at issue. A weighting factor was applied to the numbers to compensate for differential response rates from different regions and from congregations of different sizes. In no case did this weighting factor change the percentages by more than two points. For this reason, and to afford accurate estimates of statistical significance levels, the weighting factor was not used in subsequent chapters in which more detailed analyses were conducted. For further details on the weighting procedure, see *Lutheran Listening Post: Sample Design Report.*

3. In describing particular answers as "confessional" orientations, we do so in an operational sense of the term only; that is, these were the answers that the theologians we interviewed selected as most nearly representative of their understanding of confessional norms. We recognize, however (as did they), the difficulties of expressing theological understandings in briefly worded questionnaire responses.

4. Because of length considerations we have omitted some of the questions about belief from the present discussion. See appendix 1 for the complete questionnaire with percentages shown for all questions.

5. The meaning of this term ("meditating") was deliberately left ambiguous. However, a separate set of questions was included to determine how many people spent time "reflecting about your life." In all, 89% of the laity and 96% of the clergy said they did this; 27% and 38% respectively said they did this "nearly every day," with an additional 26% and 30% saying "at least once a week." The data also suggested that these times were largely devotional: 41% and 51% respectively said prayer was usually involved; 20% and 35% said Bible reading was usually involved; and 26% and 23% said the church was usually involved.

6. The ten items included in the questionnaire to measure confessional orientations were:

1. The meaning of faith: "my trust in God's grace."
2. Relation to God: "I know that I am a sinner but God loves me and is giving me new life" ("fairly well" or "very well").
3. *Best* description of one's relation to God: same as above.
4. "No doubts" that Christ was fully God and fully human.
5. This teaching (that Christ was fully God and fully human) is "very important" or "fairly important."
6. The crucifixion is meaningful: "yes."
7. The main reason why Christ was crucified: "to forgive our sins."
8. Communion: "is not essential for salvation, but it is a way of receiving forgiveness and new life."
9. Baptism: "is not essential for salvation, but it is a way of receiving forgiveness and new life."
10. Christ's presence in Communion: "Christ himself is present in the administration of the bread and wine but they remain bread and wine."

For the exact wording of these items, see the discussion in the first part of this chapter.

CHAPTER 3

1. There were ten questions in all that had been included in the data as measures of various aspects of confessionally prescribed doctrine. One strategy for constructing an index would have been simply to combine the answers to all ten of these questions. This strategy, however, did not seem as useful as the present approach of isolating five core beliefs out of the ten questions. In the first place, some of the items did not correlate very well with one another. To have combined all of them into a single index would have been something like mixing apples and oranges. In the second place, a single index would have also obscured the fact that some of the items evoked a high degree of agreement, while others manifested much disagreement. The net result of having combined all of the items would have focused attention much more on the disagreement than on the agreement. For example, only 2.6% of the lay sample gave the designated confessional response to all ten of the items, only 12% gave "correct" answers to at least nine of the items, and only 27% responded "correctly" to at least eight of the items. For these reasons we decided on the index described in the text.

2. As a means of validating the index we examined the relationships between other confessional items and scores on the index. The index proved to be a good predictor of responses on the other items. For example, only 15% of the respondents who scored 0 (low) on the salience of faith index said that "my trust in God's grace" came closest to their own definition of faith in response to the question (discussed in chapter 2) which asked respondents to say what faith meant to them. By comparison, 35% of those who scored 1 on the index gave this response. The percentage rose to 42% among those who scored 2 on the index. And it was

highest (50%) among those who scored 3 on the index (high). Other questions showed similar relationships. For example, only 40% of those who scored 0 said they believed in the Apostles' Creed, compared with 96% of those who scored 3. Or, taking a self-report measure of belief, 73% of those who scored 3 said they felt "quite certain" about their religious beliefs overall, compared with only 23% of those who scored 0 on the index.

3. The belief that "I am a sinner but God loves me" was positively associated among clergy with having preached sermons on experiencing God's forgiveness (.45), on God's love for us as sinners (.35), and on trusting in God's grace (.40). The belief that Christ was both God and man was associated with sermons on this belief (.30) and on Christ's crucifixion (.44). The perceived importance of this belief was also associated with these two sermon topics (.43 and .35). And the belief that Christ's crucifixion was to forgive sins was associated with sermons on both Christ's crucifixion (.24) and experiencing God's forgiveness (.32). The measure of association used was "gamma," which varies between 0 and (1.00).

4. Among laity who spent two or more evenings a week participating in church activities (other than worship services), 80% scored high (2 or 3) on the salience of faith index, compared with only 58% of those who spent no evenings a week participating in church activities. Among those who attended Bible study classes at least weekly, 81% scored high on the index, compared with 58% of those who did not attend Bible study classes. And 80% of those who indicated that they were "very active" in congregational activities scored high, compared with 43% of those who listed themselves as being "inactive."

5. Eighty-three percent of those who said they had been guided "many times" during the past year by "what your pastor preaches in sermons" scored high on the index, compared with 47% of those who said they had not been guided by their pastor's sermons. Those who said they were "very satisfied" with their pastors' preaching were also more likely to score high on the index than those who were dissatisfied or who had mixed feelings (75% versus 63%). Among those who felt that God spoke to them during the church service, those who felt that this usually happened "through the sermon" were more likely to score high on the index than those who felt that "God speaks to me, but not necessarily through the sermon"; and those, in turn, were more likely to score high than were those who regarded the service as "a quiet time for my reflections" (81%, 76%, and 65%, respectively).

6. Eighty percent of those who said religion was "very important" to their spouses scored high on the index, compared with 63% of those who said religion was "important" and 61% of those who said it was "not important" to their spouses. Those who had weekly Bible studies with their families were also more likely than those who had family Bible studies monthly, yearly, or never to score high on the index (88%, 80%, 70%, and 61%, respectively). The same relationship existed between the index and frequency of discussing religious convictions with one's family (91% of those who discussed every day scored high, compared with 52% of those who discussed once a year or less).

7. Other research suggests that church members frequently retain the religious styles of previous denominational affiliations. Since denominations differ greatly in the percentages of members who appear to hold firm religious convictions (for example, Baptists compared with Methodists; see Stark and Glock, 1968), we had

expected some differences to appear between respondents who, for example, had formerly been members of liberal denominations and respondents who had previously been affiliated with conservative denominations.

8. Based on synodical divisions; see *Lutheran Listening Post: Sample Design Report,* p. 1.

9. Dividing respondents into categories of higher education (at least some college) and lower education (no more than a high school diploma), we found that age differences on SFI scores still persisted. Among those with low educational levels, 55% of the young people (age thirty or less) scored high on the SFI, compared with 80% of the older people (over age fifty). Similarly, among those with high educational levels, 52% of the young people scored high, compared with 75% of the older people.

10. For example, among those who had attended church nearly every week as children there were still considerable differences between the young and old in terms of the percentages who scored high on the SFI (54% versus 80%). The same differences were evident among those who had attended church less regularly as children (55% versus 74%).

11. Without taking into account differences in attitudes toward the Bible, there was a 27 percentage-point spread between younger men (age thirty or less) and older men (over age fifty) in terms of the proportions who scored high on the SFI (49% versus 76%); there was a 22 point spread between younger and older women (60% versus 82%). But if the same proportion of young men and women had given the biblical response with respect to creation as had been given by older men and women, the percentage-point differences would have been reduced to 19 and 13 points respectively (reductions of .30 and .32).

12. Taking into account differences between the young and the old on attitudes toward smoking marijuana reduced the differences on SFI scores between the young and old by a fraction of .18 among men and by a fraction of .32 among women. Taking into account similar differences on attitudes toward trying to overthrow the government the differences were reduced not at all among men and only by a fraction of .14 among women. By comparison, taking into account differences on attitudes toward premarital sex reduced the differences by .52 among men and .41 among women.

13. The effect of changing attitudes toward premarital sex can also be estimated longitudinally. According to Gallup polls, the proportion of the American public who felt that premarital sex was *not wrong* increased from 21% in 1969 to 55% in 1979. The latter figure was exactly the same as that found in the present study (45% of the laity thought premarital sex was "always wrong"). Since we do not know what the figure might have been in the present sample in 1969, let us assume that it was the same as the Gallup figure in that year as well. Having examined the relationship between attitude and SFI scores, we can estimate the proportion who would currently score high on the index *had no change occurred* in premarital sex attitudes and compare that proportion with the actual proportion. Doing so shows that the proportion would currently stand at 75% rather than 68%. In other words, salience of faith is currently about 90% as high as it might have been had no change in sexual attitudes taken place. What "might have been" is always a dangerous gamble, of course, but the present figures suggest the possibility of such an effect.

14. Among single persons age thirty or younger, 89% of those who thought premarital sex was always wrong scored high on the SFI, compared with only 25% of those who thought that it depends on the situation—a difference of 64 percentage points. Among married persons age thirty or younger, by contrast, 79% of those who thought premarital sex was always wrong scored high on SFI, compared with 62% of those who thought it depends on the situation—a difference of only 17 points. Among young males who felt that premarital sex was always wrong, 88% scored high on the SFI, compared with 60% of the older males who felt this way. Among younger males who felt that premarital sex depended on the situation, only 26% scored high, compared with 52% of the older males. Among younger females who felt that premarital sex was always wrong, 76% scored high on the SFI, compared with 83% of the older females who felt this way. Among those who felt that premarital sex depended on the situation, 54% of the younger females scored high, compared with 72% of the older females.

15. Seventy-four percent of those who thought "a lot" about "why there is suffering in the world" scored high on SFI, compared with 53% of those who never thought about this question. Similarly, 79% of those who thought "a lot" about "what happens after death" scored high, compared with 50% of those who never thought about the question.

16. Seventeen percent of those scoring 0 on SFI said they had experienced freedom in Christ many times during the past year, compared with 78% of those who scored 3 on the index. Similar differences were evident in the proportions who had experienced more concern for others (54% versus 90%), comfort (31% versus 85%), joy (44% versus 82%), and guidance (41% versus 80%).

17. The exact question wording and percentages were reported in chapter 2.

18. As evidence, the percentages who indicated that "as long as I do the best I can, I feel that God cares for me and watches over me" and described their relation to God "very well" were: 56% among persons over age fifty, compared with 46% among persons age thirty or less; 55% among women, compared with 40% among men; and 60% among persons with grade-school educations, compared with 38% among persons with postgraduate educations.

19. Those who said that "as long as people are truly sincere in their beliefs, they show faith" constituted 16% of those age thirty or less, compared with 6% of those over age fifty; 9% of the women, compared with 14% of the men; and 12% of those in the Northeast, compared with 8% of those in the South and 8% of those in the Midwest.

20. It is bootless to ask how persons who were always members of the Lutheran Church in America (or of predecessor bodies) compared with the "average," since—representing more than half of the sample—they *were* the average in most cases. One can ask, however, about the ranking of these members compared with members who had formerly belonged to other denominations. There were nine such groups in all (always LCA, formerly ALC, LC–MS, other Lutheran, Episcopal, UCC, Methodist, Baptist, and Catholic). Of these nine, the "always LCA" group ranked fifth on "my trust in God's grace," fifth on "a life of commitment to God," eighth on "my decision to accept Christ," fourth on "truly sincere in their beliefs," seventh on "saved and going to heaven," third on "as long as I do my best," and fourth on Communion "is essential for salvation." It is difficult to argue that there are any meaningful patterns here, except perhaps that this group is rel-

atively likely to reject the "salvation" orientation, but somewhat inclined to be oriented toward works.

21. The numbers on which the percentages in this section are based are: 736 "always LCA," 183 formerly ALC, 139 formerly LC–MS, 42 formerly other Lutherans, 32 formerly Episcopalian, 39 formerly UCC, 109 formerly Methodist, 54 formerly Baptist, and 46 formerly Roman Catholic.

22. It is perhaps important to make explicit that we are not assuming that exposure to popular religious culture—through means such as watching religious television programs—"causes" people to hold particular doctrinal orientations; it is just as likely that particular doctrinal orientations "cause" people to watch certain kinds of television programs. It does seem safe, however, to suggest that the two —doctrines and exposure—reinforce one another in certain cases.

23. The question asked, "As you think about your life, how much have you learned about the meaning and purpose of life from each of the following?" A list of eleven sources followed and respondents were asked to indicate "a lot," "a fair amount," "a little," "almost nothing," or "nothing" for each one. Six percent of the lay sample said they had learned a lot "from religious TV programs"; another 18% indicated that they had learned a fair amount, and 36% said they had learned a little.

24. The relation between regarding Communion as essential and watching religious TV programs is particularly interesting since these programs generally do not stress this belief themselves. Several interpretations have been suggested. One is that both items reflect a strong but somewhat indiscriminate form of commitment to one's religion. Another is that shut-ins may watch more television than others do and independently of these programs come to attach more value to Communion because of private Communion services with pastors or visitation committees.

25. In terming these beliefs "popular religious culture," we do not mean to imply that they are majority beliefs among the general public (polls show that they are not). We mean only to suggest that they are religious positions that have come to be identified as indicators of religious commitment in the larger culture, often because of publicity surrounding particular religious debates, such as the nature of the Bible, the born-again movement, or the existence of the devil.

26. Fifty percent of those who felt they had had a "born-again" experience said they were saved and going to heaven, compared with 19% of those who had not had this experience; the former were also more likely to say that they felt God watched over them if they did their best (52% versus 47%) and that Communion is essential for salvation (29% versus 20%). On the question about the devil's existence, 52% of those who said they were sure the devil exists said they were saved and going to heaven, compared with 14% of those who thought that the devil doesn't exist. There were virtually no differences between the two groups on thinking that one should do the best he or she can (49% versus 47%); but the former group was about twice as likely to say that Communion is essential for salvation as was the latter group (31% versus 17%).

27. Only 5% of those who said they were "very active" in their congregations selected the sincerity option, compared with 21% of those who said they were "inactive."

28. The Johnson study was conducted among congregations that placed special

emphasis on the nurturing functions of the church; the present results lend generality to the findings of that study.

CHAPTER 5

1. The term "new morality" has been widely used to describe the tendency "to reject traditional moral norms," especially insofar as this implies "accepting a more liberal approach to sex, marijuana, and abortion." See, for example: Everett L. Perry et al., "Toward a Typology of Unchurched Protestants," *Review of Religious Research* 21:4 (Supplement, 1980): 338–404, from which the above quotations are taken (p. 391). While many readers may object to this term, from either the liberal or the conservative posture, it is used only to summarize the more general orientation which recognizes both the existence of and changes in traditional moral norms.

2. Here read "North American," since the statement refers to residents of both the U.S. and Canada.

3. In comparing these two indexes, it must be remembered that the political change index identified the conservative position with a high score of 3; in the human rights index, the liberal position is identified with the high score of 3.

4. It should be noted, however, that there are only limited opportunities for many Lutheran Church in America congregations to recruit minority members. This is, of course, due to the absence of minority residents in many American communities. Thus, some portion (albeit a limited one) of the undecided and negative response to the item on minority membership recruitment is probably due to the perceived lack of opportunity to engage in such recruitment.

CHAPTER 6

1. For a short review of some recent studies which utilize the Marxist explanation of apparent religion-conservatism linkages, see: Walter Broughton, "Religiosity and Opposition to Church Social Action: A Test of a Weberian Hypothesis," *Review of Religious Research* 19:2 (Winter 1978): 154–66.

2. Robert Wuthnow, "Religious Commitment and Conservatism: In Search of an Elusive Relationship," in *Religion in Sociological Perspective: Essays in the Empirical Study of Religion*, ed. Charles Y. Glock (Belmont, Calif.: Wadsworth Publishing Co., 1973).

3. The role of religious denominations in influencing social attitudes has been widely debated. See, for example, the review of the literature on this subject provided by: William A. McIntosh et al., "The Differential Impact of Religious Preference and Church Attendance on Attitudes Toward Abortion," *Review of Religious Research* 20 (Spring 1979): 195–213.

4. This report makes use of the term "orthodoxy" in similar fashion to that of Glock and Stark, who have used it to refer to "commitment to a literal interpretation of a traditional Christian dogma." The Glock and Stark "orthodoxy index"

includes the following items: the existence of a personal God, the divinity of Jesus Christ, the authenticity of biblical miracles, and the existence of the devil. Belief in life after death, belief in the virgin birth, and belief that Jesus walked on water were also tested for inclusion in the index. See Charles Y. Glock and Rodney Stark, *Christian Beliefs and Anti-Semitism* (New York: Harper & Row, 1966).

5. It was considered necessary to assess the effect of religious socialization upon these attitudinal outcomes. Measures of this type included:

    a. The importance of religion to one's spouse and close friends, indicating an interactional climate in which religious values are supported;

    b. Socialization toward church attendance, including frequency of church attendance of one's father and mother, and that of oneself as a child;

    c. Denominational history, including Lutheran denominational affiliation of one's father and mother, and any prior denominational affiliation of oneself.

Of the religious socialization variables measured, only the importance of religion to one's spouse and friends had any major effect upon attitudinal conservatism. The importance assigned to religion by such intimates of a respondent is an indicator of the extent to which the respondent lives in an environment which is supportive of religion. Also, the selection of spouse and friends, being a largely voluntary activity, indicates to some degree the importance of religion to the respondent. The findings indicate that respondents who have friends and spouses for whom religion is "very important" tend to be more conservative on matters of individual behavior, governmental change, and women's issues than are respondents to whose friends and spouses religion is not so important. While not extremely large, these differences are quite consistent in direction.

Positive socialization regarding church attendance was measured by three variables: the frequency of church attendance of one's father and mother, and of oneself as a child. The models of parents and the early behaviors of respondents regarding church attendance seem to have virtually nothing to do with current attitudinal conservatism.

Similarly, denominational history of one's father and mother, and prior denominational affiliation of oneself have virtually no effect upon any of these attitudinal outcomes. While there are many respondents who come from long-established Lutheran families, and who themselves have always been Lutherans, there is no evidence that any of these contexts produces an effect upon attitudinal conservatism. There is one exception to this pattern: respondents with Lutheran parents who have themselves always been members of this church are somewhat more positive about the church's role as an advocate for the tested public policies (national health care, higher government spending on domestic programs, redistribution of income among rich and poor nations) than are the remainder of the respondents.

6. In addition, it was necessary to assess the effects of some social background characteristics of respondents upon the attitudinal outcomes. These variables included sex, age, education, marital status, community type, and region. The latter three were dropped from the analysis when it became apparent that their effects were minor, or were convoluted with other variables' effects. In the case of marital status, single and widowed respondents tended to offer distinctive responses, but this was mainly due to their places in the age structure of the sample. Community

type was unrelated to virtually any of the attitudinal outcomes. Finally, regional effects were difficult to interpret: Canadians offered liberal responses on many indexes, but the implicit criticism of American social and political institutions contained in many liberal options may have influenced Canadians to take such positions.

The men in the sample take more liberal views than do the women on individual behavioral matters and on the foreign policy issue raised. These findings are consistent with other findings on this subject, drawn from studies of the American populace generally. Laywomen, on the other hand, are more liberal than are laymen on most of the social/socioeconomic issues raised. There is no difference between the sexes in matters of church advocacy. To be sure, differences in attitudes by gender are not extremely large, nor should they be taken as reflective of anything but the differential life experiences of men and women.

Age exerts a larger effect on these data then does sex. Older persons are consistently more likely to take conservative points of view on these matters than are younger persons. This is particularly true in individual behavioral and social/socioeconomic concerns. Again, this finding is quite consistent with those reported by other researchers. One interesting exception to this pattern is the curvilinear effect of age on attitudes toward public policies which would equalize societal resources and benefits. An explanation for this seeming contradiction to the general pattern lies in the components of the index: older persons and very young persons are far more likely than are middle-aged respondents to favor the implementation of national health care and domestic programs. For the elderly this is because, as a group, they are dependent upon such policies to insure their continued health and welfare.

Finally, education is related in curvilinear fashion to many of the attitudes tested. These include the individual behavioral indexes, attitudes toward political changes, corrective public policy, minority inclusion of congregations, and political advocacy by pastors. On all of these issues, the most liberal groups are those who have had "some high-school" education and those who possess college or postgraduate degrees. Persons with grammar-school educations and those who have completed high school, but not college, are more conservative.

Education produces clearly liberal results on some other variables, however. This is particularly true of individual attitudes toward women's rights and of attitudes regarding church efforts on behalf of women. In fact, persons with grammar-school education were about three times as likely as were persons with college postgraduate educations to be highly conservative on these matters.

7. For an analysis of the relationship of religion to morals, which makes reference to the special character of Christianity in this regard, see J. Milton Yinger, *The Scientific Study of Religion* (New York: Macmillan & Co., 1970), chapter 3.

8. This hypothesis is tested by Walter Broughton, "Religiosity and Opposition to Church Social Action," *Review of Religious Research* 19:2 (Winter 1978), 154–66.

9. This comment arises purely from a practical understanding of the problems of the aged, rather than from any data collected.

10. It has been suggested by one critic of this paper that "a halo effect, or desire to please, may be operating for the extreme responses on both religious beliefs and church attendance."

CHAPTER 7

1. T. E. Tappert, ed., *The Book of Concord* (Philadelphia: Fortress Press, 1959), p. 37.

2. Despite auditing by the Internal Revenue Service, the payment of income tax without cheating is largely a matter of self-policing. I think this helps to explain the strong negative feeling toward cheating on income tax. This does not mean that members and clergy of the Lutheran Church in America are not tempted to cheat or do not cheat. The very strength of the temptation may reinforce the sense of the moral objection to cheating under any circumstances.

3. H. Richard Niebuhr, *Christ and Culture* (New York: Harper & Brothers, 1951), p. 188. His entire chapter 5 deserves careful examination, even if one feels that the character of American Lutheranism is changing. Another portrait of the conservatism of Lutheran ethics can be found in Ernst Troeltsch, *Social Teachings of the Christian Churches* (London: George Allen & Unwin, 1931). Many of Troeltsch's individual judgments are subject to challenge but the overall portrait is an important one for Lutherans to reckon with.

4. Tappert, *Book of Concord*, p. 37.

5. An excellent example of such a revisionist account can be found in the article by William H. Lazareth, "Luther and Lutheran Ethics," in *Dictionary of Christian Ethics,* ed. John Macquarrie (Philadelphia: Westminster Press, 1967), pp. 201–2. Lazareth considers the Third Reich a total betrayal of Luther's ethical insights: "It is obvious that the authority of Luther's theology cannot be legitimately used to endorse many of the unhealthy social and political developments which have since appeared in the church bearing his name. To cite only the most notorious recent example, Luther could never have sanctioned a totalitarian regime ruling over a class-bound society in which a spiritually emasculated clergy could desist from prophetic criticism of the state in return for political and social favors."

6. Among the laity, 64% favor this and only 10% are opposed. The strength of this finding has astonished Lutherans in business, at least the several groups to whom I have presented it.

7. I do not mean this as an indictment of the quality of the LLP survey instrument. There will always be ambiguities in wording, some of which are evident only in retrospect. These can never be used to allow us to keep the findings that we do have at a distance, especially when we find such findings disappointing or surprising.

8. The entire section on homosexuality is worth citing: "Scientific research has not been able to provide conclusive evidence regarding the causes of homosexuality. Nevertheless, homosexuality is viewed biblically as a departure from the heterosexual structure of God's creation. Persons who engage in homosexual behavior are sinners only as are all other persons—alienated from God and neighbor. However, they are often the special and undeserving victims of prejudice and discrimination in law, law enforcement, cultural mores, and congregational life. In relation to this area of concern, the sexual behavior of freely consenting adults in private is not an appropriate subject for legislation or police action. It is essential to see such persons as entitled to understanding and justice in church and community." (Lutheran Church in America, "Sex, Marriage, and Family" [1970], p. 4).

This and all the other social statements are available from the LCA, Division for Mission in North America, Department of Church in Society, 231 Madison Avenue, New York, NY, 10016. Sixteen of the statements are mailed in a packet; the statement "Vietnam" must be requested separately.

9. The relevant document is *Goals and Plans for Minority Ministry: 1978–1984*. It is available on request from the LCA, Division for Mission in North America, 231 Madison Avenue, New York, NY, 10016.

10. For a more skeptical view of the origin and importance of social statements see E. Clifford Nelson, ed. "The New Shape of Lutheranism 1930—," in *Lutherans in North America* (Philadelphia: Fortress Press, 1975), pp. 525–7. I think the continued issuing of social statements by the LCA in the years since 1975 and the possible changing attitudes of the church toward them need to be weighed against Nelson's own critical judgment.

11. LCA, "Sex, Marriage, and Family" (1970), p. 5.

12. Ibid., p. 2. The quotation against premarital intercourse is found on pp. 3–4.

13. LCA, "Capital Punishment" (1966), pp. 1–2.

14. As may be expected from an academic theologian teaching at a church seminary, the issues that here emerge most forcefully involve the theological/teaching function of the church. Other interpreters of the data will be able to see implications for action in other areas.

15. I am uneasy about the implications drawn earlier in this volume about belief in the devil. Such belief is a venerable Lutheran theological tradition, not only in the writings of Luther himself, but in recent and excellent Scandinavian theologians such as Aulen and Wingren. A provocative recent treatment of Luther and the devil can be found in H. G. Haile, *Luther: An Experiment in Biography* (New York: Doubleday & Co., 1980), pp. 185–201. Whether it correlates with "conservatism" or not, belief in the devil seems to me to be continuing Lutheran theological option. And when given a chance to use the devil to solve an ethical dilemma here, few of those who claim to "believe" chose that option.

16. This would not mean an across-the-board plot to make youth more liberal. It might mean exposing them to experiences and ideas that would deepen their own ability to think theologically about the implications of their faith for social and ethical issues.

CHAPTER 8

1. Sidney E. Mead, *The Lively Experiment: The Shaping of Christianity in America* (New York: Harper & Row, 1963), pp. 103ff.

2. Abdel Ross Wentz, *A Basic History of Lutheranism in America* (Philadelphia: Fortress Press, 1964); E. Clifford Nelson, ed., *The Lutherans in North America* (Philadelphia: Fortress Press, 1975).

3. Wentz, *Basic History;* Nelson, *Lutherans.*

4. Abdel Ross Wentz, *Pioneer in Christian Unity: Samuel Simon Schmucker* (Philadelphia: Fortress Press, 1967).

5. Unpublished paper prepared by Robert Wuthnow in October 1979, entitled "Religious Belief and Experience: A Preliminary Report of Findings from the Seventh 'Lutheran Listening Post Questionnaire'" p. 35.

6. Taken from *Ranking Christian Denominations by Counties of the United States: 1971,* from data in *Churches and Church Membership in the United States: 1971* by D. W. Johnson, P. R. Picard, and B. Quinn (Washington, D.C.: Glenmary Research Center, 1974).

7. C. Richard Evenson and Robert R. Strohl, "Trends in LCA Membership, 1962–1978," *Partners* 1: 6 (December 1979): 11ff.

8. Robert Wuthnow, chapters 2 and 3. All additional references to statistics on religious beliefs and practices will be taken from tables 1–14, unless otherwise indicated.

References

Allport, Gordon. *Religion in the Developing Personality*. New York: New York University Press, 1960.

Broughton, Walter. "Religiosity and Opposition to Church Social Action: A Test of the Weberian Hypothesis." *Review of Religious Research* 19:2 (Winter 1978): 154–166.

Evenson, C. Richard, and Robert R. Strohl. "Trends in LCA Membership, 1962–1978." *Partners* 1:6 (December 1979): 11ff.

Gallup, George, Jr. *Religion in America, 1977–78*. Princeton, N.J.: American Institute of Public Opinion, 1978.

———. *The Unchurched American*. Princeton, N.J.: American Institute of Public Opinion, 1978.

Glock, Charles Y., and Rodney Stark. *Christian Beliefs and Anti-Semitism*. New York: Harper & Row, 1966.

———. *Religion and Society in Tension*. Chicago: Rand McNally, 1965.

———, Benjamin Ringer, and Earl Babbie. *To Comfort and To Challenge: The Dilemma of the Contemporary Church*. Berkeley and Los Angeles: University of California Press, 1967.

Hadden, Jeffrey. *The Gathering Storm in the Churches*. Garden City, N.Y.: Doubleday & Co., 1969.

Johnson, D. W., P. R. Picard, and B. Quinn. *Churches and Church Membership in the United States: 1971*. Washington, D.C.: Glenmary Research Center, 1974.

Johnson, Roger A. *Congregations as Nurturing Communities*. Philadelphia: Lutheran Church in America, Division for Parish Services, 1979.

———. "Learnings for Ministry from Social Survey Data," *Partners* 3:1 (Winter 1981): 22–25.

McIntosh, William A., Letitia T. Alston, and John P. Alston. "The Differential Impact of Religious Preference and Church Attendance on Attitudes Toward Abortion." *Review of Religious Research* 20 (Spring 1979): 195–213.

Mead, Sidney E. *The Lively Experiment: The Shaping of Christianity in America*. New York: Harper & Row, 1963.

Nelson, E. Clifford, ed. *The Lutherans in North America*. Philadelphia: Fortress Press, 1975.

Niebuhr, H. Richard. *Christ and Culture*. New York: Harper & Brothers, 1951.

Office for Research and Planning. *Lutheran Listening Post: Fifth Questionnaire Report*. New York: Lutheran Church in America, 1978.

———. *Lutheran Listening Post: Sample Design Report.* New York: Lutheran Church in America, 1976.

Perry, Everett L., Ruth T. Doyle, James H. Davis, and John E. Dyble. "Toward a Typology of Unchurched Protestants." *Review of Religious Research* 21:4 (Supplement 1980): 338–404.

Piazza, Thomas, and Charles Y. Glock. "Images of God and Their Social Relevance." In *The Religious Dimension,* edited by R. Wuthnow. New York: Academic Press, 1979.

Stark, Rodney and Charles Y. Glock. *American Piety.* Berkeley and Los Angeles: University of California Press, 1968.

Strommen, Merton P., et al. *A Study of Generations: Report of a Two-Year Study of 5000 Lutherans Between the Ages of 15 and 65, Their Beliefs, Values, Attitudes, Behavior.* Minneapolis: Augsburg Press, 1972.

Tappert, T. E., ed. *The Book of Concord.* Philadelphia: Fortress Press, 1959.

Troeltsch, Ernst. *Social Teachings of the Christian Churches.* London: George Allen & Unwin, 1931.

Wentz, Abdel Ross. *A Basic History of Lutheranism in America.* Philadelphia: Fortress Press, 1964.

Wuthnow, Robert. *The Consciousness Reformation.* Berkeley and Los Angeles: University of California Press, 1976.

———. *Experimentation in American Religion.* Berkeley and Los Angeles: University of California Press, 1978.

———. "Religious Commitment and Conservatism: In Search of an Elusive Relationship." In *Religion in Sociological Perspective: Essays in the Empirical Study of Religion,* edited by Charles Y. Glock. Belmont, Calif.: Wadsworth Publishing Co., 1973.

Yinger, J. Milton. *The Scientific Study of Religion.* New York: Macmillan & Co., 1970.